Now you see it, now you don't!

Now you see it, now you don't!

lessons in sleight of hand

by Bill Tarr

Vintage Books
A Division of Random House, Inc.
New York

illustrated by Barry Ross

VINTAGE BOOKS EDITION, October 1976

Copyright © 1976 by William Tarr and Barry Ross

All rights reserved under International and Pan-American Copyright Conventions. Published in the United States by Random House, Inc., New York, and simultaneously in Canada by Random House of Canada Limited, Toronto. Originally published by Random House, Inc., in 1976.

Tarr, William, 1925–
    Now you see it, now you don't.

    SUMMARY: Step-by-step instructions for sleight of hand tricks using cards, coins, balls, and other common items.
        1.   Conjuring.   [1. Magic tricks]   I.   Ross, Barry, 1938–   II.   Title.
GV1547.T33   1976b   793.8   76-12248
ISBN 0-394-72202-7

Manufactured in the United States of America

Contents:

a special note to women

I have used the masculine form in
this book, not because I wished to
exclude you, but simply because I
am not magician enough to cope
with the grammatical
complications involved.
When someone invents a better
way to say it, I'll be happy to
comply. Until then, please accept
my apologies and read on,
content in the knowledge that
these words are meant for you too.
There have been famous female
magicians in years past, there are
some today, and now that you are
reading this book, hopefully there
will be more in the future.

Bill Tarr

introduction

I think magic is far and away one of the most interesting, rewarding and enjoyable hobbies ever . . . in my estimation vastly superior to any other.

Why?

There are a great many reasons. Because it's fun, because it's exciting, because it imparts skills that make you envied and admired and sought after . . . Because you are linked by tradition both to a calling that is rich in history and to a basic form of expression as old and as mysterious as man himself! And because magic is not only psychologically rewarding, but financially remunerative as well.

But most important, I think so highly of magic beause it is a tremendously creative pursuit. Magicians are always dreaming up better ways to do things. They vary existing effects, they invent new ones. They dream up their own tricks and they write their own patter and they develop their own presentation and they put together their own routines.

Anyone can be a collector. It's essentially a matter of dollars. The more money you have to spend, the better your collection of stamps or doorknobs or paperweights. Not so with magic. It's not what you own or the people you know or the influence you wield.

It's what you can do.

Young or old, rich or poor, male or female, the success you enjoy is directly proportional to the amount of ingenuity and creativity you can muster and the time and effort you are willing to spend. The choice is yours! You can go as far as you want to go.

There are sleight-of-hand performers who have achieved fantastic proficiency . . . a degree of skill and artistry quite unbelievable even when you see it happen from inches away!

There are men who have dedicated their lives to the practice of magic . . . who have literally spent eight to ten hours a day and more, day after day, week after week, month after month, learning new moves, polishing old ones, inventing, innovating, doing everything they can to advance the state of their art.

These are men who have brought to magic the same zeal and dedication that great painters and sculptors and musicians have brought to the fine arts, and like true artists, they have done it not for fame, not for fortune, but for the sheer love of it.

When you become a magician, you become a part of this rich heritage. Photography is challenging. Wood-working is gratifying. Ceramics and model-making are rewarding, but magic is magic . . . and if you like, this book can help you to become involved.

For your sake, I hope it does.

Bill Tarr

how to use this book

Learning sleight of hand can be surprisingly easy—or terribly difficult. It all depends on you and how you choose to go about it. If you are serious about learning, proceed properly, and devote an adequate amount of time and effort to the task, there is no reason why you can't learn to do sleights really well. The key to it all is simple enough. Just start at the beginning and stay with it.

To help you do just that, I have graded all of the sleights in this book. The stars next to each move in the list of contents and on the individual pages are there to guide you. The moves and tricks with ★ are the easiest to do and the easiest to prepare and present.

★★ effects are more difficult and consequently require more time and effort, and of course the ★★★ effects are most difficult of all.

Learn the ★ first, then the ★★, and finally the ★★★, and never go on to a new sleight until you have mastered the one you are working on! That's important. Nothing is more discouraging than plunging into an effect which is too difficult and time-consuming . . . and nothing is worse than showing a half-learned move to a friend and getting caught at it!

Many of the sleights in this book are presented in two segments. For example, you begin a vanish called the French Drop by showing a small object in your left hand and removing it with your right in a very simple, natural, forthright manner (carefully observing the whole operation in your mirror).

After you have learned to do that smoothly and well, you are ready to add the secret move which will make the coin vanish.

This time you do the *same* moves in the *same* natural manner, but at the right moment you secretly allow the coin to drop into your left palm while your right continues on as though still holding it.

If you follow this important technique . . . that is, if you first perform each move in front of a mirror to see exactly how it looks before you attempt the sleight, and then you duplicate those natural motions when you actually do the secret move, you can't help but perform sleight of hand in a natural, convincing manner.

You'll notice that many of the sleights are presented without endings. They are, in most cases, moves which are meant to be used in tricks or blended into routines. You could, for example, do a Billiard Ball Color Change as a quick trick in itself, but it has really been designed as a pretty and startling effect during the course of a routine. The same holds true for a great many of the sleights that follow. You'll find that by stringing several related moves together, you have created a routine which is far more interesting and entertaining than an isolated move or two.

A Few Important Tips . . .

Be Natural

The secret to good sleight of hand is naturalness. No quick, jerky motions, no hand wagging or waving! You must work slowly, deliberately, and naturally. Then coins and balls and rings and cards will disappear and reappear at your fingertips, not because you are involved in all kinds of complicated machinations, but *magically*!

Remember that. *Slow, deliberate, natural!*

Watch Your Angles

Become aware of "angles." Those are the sight lines between the object you have palmed off and the spectator's eye. If your "angles" aren't right, your audience may glimpse the object, and for all practical purposes your trick will be exposed.

Practice Palming Wherever You Are

The most important skill of the good sleight-of-hand man—
the ability to palm an object undetectably—can be acquired
almost effortlessly if you get into the habit of palming coins
and other small objects during the course of your daily
activities. Palm an object in either or both hands while you
write, eat, watch TV, walk around, or do almost anything else.
If you are careful about your angles, no one will ever know
what you are up to, and before long, what you now approach
somewhat self-consciously will become second nature, and
you'll palm objects boldly, confidently, and successfully every
time.

Presentation Is Half The Battle!

Presentation is really what it's all about. A minor trick well
presented is infinitely superior to the most elaborate
machinations which an audience can't understand or relate to.

There are absolutely superb magicians . . . incredibly
knowledgeable and adept practitioners of the magic art,
respected and revered by their brother conjurers, who aren't
nearly as effective in front of an audience as vastly less
competent magicians who present their wares well.

What good are miracles if nobody enjoys them? Your
presentation should be simple and straightforward and easily
understood so that your audience grasps the full meaning of
what you are doing and saying.

Think about that next time you do a trick.

Never Repeat A Trick!

Never repeat a trick for the same audience. That is one of the
cardinal rules of magic. When you do, your audience knows
what to expect, and what may have looked like a miracle the
first time may be disappointingly easy to figure out the
second.

Patter is Important

Most magician's patter fits into one of two broad categories. The first, and by far the most popular, is the more or less straightforward approach. The magician simply describes what he is doing. He may do it with humor, he may do it seriously, but essentially he describes the action that is taking place.

The second type involves the use of a story-line. The magician weaves little stories around the effect he is performing. His props become the characters and places in his plot. Both techniques can be effective—or not—depending on how well they are done.

Obviously the type of patter you use is directly dependent on the type of person you are. Unless you are doing a pantomime act on stage or a short manipulative routine close-up, you do have to speak. You don't have to be super-glib, but you do have to explain what you're doing and make it clear to your audience.

That doesn't mean that everytime you make a coin disappear you have to say, "Look, I place the coin in my right hand and I take it with my left . . ," but it does mean that you have to fill in awkward pauses, keep your audience interested, and make sure there is no confusion about what you are doing.

If you feel patter is going to be a problem for you, just be descriptive. After you repeat a particular effect a number of times, you'll find that the better phrases you use will stick with you, the duller phrases will slip away, and soon you will be presenting your trick with the finesse of a pro.

Practice Intelligently

Since practice is to a great degree repetition, there is a tendency to mindlessly repeat the moves you are working on over and over again, and while this certainly helps, you will get much better results if you think about what you are doing, at least in the beginning. For example, if you are practicing a move like the Knuckle Cut, don't just slop along at a breakneck pace. Start out very slowly and deliberately, and make a conscious effort to do it as neatly and as smoothly as you can.

Continue at an exaggeratedly slow rate until your hands become thoroughly accustomed to the move, and then gradually increase your speed until you are proceeding at a natural pace.

Even when you are practicing while you are involved in doing something else—watching TV, for example—work slowly and the end results will be far more gratifying.

Never Show Anything You Can't Do Perfectly!

Never show *anything* to *anybody, ever,* unless you are thoroughly prepared. Performing a sleight well enough to fool people requires self-confidence, and that comes only when you have practiced sufficiently to do your moves smoothly and without hesitation. If you don't do them perfectly in front of your mirror, you are certainly not going to do them well in front of an audience, and nothing is more discouraging than flubbing in front of your friends.

Don't Tell!

Never expose a trick. Never tell how it's done . . . not to friends, not to family, not to anyone! Magicians never do. You will be admired and respected much more if you don't. If your friends really want to know, let them learn the hard way, as you did.

You Can Learn Sleight Of Hand!

Most sleight-of-hand experts learned from books, and if they could do it, so can you. It doesn't take any inborn skills or special physical characteristics to do sleights well. If you can read this page, you certainly have enough intelligence to proceed, and if you can tie your own shoelace, you surely have enough coordination to do any move in this book, and then some! Just remember that sleight of hand, like any skill, should be learned from the beginning, so start with the easiest effects first. Practice long and hard, and never proceed to the next sleight until you have mastered the one you are working on!

Stay With It!

Don't be discouraged! Sleight of hand isn't nearly as difficult as it may seem. Just remember that the first move is always the toughest, but once you get to do it well—and start to fool people with it—the rest will come easy. Just relax, follow the instructions carefully, and you're on your way to what is far and away the most fascinating hobby ever.

Don't Neglect Your Hands

Take care of your hands. They don't really have to be in exceptional condition to palm coins or cards or thimbles, but you can't really palm smooth objects well—billiard balls, for example—if your hands are too dry or too moist. If your skin is dry, a good hand cream or a few drops of glycerine every day will probably help. If they are too moist, however, there may not be anything you can do about them. Some sleight-of-hand people with that problem reportedly wash in icy water before performing, but the benefits, if any, are probably of very short duration.

In any case, keep your hands clean, your nails neatly clipped, and avoid calluses if you can.

Practice Is What It's All About

Remember, the three basic rules in magic are *practice*, *practice*, and *practice* again!

Misdirection

If there is one word which sums up the very essence of sleight of hand, that word is *misdirection*. The hand isn't quicker than the eye, but it is—or can be—far more clever, and that's what sleight of hand is all about.

Sleight of hand depends, not on quickness, but on *misdirection*, which is the process of diverting the spectator's attention from that which you don't want them to see, to that which you do.

In the movies, when the heroine doesn't want her boss to see something, she dumps a bowl of soup into his lap. Not very subtle, but it works. In real life, the pickpocket bumps the victim on the shoulder at the same instant he lifts his wallet, or the quarterback *pretends* to hand off to the halfback. That's misdirection too.

The magician uses similar techniques to direct his audience's attention to wherever he wants it to be. He gazes intently at the hand that pretends to be holding the coin . . . and so does his audience. Sometimes he merely points in the direction he wants his audience to look, sometimes he tells them where to look in words ("keep your eye on the little ball"), and often he does all three.

Disguise is another part of misdirection. The magician disguises his hands. He puffs out the empty hand to make it appear to be holding the ball, and he holds the hand that is palming the ball in a natural position to make it appear empty. He never sneaks a glance at the hand that is palming the object because if he does, his audience will too, and he never moves that supposedly empty hand rapidly because that focuses the audience's attention where it shouldn't be. As you gain skill you will find yourself misdirecting your audience easily and naturally, without even trying!

cards

Of all the branches of magic, card effects are by far the most popular. There are literally hundreds of sleights with cards and thousands of tricks. Some are so simple they work by themselves. Others are so bewilderingly complex that they are accomplished only by means of the most subtle, ingenious, and difficult sleights . . . but all of them are fun to do.

about cards

Regular playing cards come in two sizes ... standard (poker) and bridge

Standard cards are one quarter of an inch wider than bridge cards. Most magicians work with standard cards, but if your hands are small, don't hesitate to use bridge cards. Try to avoid one-way patterns, however. They can make certain sleights like the double-lift obvious.

Plastic cards or plastic-coated cards are difficult to handle well, and are generally shunned by magicians.

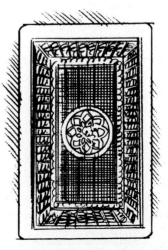

Fox Lake cards are bridge-sized but have overall patterns like poker decks. They are available at magic shops.

types of shuffles

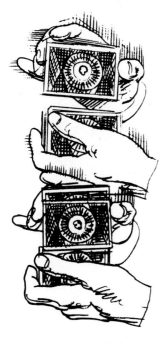
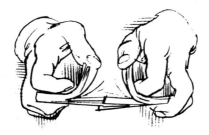

overhand   riffle   poker

self-working card tricks

There are literally thousands of card tricks which require no sleight of hand. Most are dull, long-winded, boring affairs, but some are absolute gems . . . ingenious, baffling and, when properly presented, great reputation-builders. The Spelling Trick is one such example, although it requires some manipulative help.

There is no onus in doing self-working tricks. The ultimate effect on the spectators is all that counts. Many card experts intersperse self-working tricks and sleight-of-hand effects with devastatingly good results, and their audiences attribute all their efforts to pure skill.

stripper decks

A stripper deck is shaved to a keystone shape. Any card reversed in a stripper deck is easily located by feel. For example, an ace reversed in the deck may be easily cut to, and four reversed aces may be slid out of the deck with ease.

Stripper decks can also be trimmed on the ends.

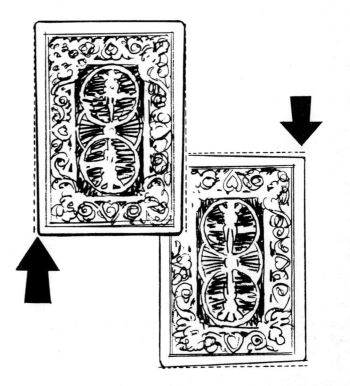

palming ★★★

Cards can be palmed in a number of ways . . . The classic palm is the most widely used, the pinkie is probably the most deceptive, and the back-palm is rarely used except during certain types of card manipulations.

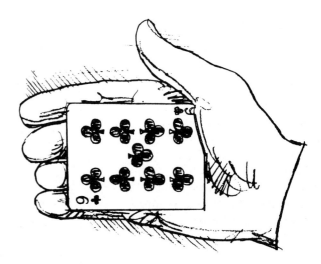

Palming a card is a simple process . . . provided your hands are large enough. The real problem is getting it into your palm in the first place! To achieve this without getting caught, magicians have, as usual, worked out a number of ingenious methods for stealing a card from the top, bottom and even the middle of the deck.

For your purposes, the top and bottom palms presented here will be more than sufficient for the moment, but again, a word of caution. It takes a good deal of practice, confidence and, especially, misdirection to palm off a card successfully. Don't do it until you can do it superbly well. It would be a shame to expose a perfectly good move, and it certainly won't do your reputation any good either!

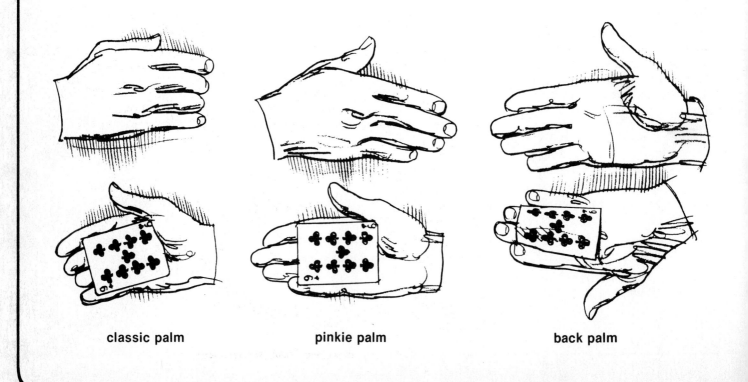

classic palm   pinkie palm   back palm

top palm

Hold the deck in the L. hand in dealing position. In act of squaring the cards with the R. hand, push top card about one half inch to the right with the L. thumb. L. 2 presses up under the upper right corner of the card, snapping it up into the R. palm.

At this point the R. hand should not take off with the card! Instead, grasp the deck with the R. hand and offer it to the spectator for shuffling. When he takes the deck, you go to your pocket where you leave the card or you do whatever else is called for by the trick.

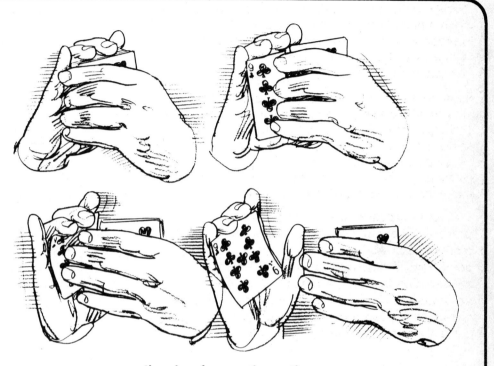

the view from underneath

bottom palm

As cards are squared up L. 2 and 3 push bottom card to right. Tip of R. 4 presses down on upper right hand corner of card and tip of L. 2 presses card up into R. palm.

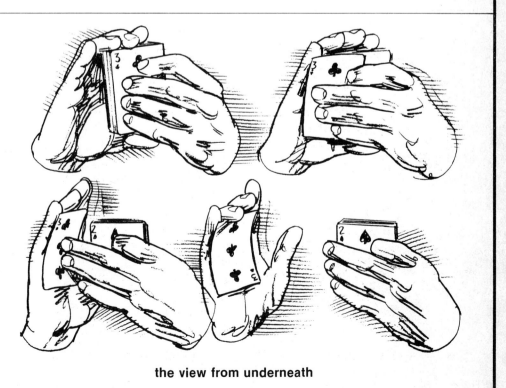

the view from underneath

the pass ★★★

the classic but very difficult method of secretly bringing a selected card to the top of the deck

what the spectator sees . . .

The magician riffles the deck until the spectator tells him to stop. The spectator replaces the selected card at that point, the top portion is replaced, and the card is apparently lost in the deck.

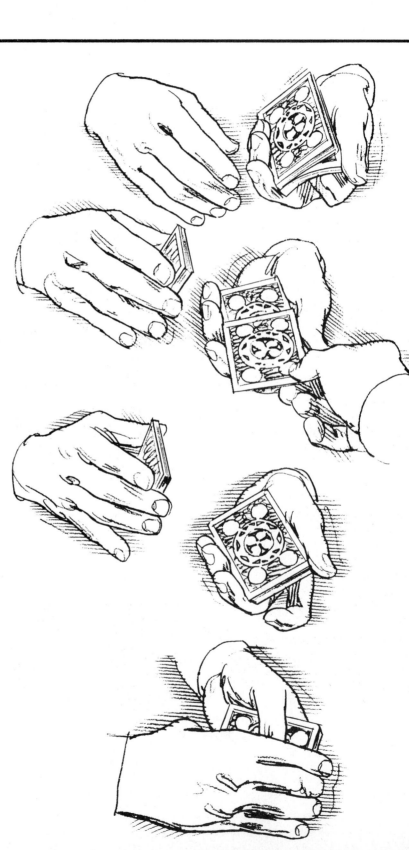

what really happens . . .

Selected card is replaced on top of lower portion B of deck.

Tip of L. 4 holds break over selected card.

R. approaches to replace upper portion A. Tip of R. thumb takes position on near side of A and tip of R. 2 rests on side of A.

L. 4 on bottom of A and L. 3 and 2 on top of A straighten out just enough to allow B to be pivoted over A. (Tip of R. thumb and R. 2 act as axis for the pivot).

B slips over A

cards are squared, and

selected card is on top of deck.

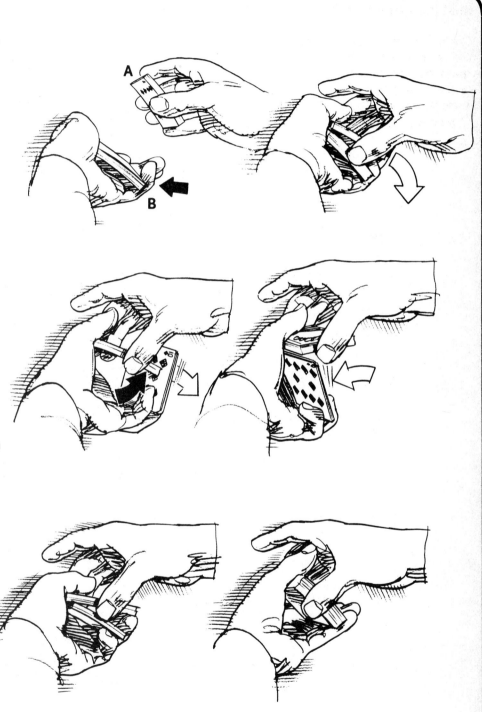

This is one of the few moves which should be executed rapidly, and never while spectators are gazing at your hand because there really is no sure-fire way to completely hide the resulting flash. The success you have with this move depends in large measure on your ability to misdirect your audience. One way to distract their attention is by speaking to them as you replace A on B. The instant your gazes meet, pass!

"say when" pass ★★

*an easy, undetectable way to bring
a selected card to second from the top*

A freely selected card is held by spectator.

Say "Tell me when to stop" as you slowly riffle deck in L. hand.

The instant spectator says "Stop", do so and then reach down and

appear to remove top portion down to where riffle was stopped, and

have selected card replaced at that point. Replace top portion and square up deck. Selected card appears to be at center of deck at spot chosen by spectator.

what you really do

Riffle until told to stop.

Bring R. hand across face of deck. Under cover of R. fingers L. thumb releases its grip on riffled cards, and with R. fingers at bottom and R. thumb at top, remove the top card only and unobtrusively hold it fairly close to your body and at such an angle that your audience can't detect it is only one card.

L. hand comes forward so selected card can be placed on top of lower portion of deck.

L. hand then comes back and R. drops single card on top of selected card and squares up deck.

Selected card appears to be in center of deck but is actually second from top.

From this position you can bring it to the top during a false overhand shuffle or you can simply execute a false shuffle (riffle or overhand) and then, showing your audience the top, indifferent card, say, "Your card is not on the top of the deck . . . but somewhere in the middle" as you casually push it into the deck.

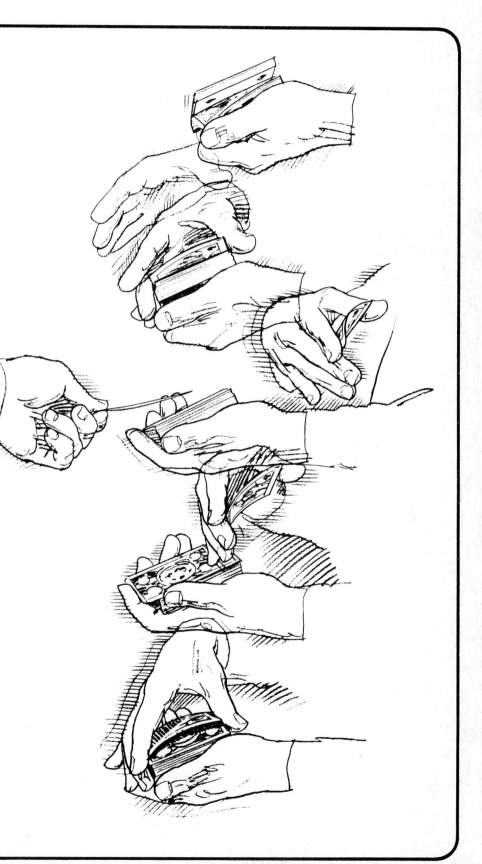

pass flourish ★

*an easy way to bring a selected card to the top,
useful when you can't get away with the pass . . .*

**looking down . . . forearms
parallel with floor**

Deck riffled and spectator
asked where to stop.

Cards separated at that point and

selected card placed on top
of portion B.

Portion A tossed on B and
break held with thumb.

L. hand immediately tilted to
right. A dropped on R. fingertips
and

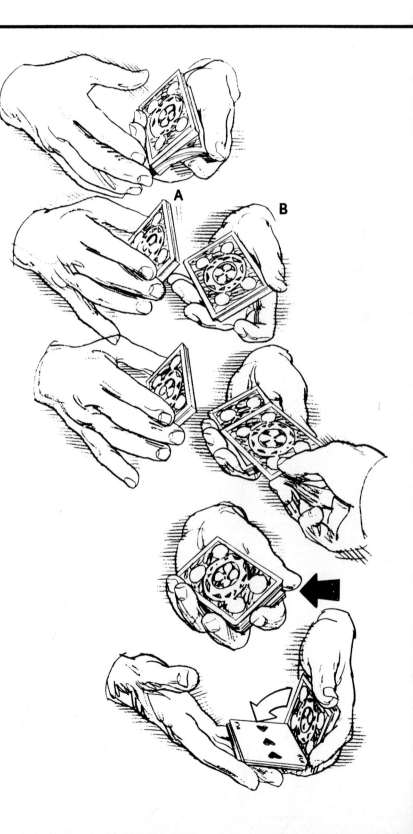

flipped over face down on R. palm by L. fingertips.

In same motion B dropped face up onto R. fingertips with L. fingers and

A flipped face up on top of B by R. fingertips.

Deck flipped face down onto L. hand with R. fingertips.

One segment blends into the other in rapid succession, so that the entire move appears to be no more than a little flourish.

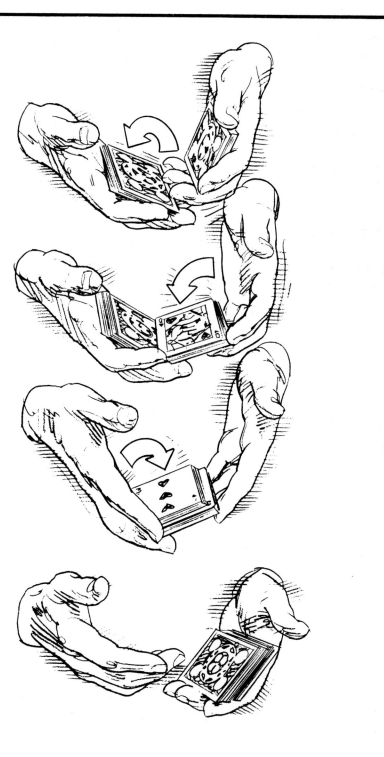

double-lift ★★

*far and away one of the most useful
of the many, many card moves . . .*

The object is to pick up two
cards and show them as one.
There are various methods for
accomplishing this. Try the few
that follow and settle on the one
that is best for you.

first method

Deck held in L. palm, thumb on left
side, L. 1 on top and L. 2, 3 and 4
on the right side.

R. thumb-tip pulls up two top cards
at lower left corner and holds them
as one between the R. thumb and
R. 1 and 2.

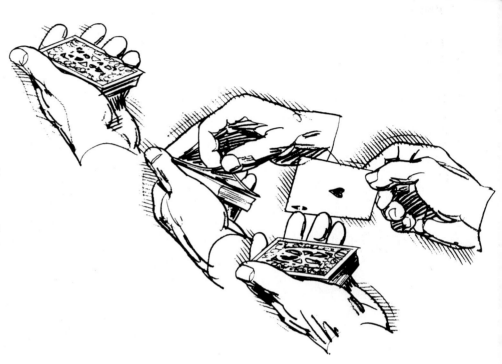

second method

Since it takes a good deal of
practice to pick two cards off the
deck every time, a more reliable
method is to secretly riffle-count
two cards with the tip of the L.
thumb and then hold the break at
the back with the fleshy part of the
L. thumb until you are ready to
actually do the double-lift.

Of course, the riffle-count must be
done while the spectator's
attention is diverted away from the
deck.

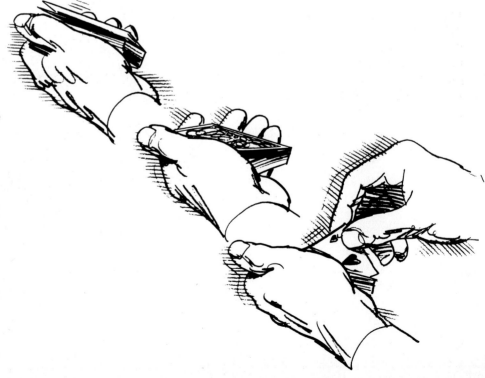

third method

Hold the deck with L. thumb on left side, L. 1 at top and L. 2, 3, and 4 on right side.

Riffle top ten or so cards until you are down to the last two and grasp those as one between R. thumb and R. 1 and 2. (Note that during riffle R. 2 and 3 are resting on top of pack.)

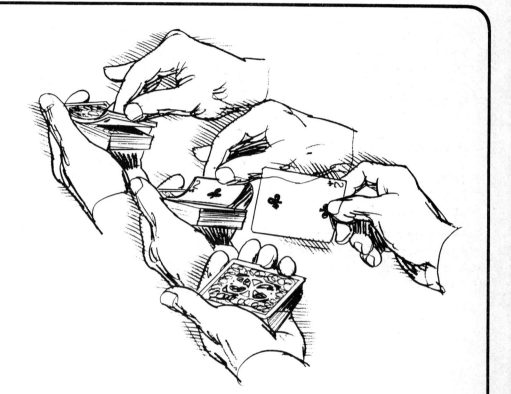

fourth method

While speaking to or otherwise occupying the attention of your audience, secretly riffle the top few cards of the deck, stopping at the top two, and hold the break with the tip of L. 4. until you are ready to do the double-lift.

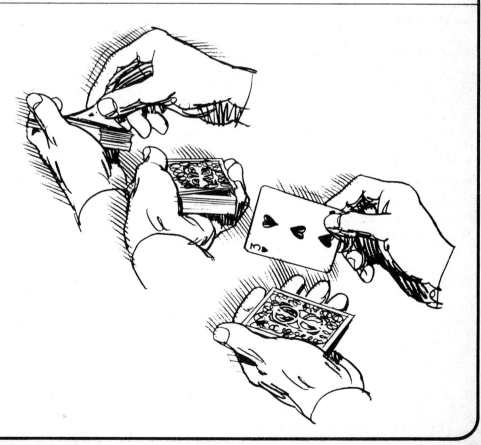

false shuffle number one ★

*an easy method for keeping the
bottom card(s) undisturbed*

1 Hold deck in position for conventional overhand shuffle. R. grasps center portion of deck between thumb and fingertips of R. 1 and 2 and

2 slides that portion up and out of deck.

3 Fingertips of L. 2 and 3 keep bottom cards in place and L. thumb keeps top card or cards in place.

4 Center portion in R. is shuffled off on top of cards in L. hand, and this sequence is repeated several times.

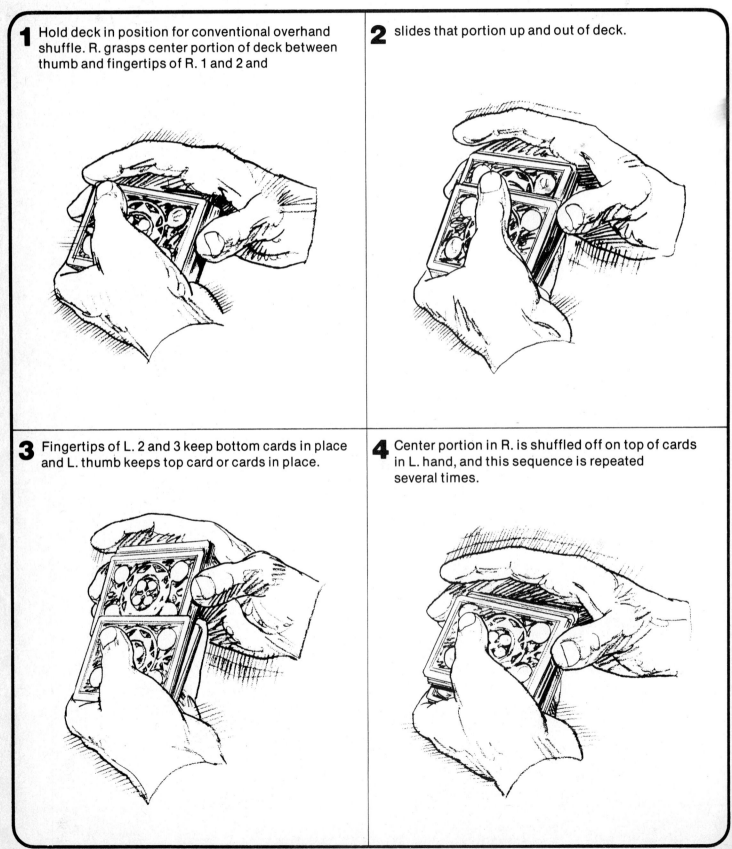

false shuffle (two) ★★

a fairly easy way to shuffle the cards without disturbing the order of the top portion . . .

Hold deck as for ordinary overhand shuffle.

Undercut about half the cards.

Slide the top card of the undercut portion onto the top of the deck but about ½″ to the left.

This is called an in-jog.

Without any hesitation, continue to shuffle the rest of the undercut portion on top of the in-jogged card.

Cut to the in-jog with your thumb and throw the entire portion underneath it on top of the deck.

Repeat the same series of moves several more times.

a more deceptive, but more difficult method

Proceed as above, but instead of cutting to the in-jog and throwing the bottom portion on top of the deck, hold a break at the in-jog, shuffle off those cards on top of the break and throw the remaining cards on top of the deck.

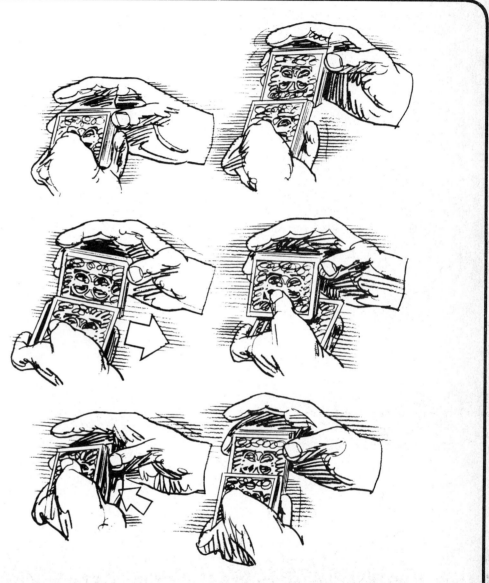

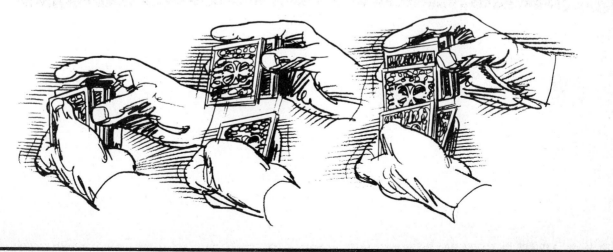

false triple cut ★

an easy and quite convincing triple cut that effectively keeps the order of the pack intact

1 Deck held in L. hand parallel to floor.

2 R. cuts away bottom third A between R. thumb and second joint of R.1 and

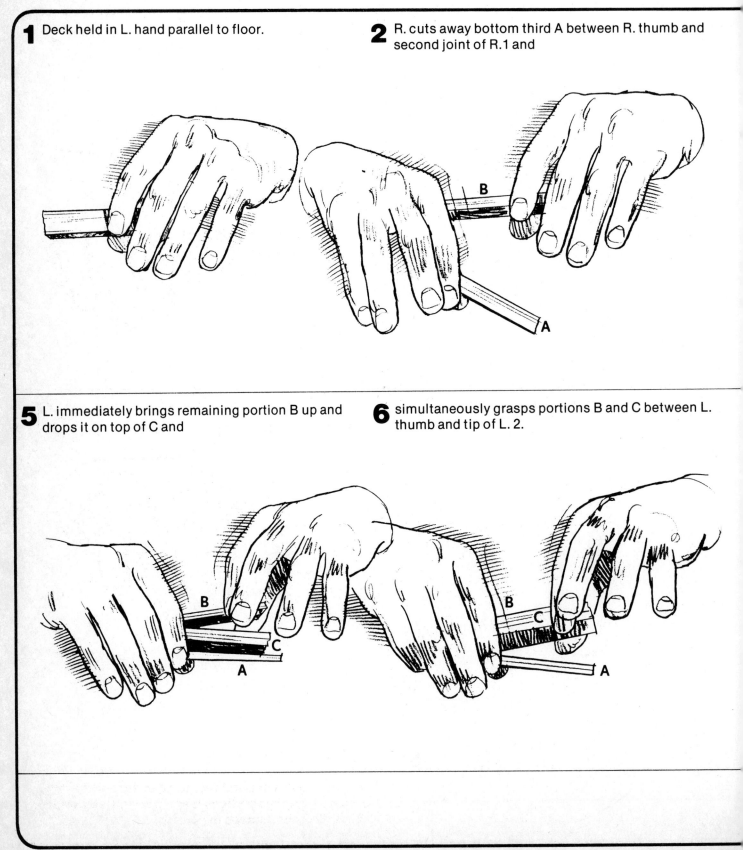

5 L. immediately brings remaining portion B up and drops it on top of C and

6 simultaneously grasps portions B and C between L. thumb and tip of L. 2.

3 brings it up over top of deck.

4 While still holding A, top portion C is grasped between R. thumb and tip of R.1.

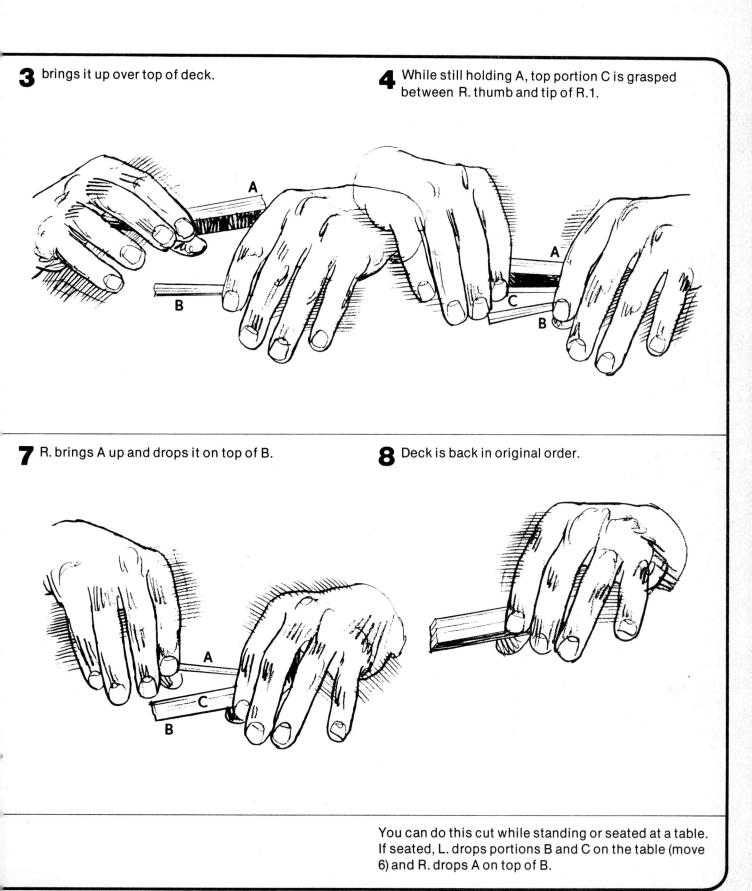

7 R. brings A up and drops it on top of B.

8 Deck is back in original order.

You can do this cut while standing or seated at a table. If seated, L. drops portions B and C on the table (move 6) and R. drops A on top of B.

hindu shuffle ★★

*an easier way to bring the selected card,
or cards to the top of the deck*

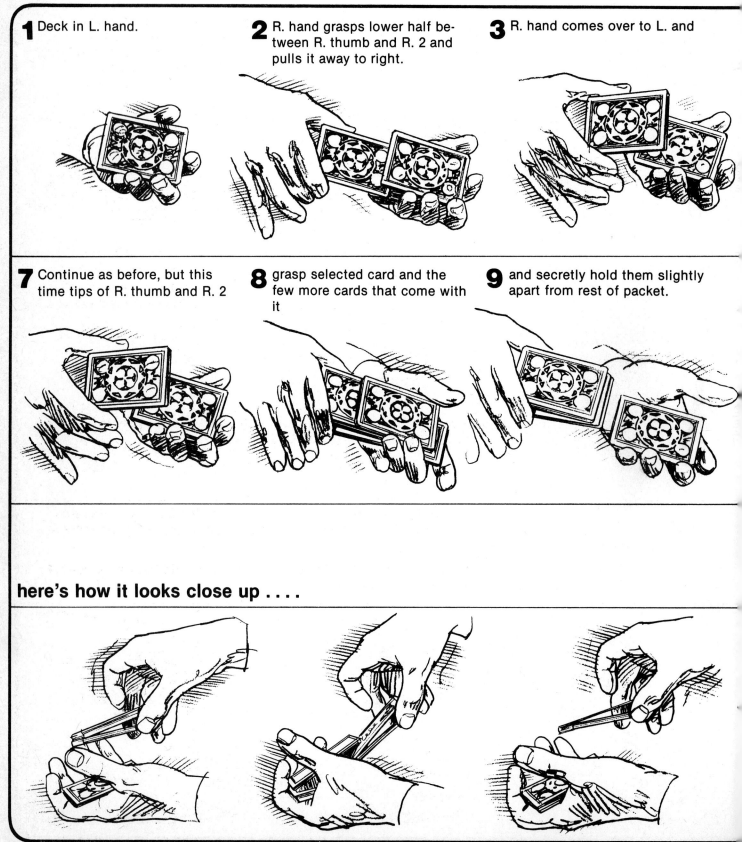

1 Deck in L. hand.

2 R. hand grasps lower half between R. thumb and R. 2 and pulls it away to right.

3 R. hand comes over to L. and

7 Continue as before, but this time tips of R. thumb and R. 2

8 grasp selected card and the few more cards that come with it

9 and secretly hold them slightly apart from rest of packet.

here's how it looks close up . . . .

4 base of L. thumb and tip of L. 3 pulls small packet off top of R. hand portion

5 on to top of L. hand portion. Repeat several times.

6 Allow spectator to replace selected card on top of L. hand portion whenever he or she desires to do so.

10 Continue to slide top portions off with L. hand

11 until you come to break.

12 Throw top card (and the few that may have come with it) onto top of L. hand portion.

Selected card (or cards) are now on top of deck. You can continue to shuffle this way for as long as you like without disturbing the order of the top cards.

If you use the Hindu Shuffle often, then you should frequently use it for legitimate shuffling as well.

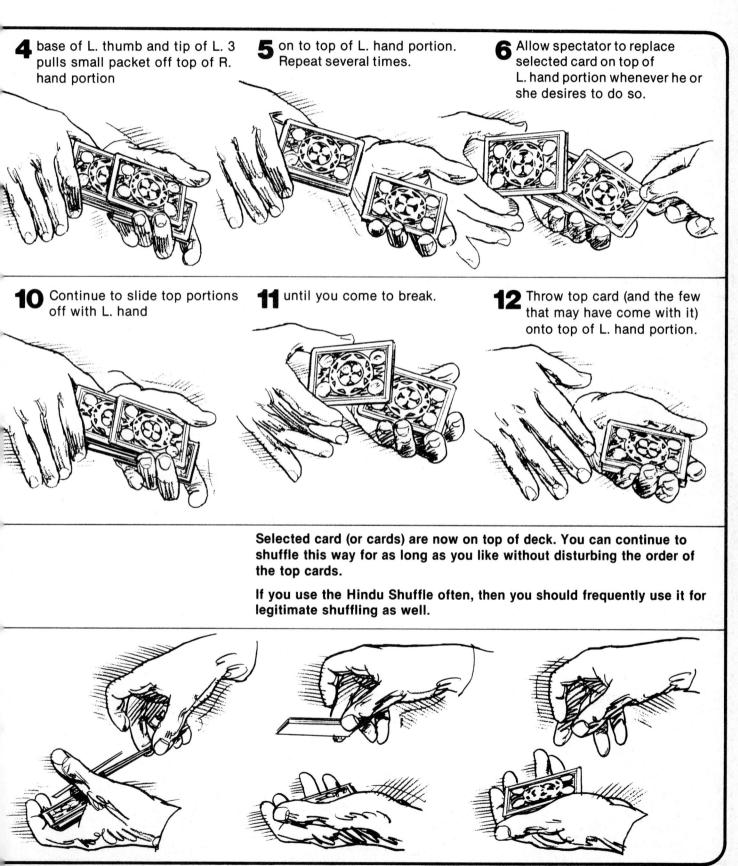

force ★★

the classic method of "forcing" a spectator
to select the card you want him to take

1 Secretly glimpse bottom card.

2 Cut glimpsed card to center of deck

5 Keep track of card to be forced, and

6 time the selected card to appear as spectator's fingers near deck,

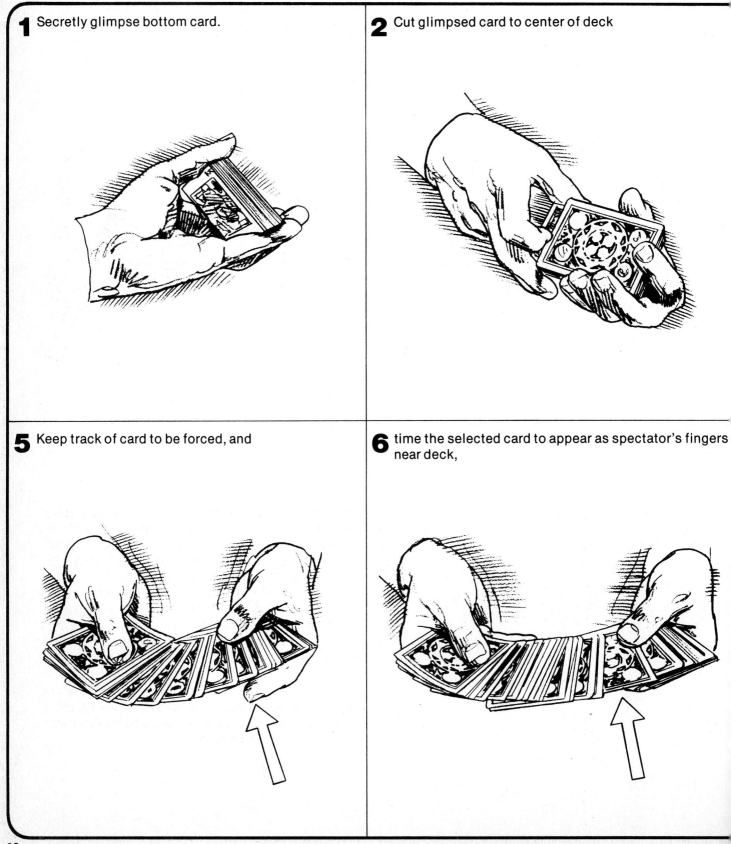

3 and hold break with tip of pinky.

4 Spread cards for spectator's selection.

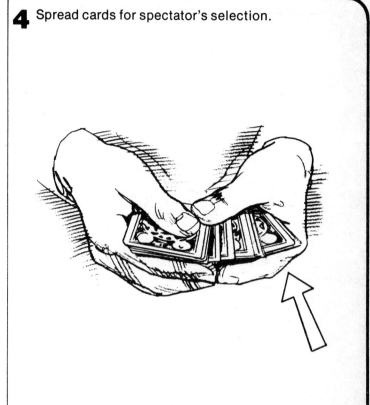

7 subtly forcing him to grasp desired card.

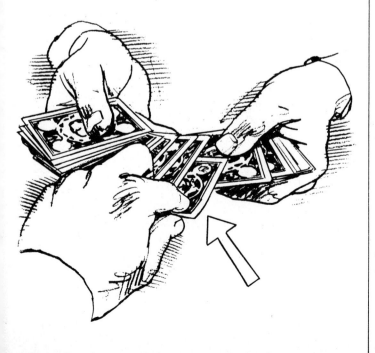

Practice and experience will enable you to force a card almost every time. Most people are docile and cooperative and you rarely miss with them. Some are insecure and don't like to be fooled. They are difficult. If you recognize the selector to be a skeptic or wise-guy type bent on showing you how clever he is, undercut a larger portion of the deck because he'll probably want to wait until the last instant to select a card. Better yet, use a sure-fire method like the Riffle Force.

Incidentally, the force is not meant to be a trick in itself. It is merely one of many moves designed to contribute to the successful conclusion of any one of a number of card effects.

riffle force ★★

not as natural as the classic force but it works every time

Secretly glimpse top card of deck.

Riffle deck with L. thumb.

Say, "Tell me where to stop . . . anywhere you like."

Stop precisely where spectator requests.

Right hand grasps top portion A of deck between thumb and R. 2. and 3.

L. 2, 3 and 4 remain along top right edge of deck.

Both hands pivot to right and as they do

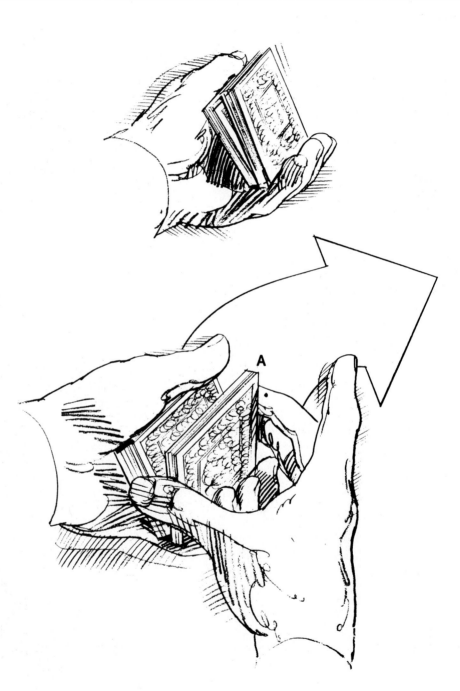

L. makes half turn toward body, taking bottom portion B of deck *plus* top card and

R. makes turn in opposite direction, retaining top portion A of deck *minus* top card.

As turn is made, L. 1 is extended and points to bottom card of packet A as you say, "You asked me to stop next to the ____ of ____" (name whatever the card happens to be).

Pivot both hands back to the left, and with R. 1 point to top card on portion B as you turn your head away, and say, "Take the next card, but don't let me see it," the next card being the force card.

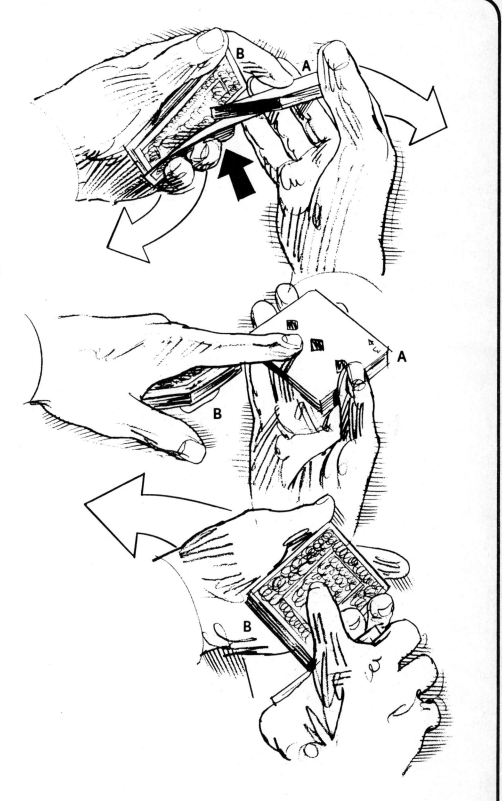

the glide ★★

a basic and not too difficult method for changing or switching one card for another

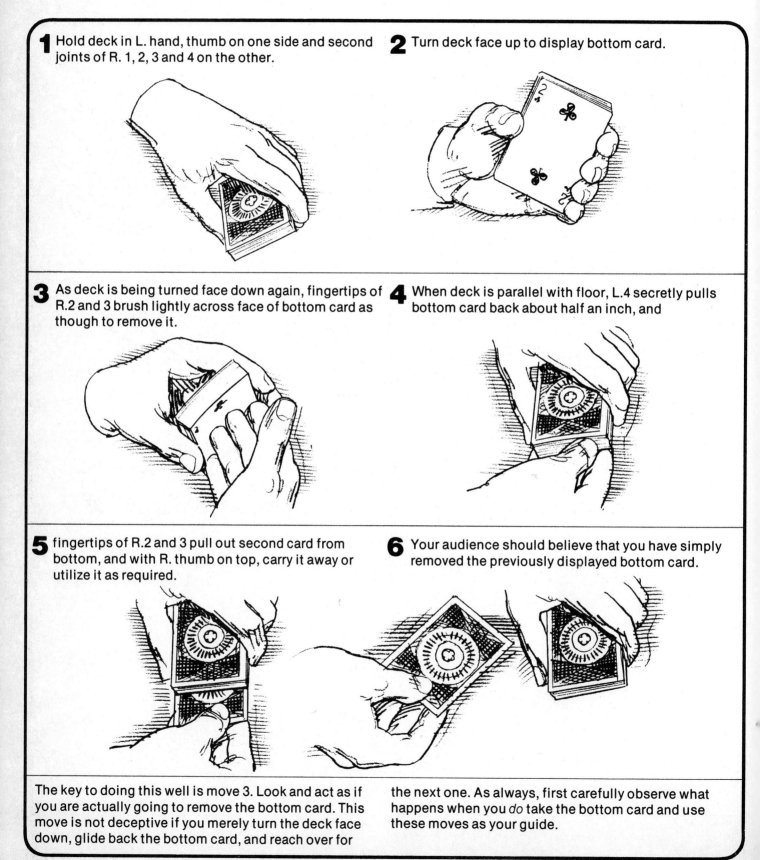

1 Hold deck in L. hand, thumb on one side and second joints of R. 1, 2, 3 and 4 on the other.

2 Turn deck face up to display bottom card.

3 As deck is being turned face down again, fingertips of R.2 and 3 brush lightly across face of bottom card as though to remove it.

4 When deck is parallel with floor, L.4 secretly pulls bottom card back about half an inch, and

5 fingertips of R.2 and 3 pull out second card from bottom, and with R. thumb on top, carry it away or utilize it as required.

6 Your audience should believe that you have simply removed the previously displayed bottom card.

The key to doing this well is move 3. Look and act as if you are actually going to remove the bottom card. This move is not deceptive if you merely turn the deck face down, glide back the bottom card, and reach over for the next one. As always, first carefully observe what happens when you *do* take the bottom card and use these moves as your guide.

a quicky card trick ★★

*one of the very best
quick card tricks ever*

Do a brief shuffle, execute the double lift, show the card(s) as one and say, "The six of hearts," or whatever, and place the card(s) back on the deck face down.

Say, "Watch. We place the six of hearts into the center of the deck." Slide the top card into your R. hand and place it in the center of the deck.

Push it in flush with L. 1 and say, "A tap of the finger (as you tap the top card) and the six of hearts comes right up to the top."

Turn over the top card (using the same moves as when you did the double lift) and show the six of hearts back on the top of the deck.

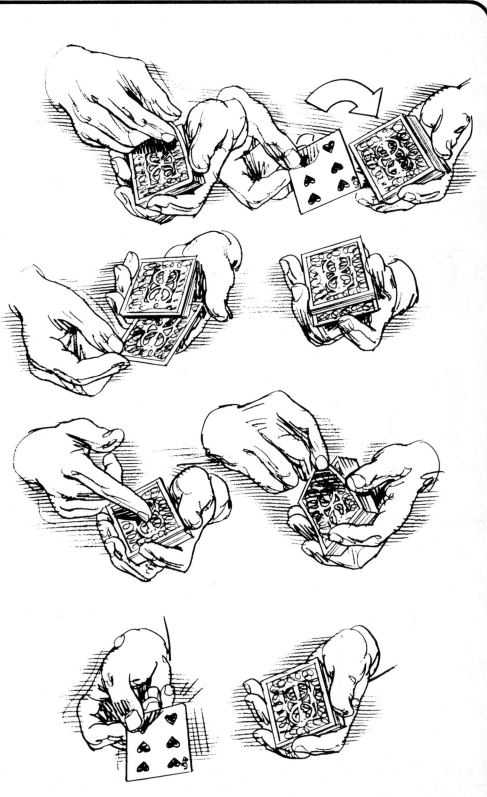

card transposition ★★★

a terrific effect, quick, startling, almost magical, but don't try it until you have had lots of experience . . .

the effect

Magician shuffles pack, shows top card and places it in his pocket. He shows the next card, places it face down on the table and asks spectator to hold his hand over it. Magician removes his card from pocket face down. He and spectator turn their respective cards face up at the same instant, and lo and behold, the cards have changed places!

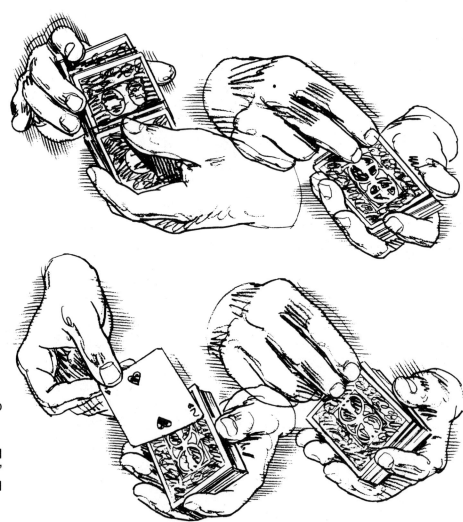

how to do it

Shuffle pack.

Do Double Lift.

Show spectator face of card(s) and say, "Two of hearts," or whatever card happens to be.

Replace card(s) face down on top of deck.

Remove top (indifferent) card and say, "I'll take the two of hearts," and place card in your right-hand jacket or trouser pocket.

Do Double Lift again.

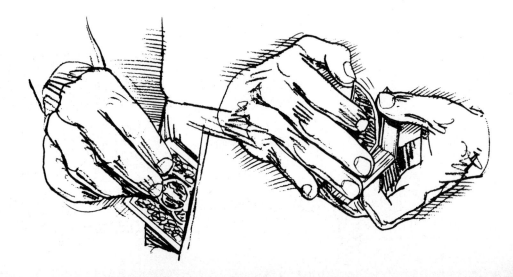

Show card and say, "Six of clubs," or whatever card happens to be.

Place card(s) face down on top of deck.

Remove top card and place it face down on table, saying, "You get the six of clubs. Place your hand on top of it so it can't get away."

While spectator places his hand over card, palm off the top card (actually the six of clubs), and immediately reaching into your pocket, say, "I'll get my card." Appear to be obtaining card previously placed in pocket, but actually come out with the six of clubs held face down.

Say, "O.K. Now what card do you have?" Spectator will answer, "Six of clubs."

You say, "Right. You have the six of clubs and I have the two of hearts. Let's each hold our card face down, and when I count to three we'll turn them over together . . . One, two, THREE!"

You both turn your cards over and they are seen to have changed places!

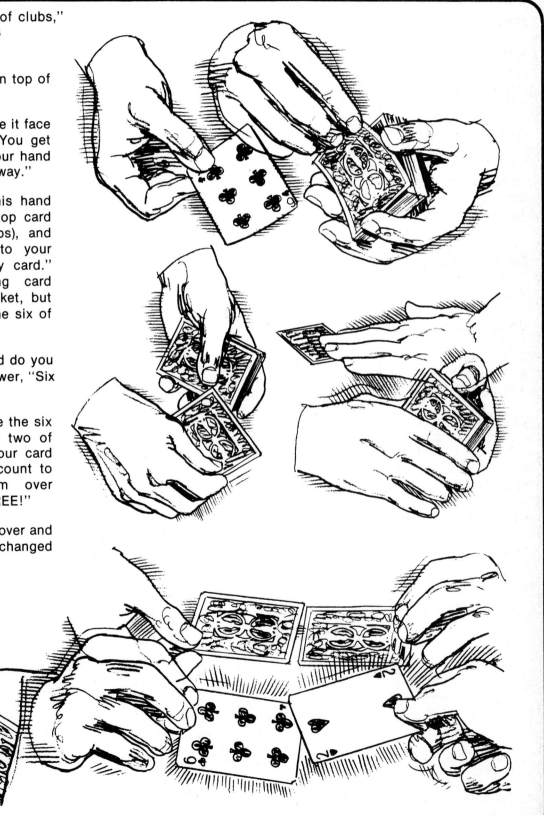

five card trick ★★★

*an absolutely dynamite effect . . . one of
the best club or stage card tricks ever*

the effect

Magician carefully counts five cards, one at a time,
distinctly discards three, and discovers to his
surprise that he still has five cards left. He repeats
this procedure three more times and on each
occasion, still has five cards left!

important note

This is a superb professional trick, and not that
difficult to do well, but don't expose it! Practice it to
perfection before you show it to a single person, and
don't do it close-up!

learn this first

false count

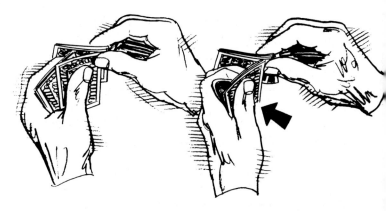

Hold eight cards vertically in the L. hand, thumb on
back and L. 1, 2, 3 and 4 on the front.

Say "One," and as you slide the top card (nearest to
you) to the right with L. thumb, bring your R. hand
over and grasp the card at the upper right corner with
the R. thumb behind and R. 1 and 2 in front, and carry
it several inches to the right.

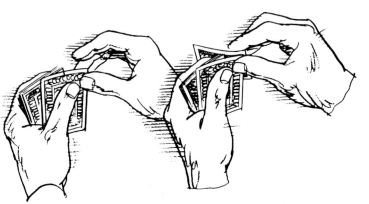

Say "Two" as you slide second card to the right.
Bring card in R. hand in front of cards in L. and slide
upper right corner of card behind first card and under
R. thumb. Carry R. hand and cards several inches off
to the right.

Say "Three" and repeat identical moves with third
card.

Say "Four" but this time as cards in R. hand cover
cards in L. hand, L. 1 buckles the bottom card
(nearest audience) and places the balance of the
cards as one, under the R. thumb just as with the
previous single cards.

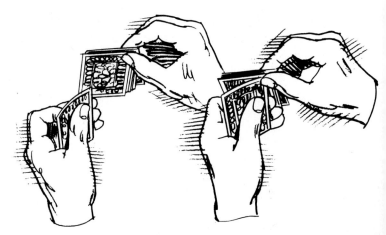

Say "Five" and remove the last card in the same
manner.

You held eight cards but they appeared to be five.
When you can do this smoothly and unhesitatingly,
add more cards and continue practicing until you can
make seventeen cards appear to be five . . . and do it
perfectly.

doing the trick

The patter that follows is just for purposes of illustration.
Use it if you like or dream up
your own.

Pull or roll back your sleeves, take packet of 17 cards
from your table or from your upper breast pocket and
say,

"I saw an amazing trick the other day. A magician I
know took five cards ... One (do the false count),
two, three, four (buckle bottom card and remove all
but it), five cards. (Place packet of cards back in L.
hand and square.) He threw away one, two, three
cards. (Count off just as before with same moves,
and throw away each card individually, as you count
it.) When he counted them again, there were still one,
two, three, four, and five cards (do false count as
before). When I saw that I was amazed. I took the
cards and I said, how can you possibly take five
cards and throw away one, two, three (discard three
cards as before), and expect to have left one, two,
three, four, five cards? (Do false count.) Very simple,
he said. You simply take the five cards, throw away
one, two, three (discard three cards), and then you
snap your fingers! It's all in that little snap. When
you count them again, you still have left one, two,
three, four, and five cards. (Do false count.) Now I
find that I can do the same thing. I take five cards, I
throw away one, two, three (discard three cards), and
I remember to snap my fingers! When I count them
again, I find that I still have **one, two, three, four, and
five cards**!"

spelling trick ★★

*an absolutely stunning effect and of the many methods,
probably the simplest and the best*

the effect
A card is freely selected and returned to the middle of
the deck. Magician proves the spectator's card is
buried in the pack and then, handing the cards to him,
requests that he spell out the name of his selected
card, one card for each letter. Spectator does so and
the last card spelled out is the selected card.

required sleights
False Shuffle #1
False Shuffle #2 or
The Pass

doing the trick

Glimpse the bottom card of the deck.

Casually execute False Shuffle #1 as you say, "I'd like
someone to pick a card . . ."

Spread cards and allow spectator to freely select
a card.

Square deck in L. hand, cut off bottom half of deck in
R. hand and ask spectator to replace card on top of L.
hand portion.

Throw cards in R. hand on top of selected card, thus
completing cut and bringing previously glimpsed
"key" card on top of selected card.

Square cards well so nothing protrudes, and say,
"Your card is somewhere in the middle of the deck.
Just to prove it's still there, I'm going to run through
the cards. Make sure you see your card, but don't tell
me where it is."

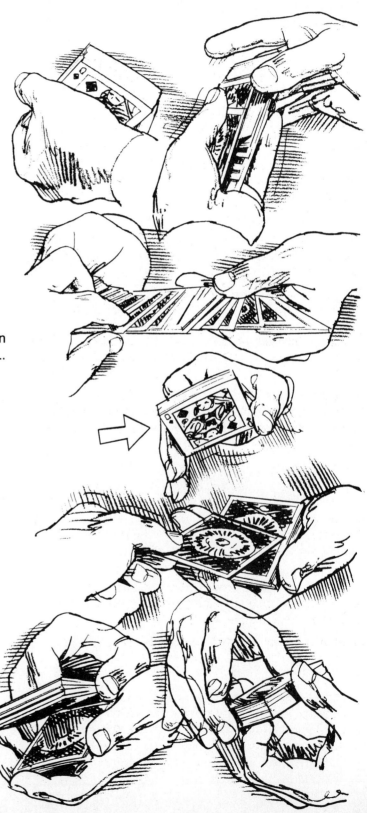

Turn deck face up and spread the cards, one at a time, with the L. thumb, but move rapidly or you'll bore your audience to sleep.

The instant you spot your "key" card you know that the card immediately to its right is the selected card, but don't hesitate or change your pace.

As you continue to spread the cards, mentally spell out the name of the selected card, one card for each letter. For example, if the selected card was the ace of clubs, spell to yourself, A for the ace, C for the next card to the ace's left, E for the next, and so on until you have spelled out A-C-E-O-F-C-L-U-B-S.

Hold a break with L.4 between the "S" and the next card, but continue to spread cards for a bit so as not to arouse suspicion. Say, "O.K., you must have seen your card somewhere in the deck by now. Right?"

At this point you must get all of the cards on top of the break to the bottom of the deck. If you can do the Classic Pass well, and if you have succeeded in diverting the attention of your audience away from the cards for a second, this would be the perfect moment to do it.

If you can't pass well, however, grasp the deck in the R. hand, holding the break with the R. thumb, shuffle off to the break, and throw the balance of the deck on top.

Say, "You saw your card somewhere in the middle. Right? Here you take the deck. You're going to be the magician. Spell out the name of your card, one card for each letter . . . For example, if you selected the two of hearts, you spell out T-W-O-O-F-H-E, etc., and call each letter out loud so we can all hear you . . .

Spectator takes cards and spells out A-C-E-O-F-C-L-U-B-S, removing one card from the top of the deck face-down for each letter he spells out, and placing it face down on the table.

When he comes to the last letter, "S" (for the S in clubs), he turns the cards face up, and that card is the ace of clubs!

The patter suggestions are only approximate . . . more or less of a guide to help you along, but do bear in mind that your explanation has to be very clear if you expect the trick to go smoothly.

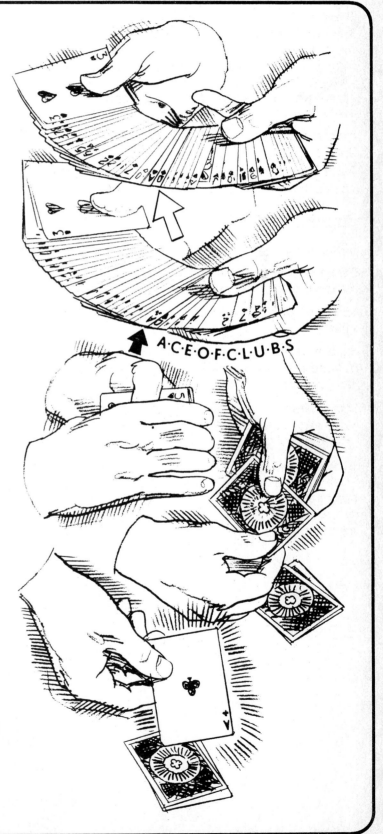

A·C·E·O·F·C·L·U·B·S

the upside-down card ★★

a very simple, very baffling trick

the effect

Spectator returns his selected card to the center of the deck. The magician fans the deck, and the one face-up card in the face-down pack is the selected card!

required sleights

The Pass or any other method to bring the selected card secretly to the top of the deck, and the Double Lift.

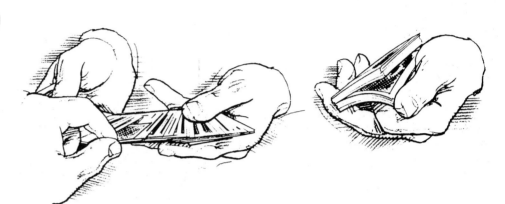

doing the trick

Spread the cards and allow the spectator to select a card freely.

Close the deck in the left hand, riffle deck with L. thumb, and say, "Tell me where to stop . . . anywhere at all . . ."

Allow card to be replaced in the deck at requested spot and secretly bring it to the top by your favorite method.

With deck squared and lying face down on left palm, look squarely at spectators, while you say, "I want you to see that your card isn't on top of the deck...", and prepare to do the Double Lift.

Pick up the top two cards as one and place them face up on top of the face-down deck. Say, "See, not on the top of the deck . . ."

With R. thumb on bottom and R. 2 and 3 at top, turn deck face up on your L. palm.

Reach under deck, remove bottom card, and use it to point to indifferent card on the face of the deck, and say, "...and not on the bottom . . ."

Place pointer card face up on the top of the face-up deck and say, ". . . but somewhere in the middle . . ." and

with that, cut the cards and, completing the cut, say,

"Now watch . . . nothing tricky. No manipulation. No sleight of hand. We fan the cards" (Fan them face up. If you can't fan well, spread the cards,) "and amazingly enough, one card is reversed in the deck." If the reversed card isn't obvious, spread the deck with your thumb to reveal it more plainly, and say,

"What was the name of your card? Please name it out loud so we can all hear it."

As the spectator names the selected card, turn over the fan or the spread cards to reveal that the reversed card and the spectator's card are the same!

An important note: Don't merely learn the secret and then dash off and attempt to show this trick (or any other) to the first likely prospect that passes by. The moves that follow have been carefully worked out for you. Learn and do them exactly as they appear here, and practice them to perfection. Later on, when you're an expert, you can modify and amplify and even improve, but for now, please follow the instructions precisely.

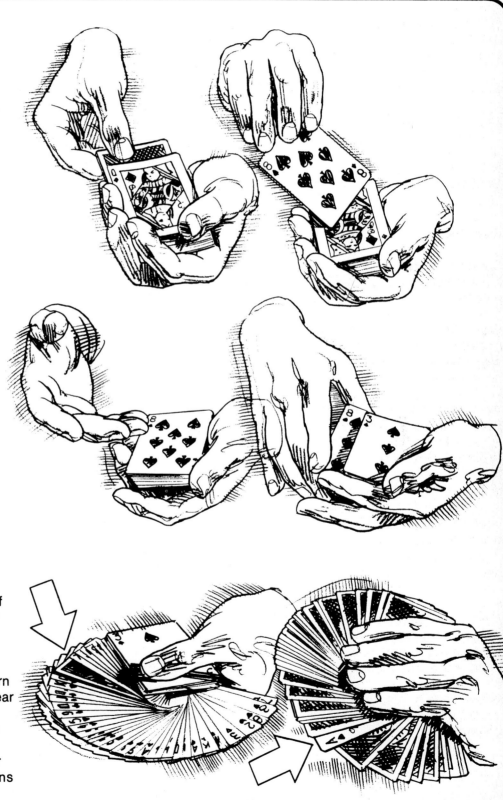

the changing card trick ★★

a spectacular trick that always wins an enthusiastic response

A card has been freely selected by a member of your audience, returned to the deck and secretly brought to the top by your favorite method.

Riffle-shuffle the deck several times keeping the selected card on top and explain that you are shuffling to be sure that the card is hopelessly lost somewhere in the deck.

Say, "Now watch closely as I bring it to the top." Riffle the cards with your L. thumb and say, "Believe it or not, your card has just come through the deck right up to the top, and here it is."

Do the double lift and show the indifferent card. Say, "That was your card—The nine of hearts" as you replace the card(s) face down on the deck.

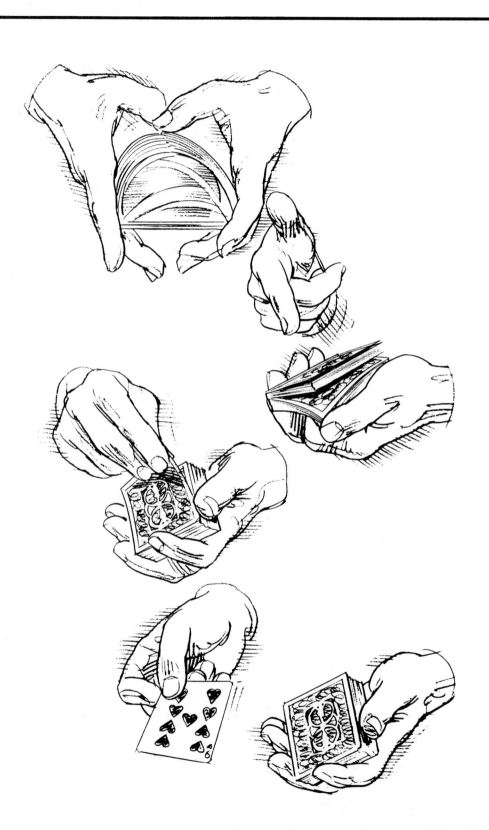

The person of course denies
that you showed him his
selected card, but you maintain
that you did as you openly slide
the top card into your R. hand
and hold it face down.
He continues to protest that you
did not show him his card and
you insist that you did.

Finally, you ask, "Okay then,
what was the name of your
card?"

He answers, "The three of
diamonds," and you say, "That's
exactly what I showed you, . . .
the three of diamonds."

As the spectator gleefully insists
you mistakenly showed the nine
of hearts, you slowly turn over
the card over to reveal that it is,
indeed, the three of diamonds.

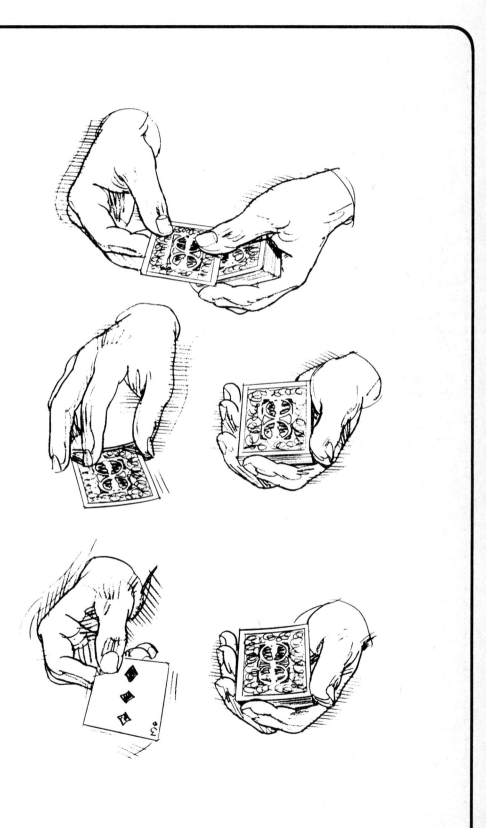

three-card monte ★★

*an old carney-type hustle currently being
revived on the streets of New York . . .*

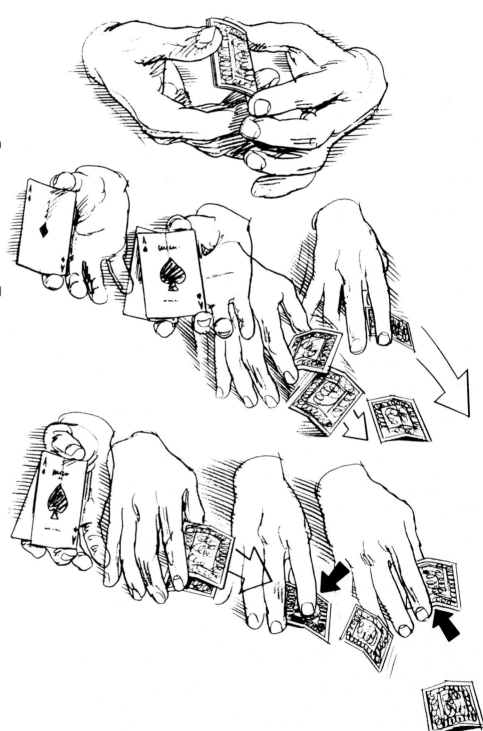

the effect

The operator shows three cards, generally two red aces and a black one. He throws them face-down on his table (or the ground), mixes them up, and you bet you can pick out the black ace. If you do — a rare occurrence — he pays off at two to one.

The operator usually has at least one shill (confederate) working with him. They place bets, win easily, and in so doing, induce spectators to take a chance. One classic ploy occurs when the operator looks away and his shill bends up a corner of the black ace. The operator, not noticing, throws the cards, and the crowd bets heavily. When the bent corner card is turned over, it proves not to be the black ace. The operator had secretly removed the bend and placed it on another card.

to prepare

Bend three cards, the ace of hearts, diamonds and spades, as illustrated.

the secret move

Hold a red ace between the R. thumb and R. 1. Pick up black ace in same hand between R. thumb and R. 2. Throw black card down as illustrated. Now, in the same way, throw red ace to the left of black ace. Do this a number of times until you get the feel of it.

now try the switch

Make the identical throw, but this time release the grip on the top (red) ace allowing it to fly off, and quickly replace R. 2's grip on the black ace with R. 1. This finger transfer must be done imperceptibly or the move will be detected.

typical series of moves

Line up three aces, black ace in middle.

Pick up C between R. Thumb and R. 1, show, and say "Red ace".

Pick up A between L. thumb and L. 1, show, and say, "Red ace."

Pick up B between R. thumb and R. 2 and say, "Black ace".

Throw C to left (switch).

Throw A about eight inches to right of C.

Throw B in center.

Pick up A in R.

Pick up C in L.

Throw A to the left of B.

Throw C to the right of B.

Pick up B and throw to the right of A.

Allow one spectator to point to the card he thinks is the black ace.

Repeat with various combinations of moves and always use clean, unmarked cards.

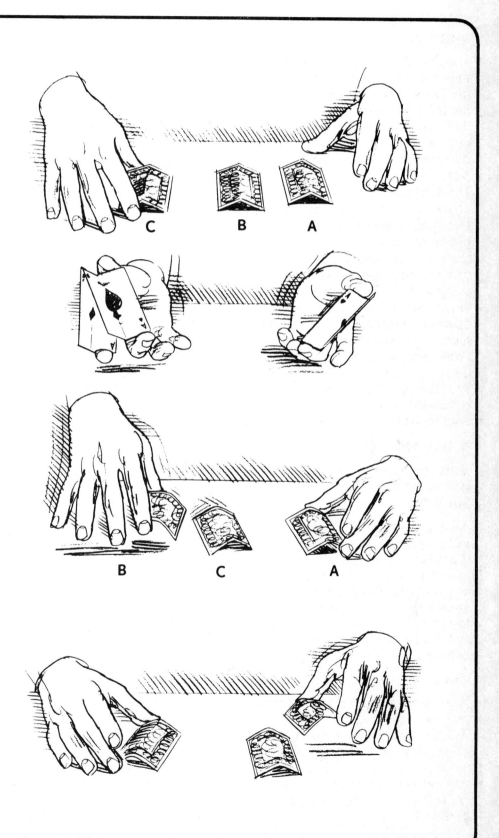

To make matters more confusing, you can use multiple switches. For example, after you make the first series of throws, you can pick up the cards again, without showing the faces, and do the switch one or more additional times.

If you think the spectators are becoming aware, you can fake doing the switch occasionally. Sometimes you can do the switch under cover of the L. hand which crosses over the R. to throw its card. In any case, if you practice the move sufficiently, no one, even those in the know, will be able to detect it.

flourishes

Although more akin to juggling than magic, card flourishes have always been the special province of the magician. They are fascinating to watch, fun to do, look like they require great skill (and they frequently do), but are often not as terribly difficult as they seem at first trial. Like everything else in magic, however, if you don't do them well, best not to do them at all.

riffle shuffle ★

*a common but attractive way to shuffle
the deck, and it sounds good too . . .*

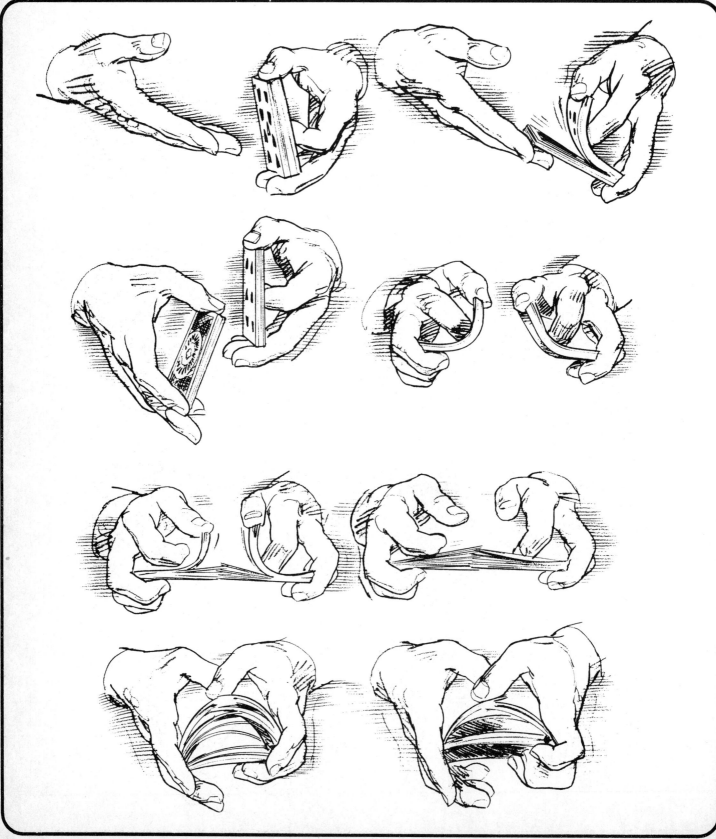

weave shuffle ★★

*a unique and interesting way to shuffle the
deck, and it's easier than the riffle shuffle . . .*

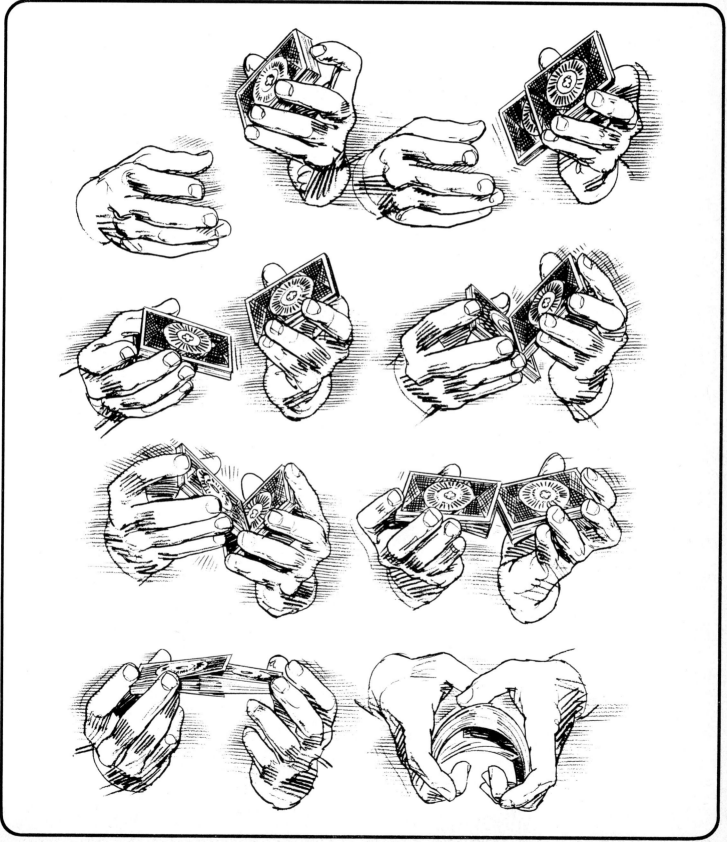

tips on fanning

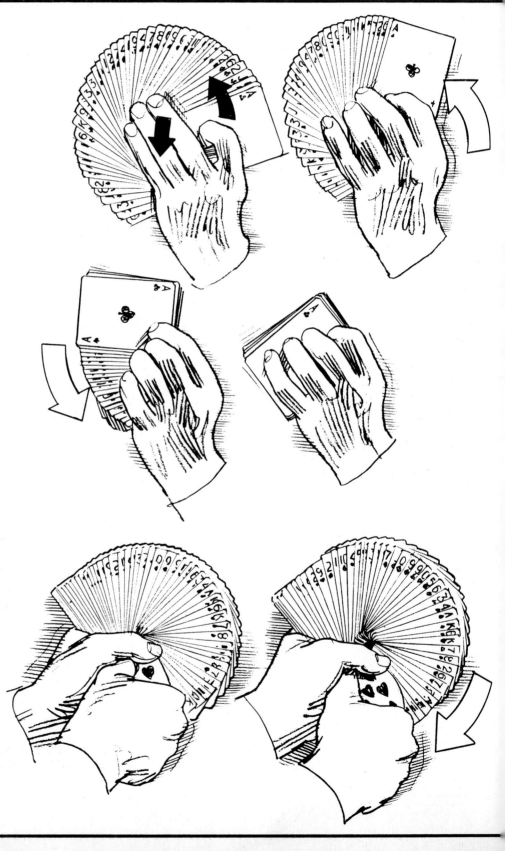

the snapback

a beautiful way to close the fan, but almost as difficult to describe as to do . . .

L. thumb on front and tip of L. 2 on back form axis around which L. 1 (snapping forward) and L. 2 (snapping backward) close fan.

If the fan is held horizontally, the momentum of the moving cards helps to close the fan. If the fan is held vertically, gravity supplies the extra impetus sometimes required.

It may take a bit of experimentation to find the right combination, but when you do, the cards will snap back in one crisp, rapid motion . . . never by degrees.

A fan made with a poker deck looks better with its face to the audience.

You can make a large fan by moving your R. hand in a wider arc and your L. thumb in a small one.

Poorly made fans look awkward and amateurish. If you don't fan well, you are better off not fanning at all.

exhibition card fans

Exhibition card fans are precisely what the name indicates . . . an exhibition of fancy card fanning and associated flourishes blended into a routine, and often presented in conjunction with the production of fans of playing cards from the air.

Exhibition fanning decks are bridge-sized, generally borderless and brightly colored and patterned. They are usually treated with zinc stearate and used only for fanning. (Cards used for tricks should never be treated.)

Plastic-coated cards are impossible to fan well.

The one-handed reverse fan is probably the prettiest of all the fans to watch happen because it slowly develops with no visible hand motion. It is also the most difficult fan to do well.

how to treat an exhibition fanning deck

Purchase a small quantity of pure zinc stearate at your druggist's. Dip a wad of cotton into the zinc stearate and wipe a uniform amount—the equivalent of a little mound about one-sixteenth of an inch high—on the back of each card.

Thumb-fan the deck until it fans evenly, and try not to upset their order once they are fanning well. If you should happen to drop them, wipe each card lightly to remove any traces of grit they may have picked up.

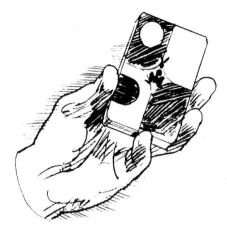

One popular professional fanning deck looks very similar to this . . .

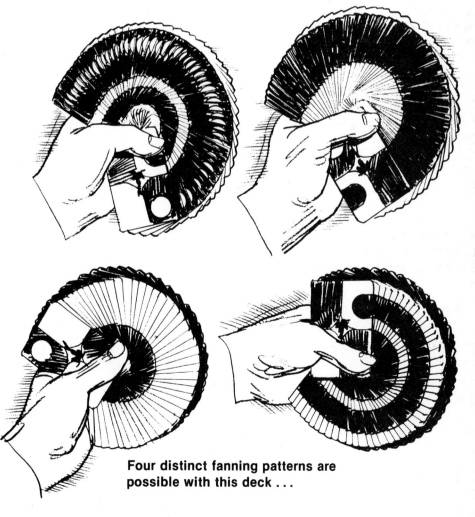

Four distinct fanning patterns are possible with this deck . . .

thumb fan ★

*not really as effective as a spring fan
but easier and less damaging to the cards*

Start with half a deck and add cards as your skill increases.

1 Hold deck between L. thumb and palm.

2 R. thumb on upper-left edge of cards

3 slowly arcs to right,

4 making fan as large and as even as possible.

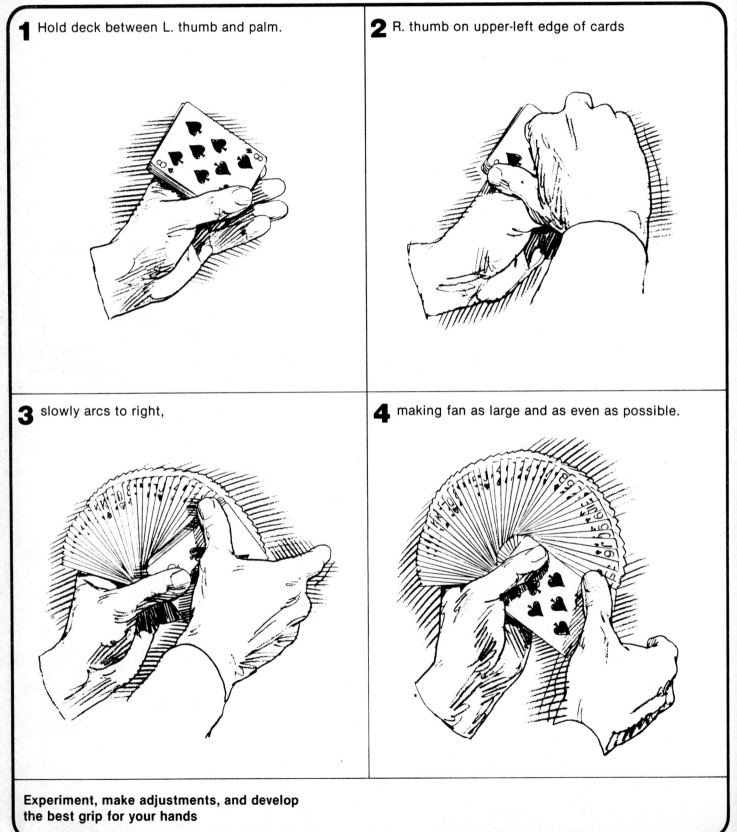

**Experiment, make adjustments, and develop
the best grip for your hands**

spring fan ★★

*the most popular flourish, and easy once you get the
knack of it, but you need a reasonably new deck*

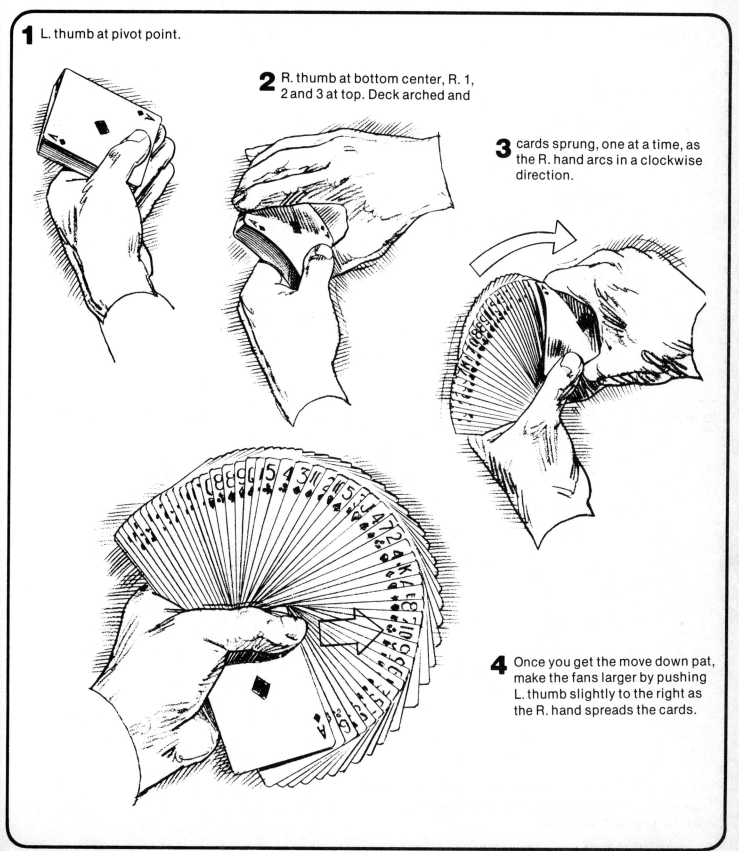

1 L. thumb at pivot point.

2 R. thumb at bottom center, R. 1,
2 and 3 at top. Deck arched and

3 cards sprung, one at a time, as
the R. hand arcs in a clockwise
direction.

4 Once you get the move down pat,
make the fans larger by pushing
L. thumb slightly to the right as
the R. hand spreads the cards.

reverse fan ★

interesting because the face of the fan is blank . . .

Hold deck as illustrated, place R. thumb in lower left corner and spread cards in a counterclockwise direction.

It is also possible—but more difficult—to do a reverse Spring Fan.

If you want the face of the reverse fan to look completely blank, use an ace as the face card and hide the pips behind your hand as illustrated.

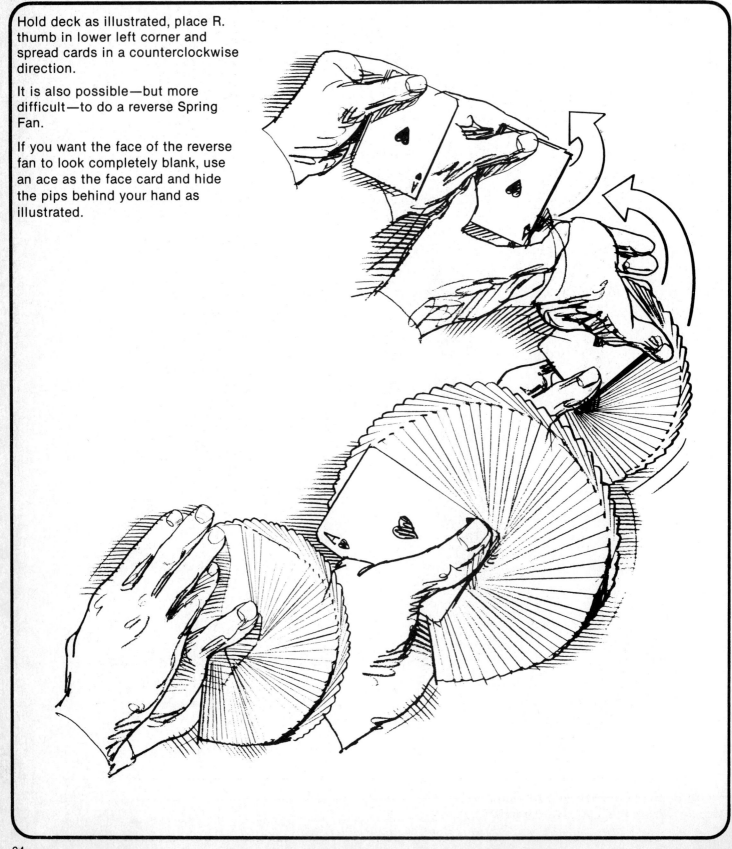

one-hand fan ★

an easy move—and essential for the card manipulator—
but you must have a good deck to work with

Start with a third of a deck and add cards as your skill increases.

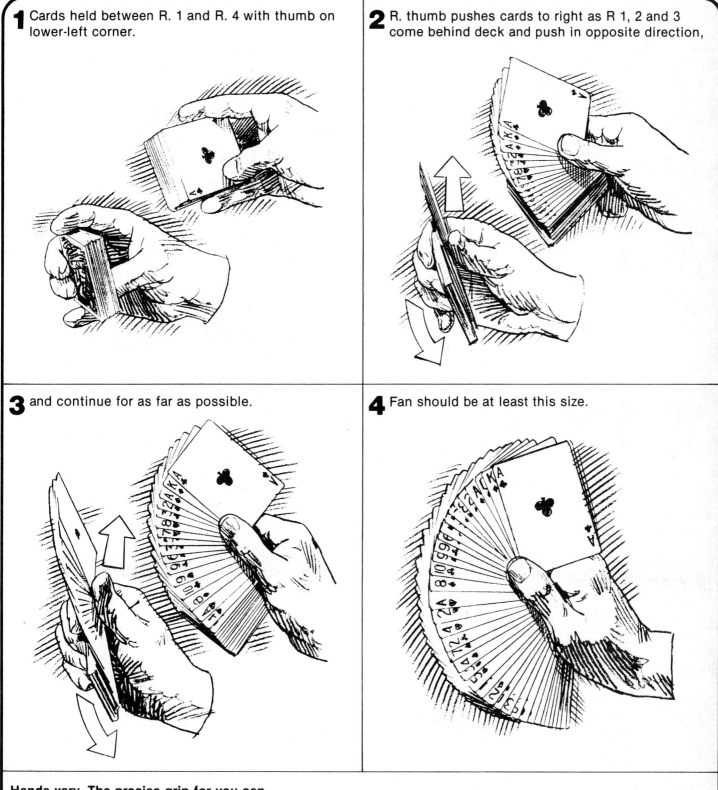

1 Cards held between R. 1 and R. 4 with thumb on lower-left corner.

2 R. thumb pushes cards to right as R 1, 2 and 3 come behind deck and push in opposite direction,

3 and continue for as far as possible.

4 Fan should be at least this size.

Hands vary. The precise grip for you can only be determined by experimentation.

one hand reverse fan ★★

the prettiest fan because it develops slowly, with almost no perceptible hand motions . . .

This move is very difficult to describe—and do—because there are no specific directions to give. It's really a trial-and-error situation. Hold the deck in the L. hand as illustrated and bring your thumb down and your fingers up in the direction opposite that used in the conventional one-hand fan, and spread the cards evenly.

Try, experiment, be patient, and with a bit of extra effort you will have added a very pretty flourish to your repertoire.

Needless to say, you must have a good deck for this effect.

Note that this fan is rounder than the conventional one-hand fan.

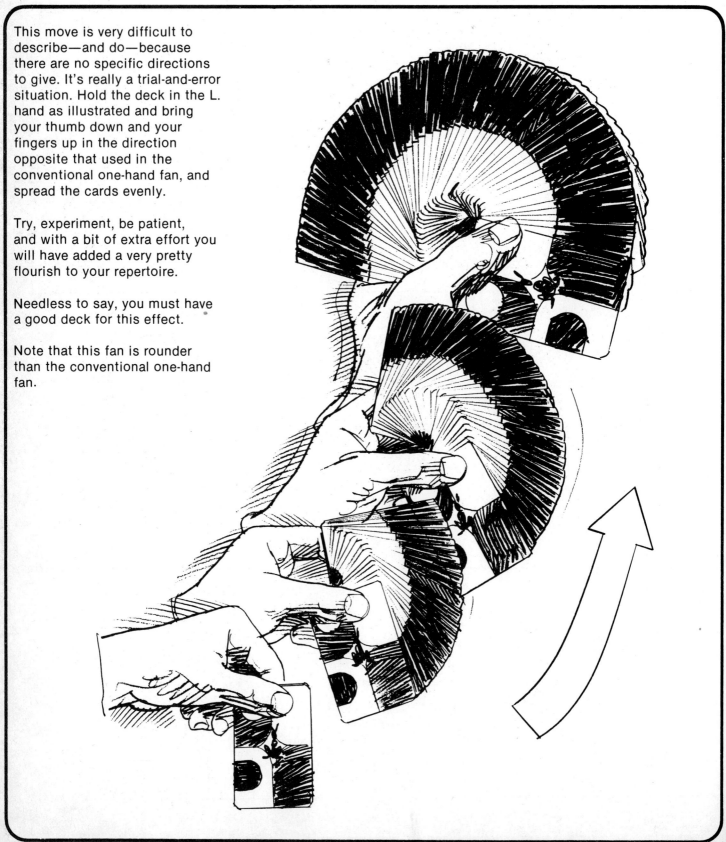

diminishing fan ★★

a pretty—and amusing—series
of fans for use in a routine

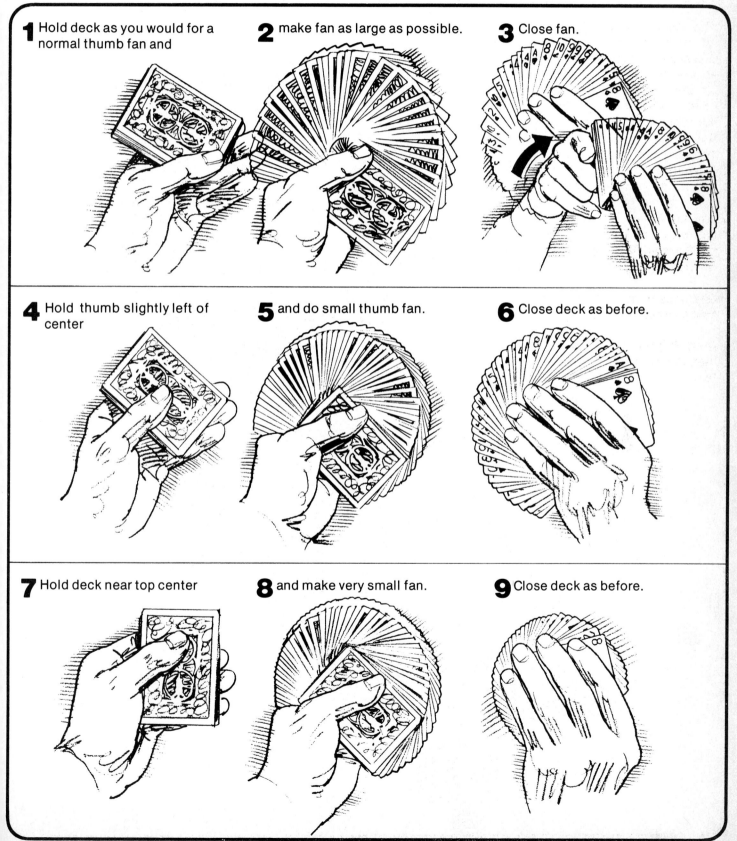

1 Hold deck as you would for a normal thumb fan and

2 make fan as large as possible.

3 Close fan.

4 Hold thumb slightly left of center

5 and do small thumb fan.

6 Close deck as before.

7 Hold deck near top center

8 and make very small fan.

9 Close deck as before.

twin fans ★★

*a pretty flourish, provided
it is done neatly and well*

Deck held in L. hand in position to
do one-handed fan.

Bottom half dropped on R. fingers,
which grasp cards in position to do
one-handed fan.

R. and L. do simultaneous one-
handed fans.

Backs shown to audience.

Fans raised, faces toward
audience, right-hand fan higher
and behind left-hand fan, and both
closed from top down and

squared away at the fingertips.

giant fan ★★

*with a nicely patterned, borderless deck
you can make a variety of beautiful fans . . .*

weave the cards

thumb fan just as you ordinarily
would, but be careful not to
knock any cards loose

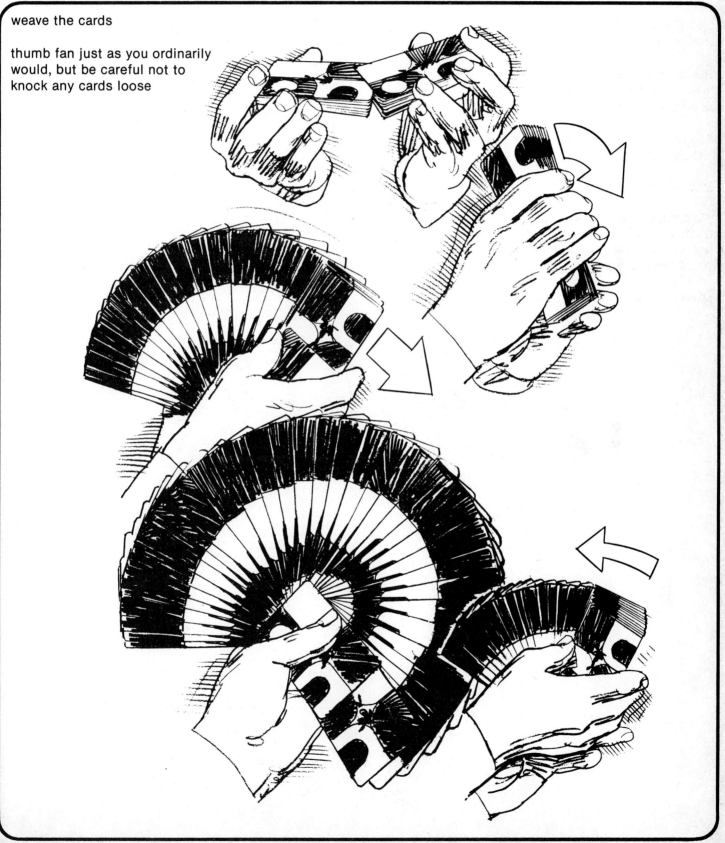

peel away fan ★★

fan changes color and is peeled into two fans

Make a thumb fan but spread only half the deck. Balance of cards are stacked at bottom of fan (see arrow).

Fan the stacked portion back over fan in counterclockwise direction.

To peel top fan away from bottom fan, place R. 1, 2, 3 and 4 on outside of fan, remove L. thumb, insert R. thumb between fans at bottom, and remove top fan, simultaneously replacing L. thumb. Replace top fan and close both fans as one.

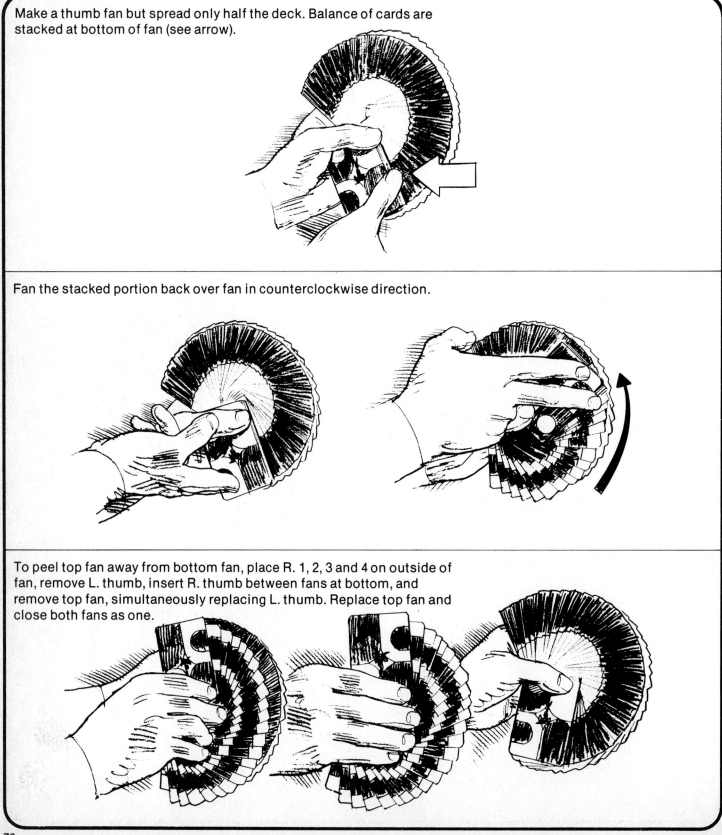

peel away fan in reverse ★★

*substantially the same color-changing peel-away fan as #1, but
reverse fan is made first*

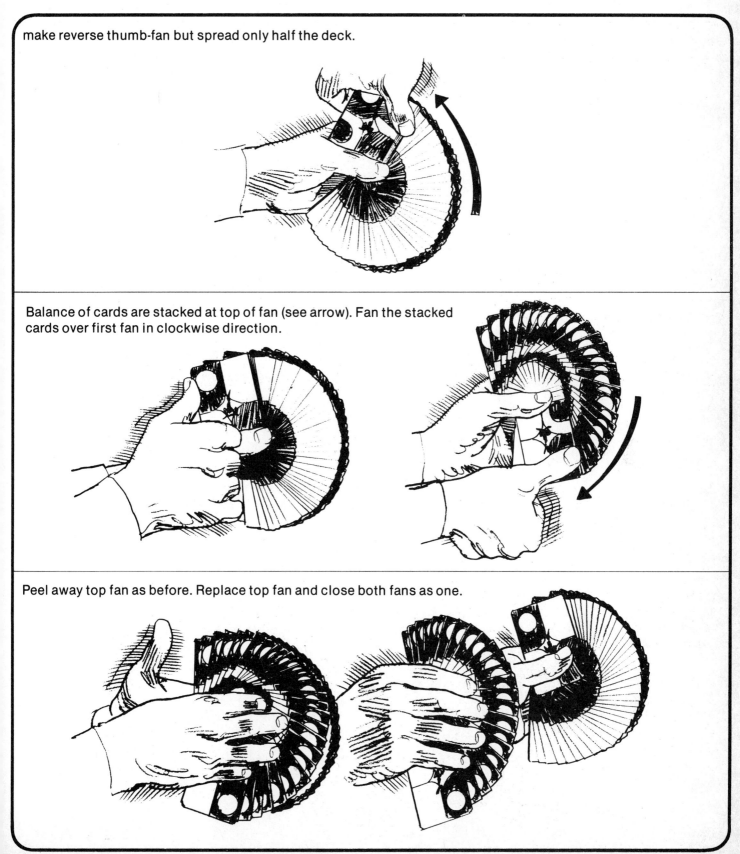

make reverse thumb-fan but spread only half the deck.

Balance of cards are stacked at top of fan (see arrow). Fan the stacked cards over first fan in clockwise direction.

Peel away top fan as before. Replace top fan and close both fans as one.

fan away pack ★★★

*A superb flourish for use during
an exhibition fan routine.*

1 Deck in L. hand.

2 L. thumb breaks deck in half.

3 R. grasps top half in position for one hand fan.

7 Once, and

8 once again

9 as shown.

as seen from the side

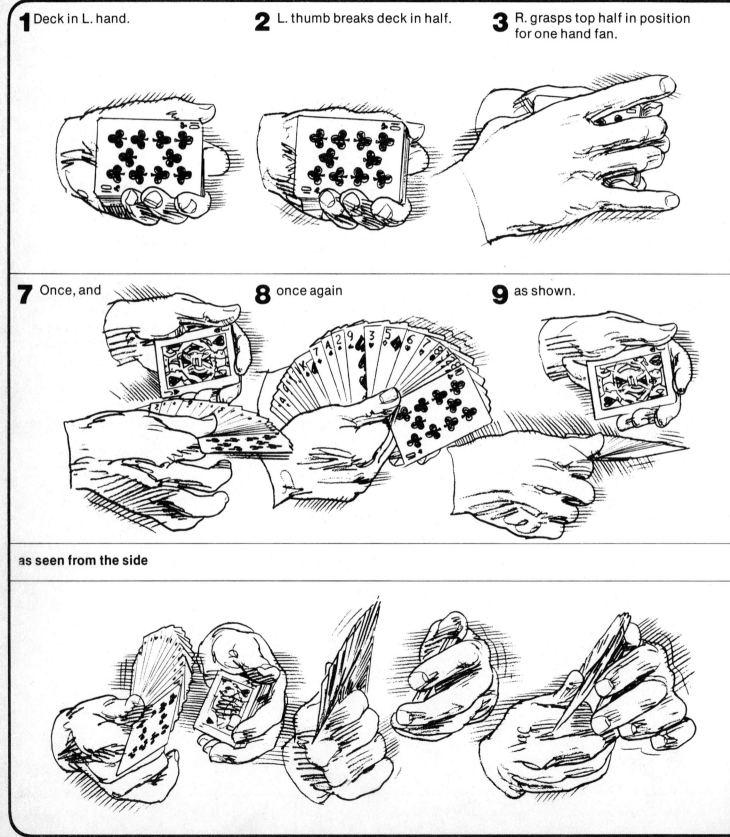

4 R. makes

5 one-hand fan.

6 R. fans pack in L. hand.

10 Fanning motion is repeated a third time, but this time, on down motion, pack is stolen between R. 2, 3, 4 and R. 1 and

11 L. is turned back to audience and fanned twice more by R. as

12 it turns over again and reveals pack has vanished.
At this point, fan may simply be closed or pack stolen for the production of more fans.

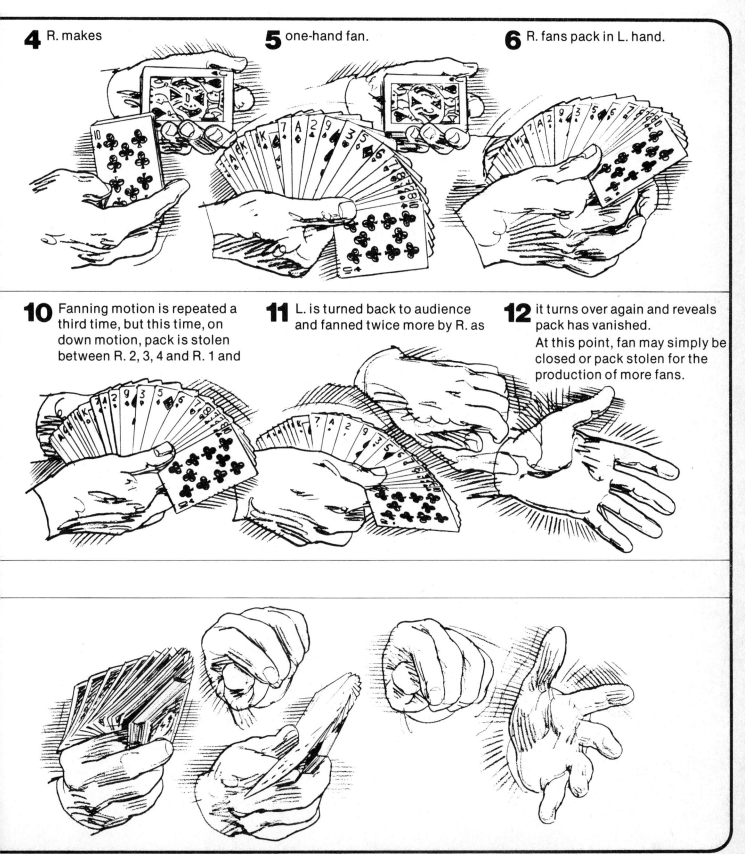

the waterfall ★★★

*a classic flourish, somewhat difficult,
but very beautiful and fun to do*

Object is to release the cards singly, in rapid
succession, so that they actually fall, one after
the other at about ¼″ intervals, into the
L. hand, which catches them in a neat packet.

Start with half a deck held in the R. hand between
thumb and R. 1, 2, and 3 and flex the cards inwards.

Hold the L. hand about 4 inches below, poised to
catch cards.

Release cards one at a time from the front by slowly
relaxing the pressure at the fingertips.

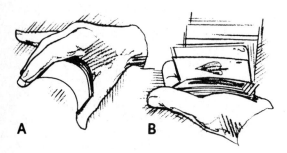

A   **B**

The cards should hit diagonally across the roots of
the fingertips (see B above) and fall forward, one on
top of the other, against the base of the thumb.

As your skills increase, lengthen the distance
between your hands until you are doing a foot or
more.

An alternate method of achieving greater distance
between hands is to start about 8 inches apart, and as
soon as the cards start to fall, rapidly increasing the
distance by raising R. and/or lowering L.
simultaneously.

Experiment. Try different positions, different cards
and different techniques until you discover the right
combination for you. If your cards are new and too
stiff or springy, press them inwards until they retain a
permanent bend.

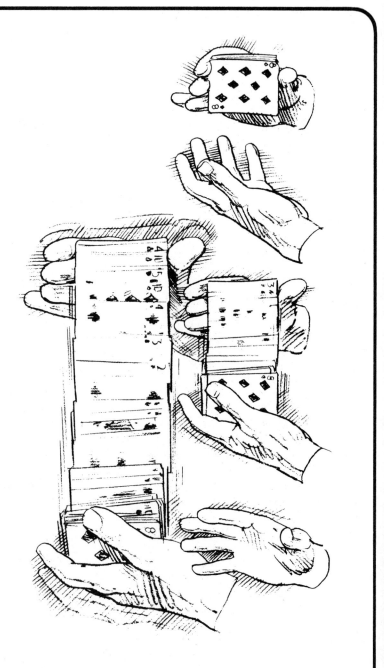

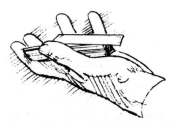

springing the deck ★★★

the most spectacular of the flourishes, this moves sounds as good as it looks . . .

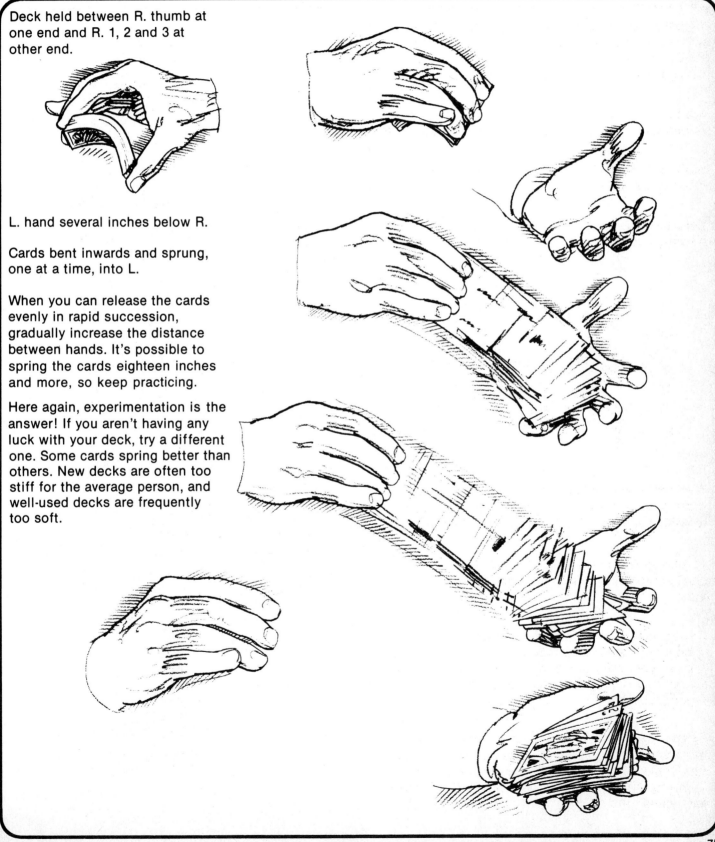

Deck held between R. thumb at one end and R. 1, 2 and 3 at other end.

L. hand several inches below R.

Cards bent inwards and sprung, one at a time, into L.

When you can release the cards evenly in rapid succession, gradually increase the distance between hands. It's possible to spring the cards eighteen inches and more, so keep practicing.

Here again, experimentation is the answer! If you aren't having any luck with your deck, try a different one. Some cards spring better than others. New decks are often too stiff for the average person, and well-used decks are frequently too soft.

charlier pass ★

the best known of the one-handed cuts once used to bring selected card to top of deck

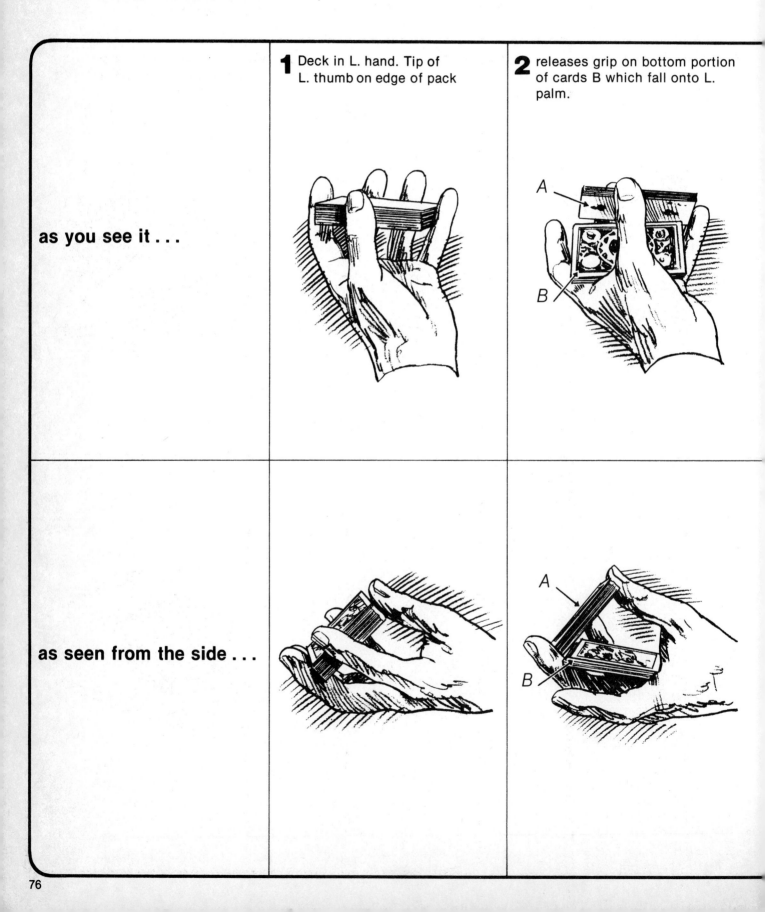

as you see it . . .

1 Deck in L. hand. Tip of L. thumb on edge of pack

2 releases grip on bottom portion of cards B which fall onto L. palm.

A

B

as seen from the side . . .

A

B

3 L. 1 pushes B up and

4 over A.

5 B drops on A and cards are squared in L., as in illustration 1.

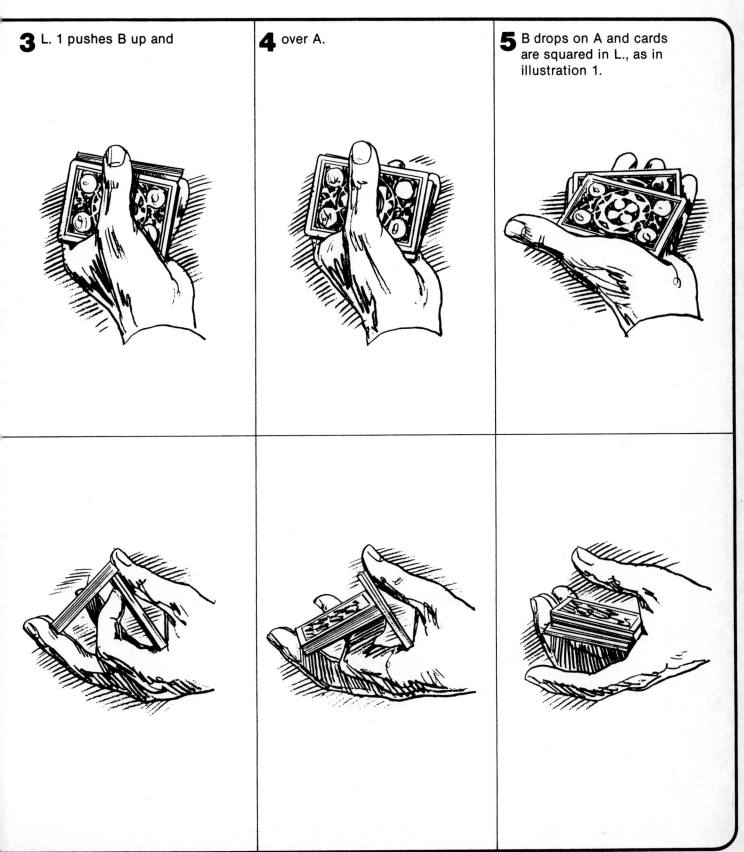

knuckle cut ★★

*a one-handed cut that looks good
but has no particular function*

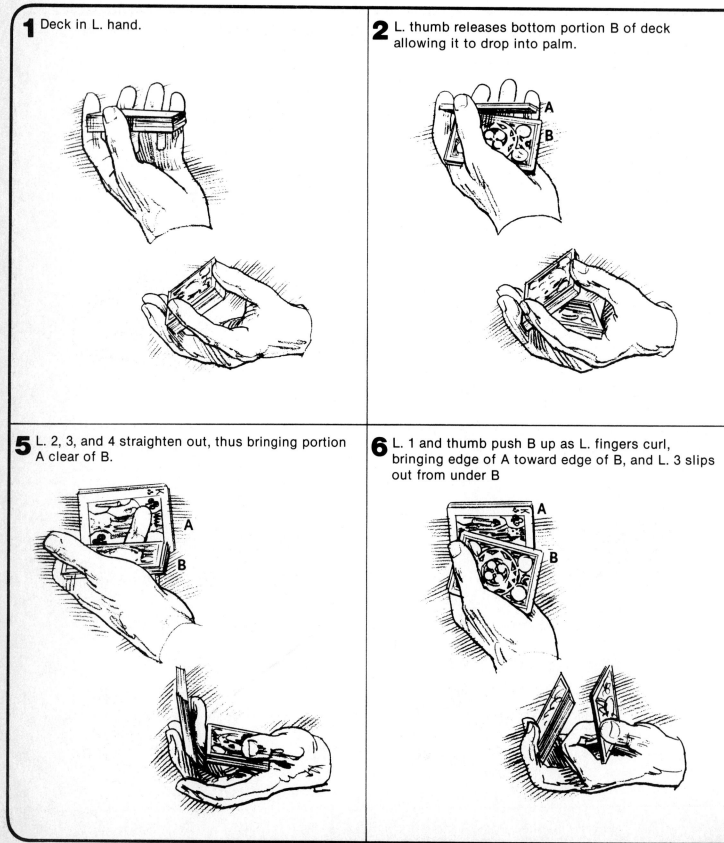

1 Deck in L. hand.

2 L. thumb releases bottom portion B of deck allowing it to drop into palm.

5 L. 2, 3, and 4 straighten out, thus bringing portion A clear of B.

6 L. 1 and thumb push B up as L. fingers curl, bringing edge of A toward edge of B, and L. 3 slips out from under B

start with half a deck, work slowly, deliberately and neatly, and no arm waving or wagging!

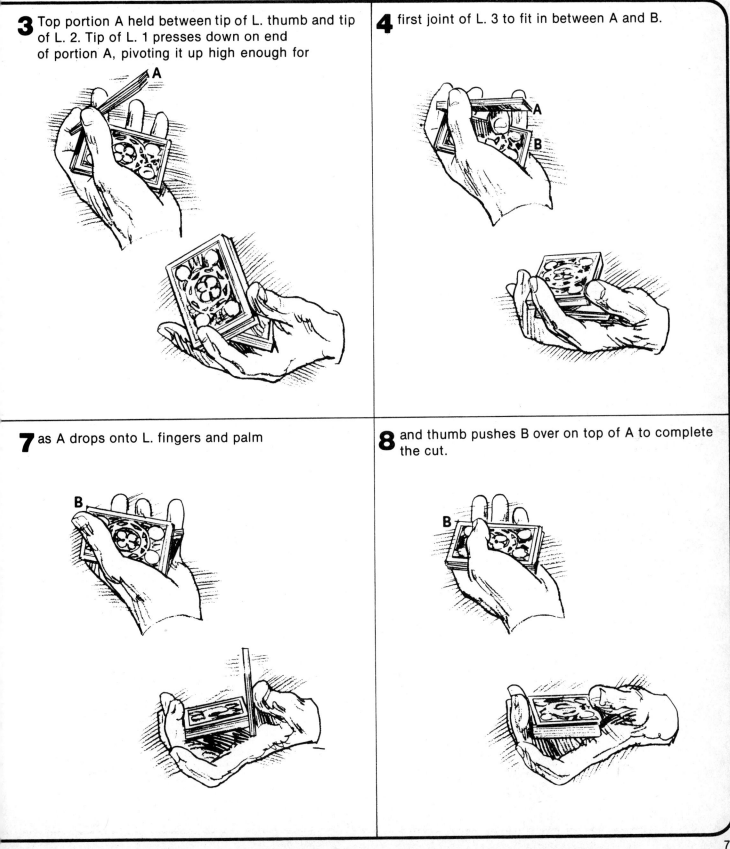

3 Top portion A held between tip of L. thumb and tip of L. 2. Tip of L. 1 presses down on end of portion A, pivoting it up high enough for

4 first joint of L. 3 to fit in between A and B.

7 as A drops onto L. fingers and palm

8 and thumb pushes B over on top of A to complete the cut.

a new changing card ★★★

*not easy to do, but a dynamite color change and
well worth the time and patience it takes to perfect*

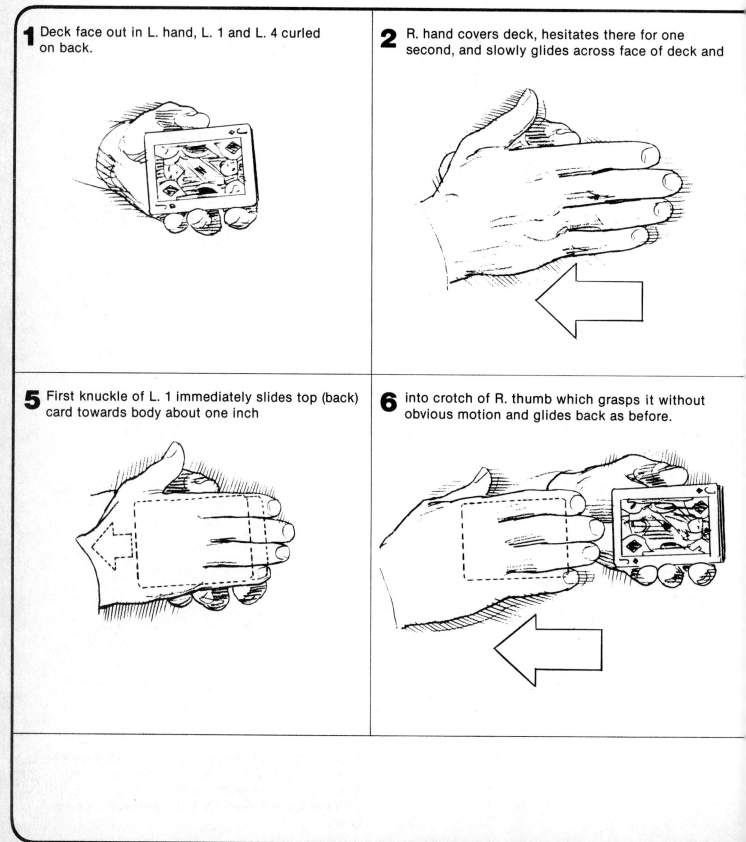

1 Deck face out in L. hand, L. 1 and L. 4 curled on back.

2 R. hand covers deck, hesitates there for one second, and slowly glides across face of deck and

5 First knuckle of L. 1 immediately slides top (back) card towards body about one inch

6 into crotch of R. thumb which grasps it without obvious motion and glides back as before.

3 back, again hesitating for a count of one over face.

4 Fingers curve slightly and hand glides down three inches below deck and up again, hesitating for count of one over face.

7 R. hand glides forward depositing card on face of deck, and remains there for count of one.

8 Hand curves slightly as before, glides down over deck, stops dead for the count of one, and slowly turns over to reveal that it is empty.

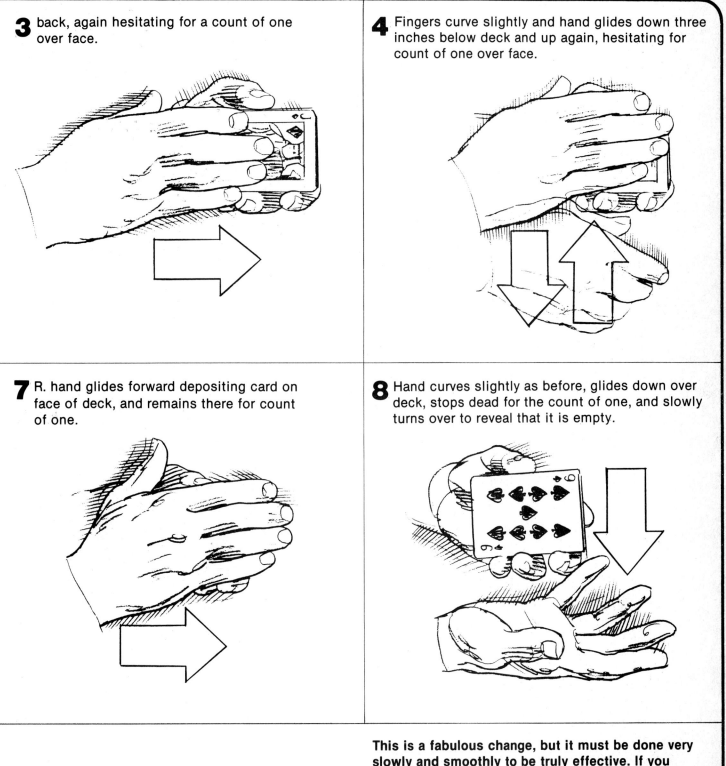

This is a fabulous change, but it must be done very slowly and smoothly to be truly effective. If you move your thumb when the card is picked up, the effect is spoiled. Smooth, fluid, graceful motions count!

card bits ★★

*little bits of business that
card men use to perk up their work*

snap change

Selected card is face down on deck, second from top. Turn top, indifferent card face up on deck. Lift top two cards as one at lower left corner and pick up with R. thumb on left edge and R. 2 and 3 on right. Bring R. thumb and R. 2 and 3 closer together, bending card inward.

Grasp card with tip of R. 1 at edge behind thumb and at same time release R. 2 and 3 with a snap. Bring R. 2 and 3 alongside R. 1 and pivot hand slightly to right, thus showing other side of cards which are still held as one. Place cards on top of deck with selected card face up.

The top, indifferent card has instantly, visibly turned into the selected card with an audible snap.

card count flourish

Deck held in position for dealing. L. thumb pushes top card slightly to right. Tip of R. 1 curls under top right corner and R. 2, 3 and 4 come to rest along right edge of card. Fingers straighten out and top card is turned face up.

rising-card bit

Selected card is on top of deck. Magician extends R. 1 and rubs it against his sleeve to "magnetize" it. He holds it on top edge of deck, raises his finger and selected card rises with it.

Back view shows how extended R. 4, unseen from front, actually makes card rise.

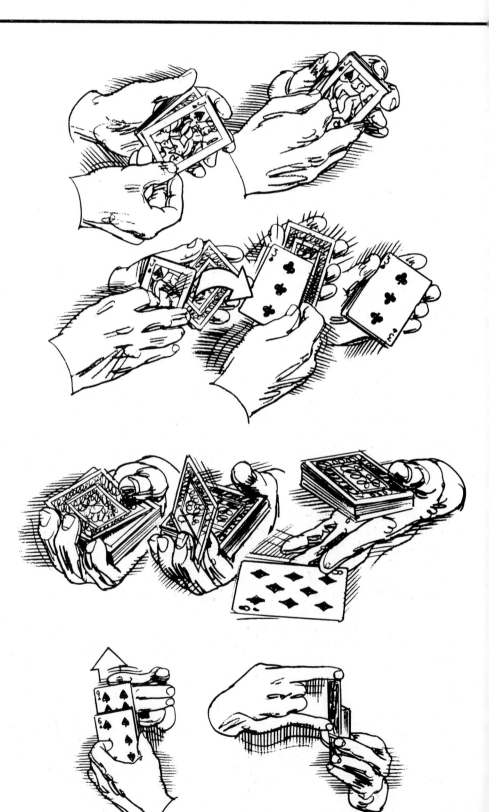

rising-card two

Selected card on top of deck, which is held the long way, face toward audience. Magician breaks an "invisible" hair from his head, mimes lassoing top card and pulls up on "invisible" hair. Selected card rises as though attached.

Back view shows action of thumb which makes card rise.

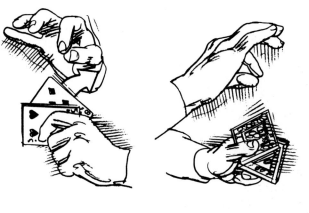

comedy cut

Ask someone to cut the cards. As they extend their hand to do so, sharply tap bottom portion of loosely held deck and bottom half will fly toward you. Catch in R. hand, place on top of portion remaining in your hand, and thank spectator for his help.

With a bit of practice you can get the cards to fly back in a neat package for a foot or more.

visible card change

Deck held in position for dealing. Selected card is second from top. Remove top card with R. 1 and 2 on top and R. thumb underneath card. Pivot R. hand to right, showing face of top card. As you do so, push selected card about an inch to right so that bottom right corner comes above tip of R. 3 and under tip of R. 4.

Say, "Is that your card?" and when spectator says "No," say, "That's strange. I thought it was," and pivot R. hand back to left, replacing visible card on top of deck and exposing the actually selected card to view.

the boomerang card ★★★

this is a cute bit, not particularly earth-shaking,
but amusing and fun when it's done well . . .

Magician throws card into air. It
arcs out for about six or eight
feet
and then boomerangs back to the
performer, who catches it.

Card is held like this and then
launched with a hook-type
motion.
Experiment until you get the
knack. It is possible to exert a
surprising amount of control
this way.

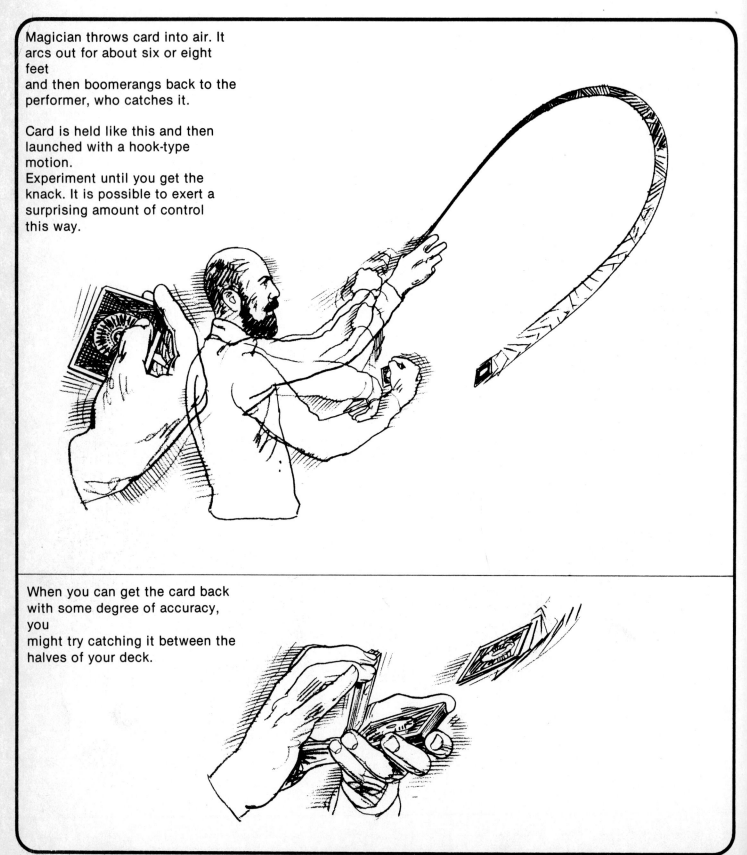

When you can get the card back
with some degree of accuracy,
you
might try catching it between the
halves of your deck.

card throwing ★★

*not magic, but a skill that card
workers frequently acquire*

The late illusionist, Howard
Thurston, used to throw cards
up to the balcony from the
stages of the largest theatres,
and, it is said, with amazing
accuracy. The secret is in the
grip. Hold the cards as
illustrated, bring the hand back
until the card almost touches
the wrist, and then straighten
out very rapidly like a taut spring
uncoiling.

Throw easily at first, release the
card on a level plane, and
follow through smoothly. When
you achieve fairly level flight you
can gradually increase the force
of your throws. In a short while
you should be able to throw a
card into a wall twenty feet away
with enough force to break the
card's corner.

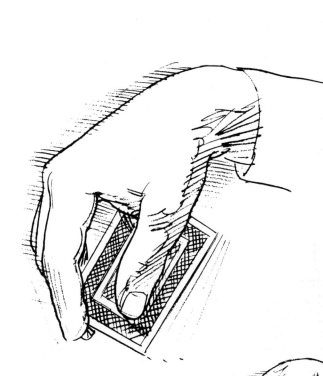

card spreads ★★

*very pretty flourishes, and easier
to do than they appear . . .*

Spread the cards in a straight line
or in an arc.

Spread the cards in one fast
motion, using the fingertips of R.
2 and 3 (or R. 1 if you prefer). If
your deck fans well, it will spread
well too. Don't attempt the move
if the table surface is too smooth.

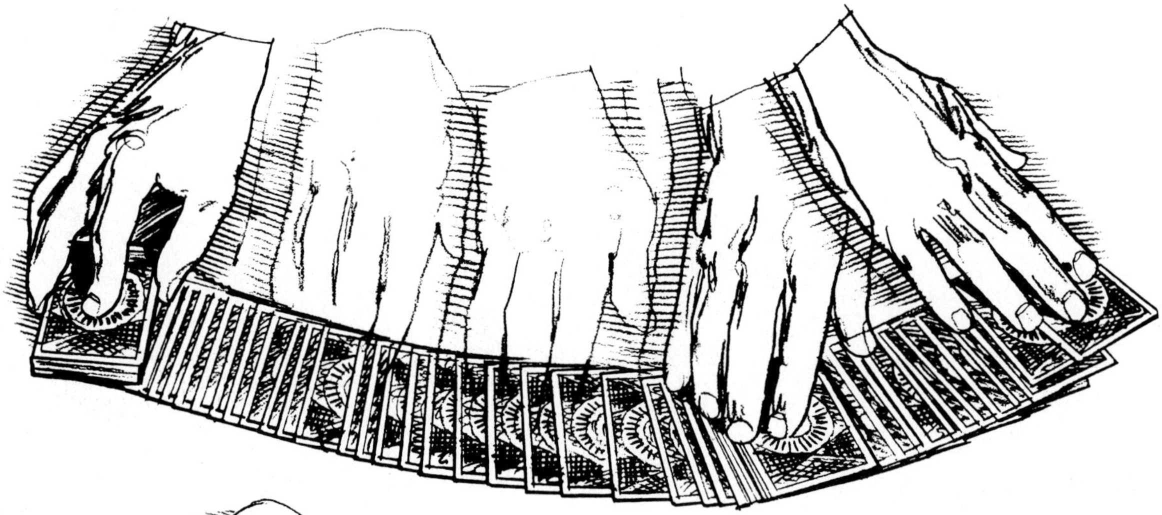

Turn over the first card
and the rest will follow. The
slower the turnover, the
prettier the effect.

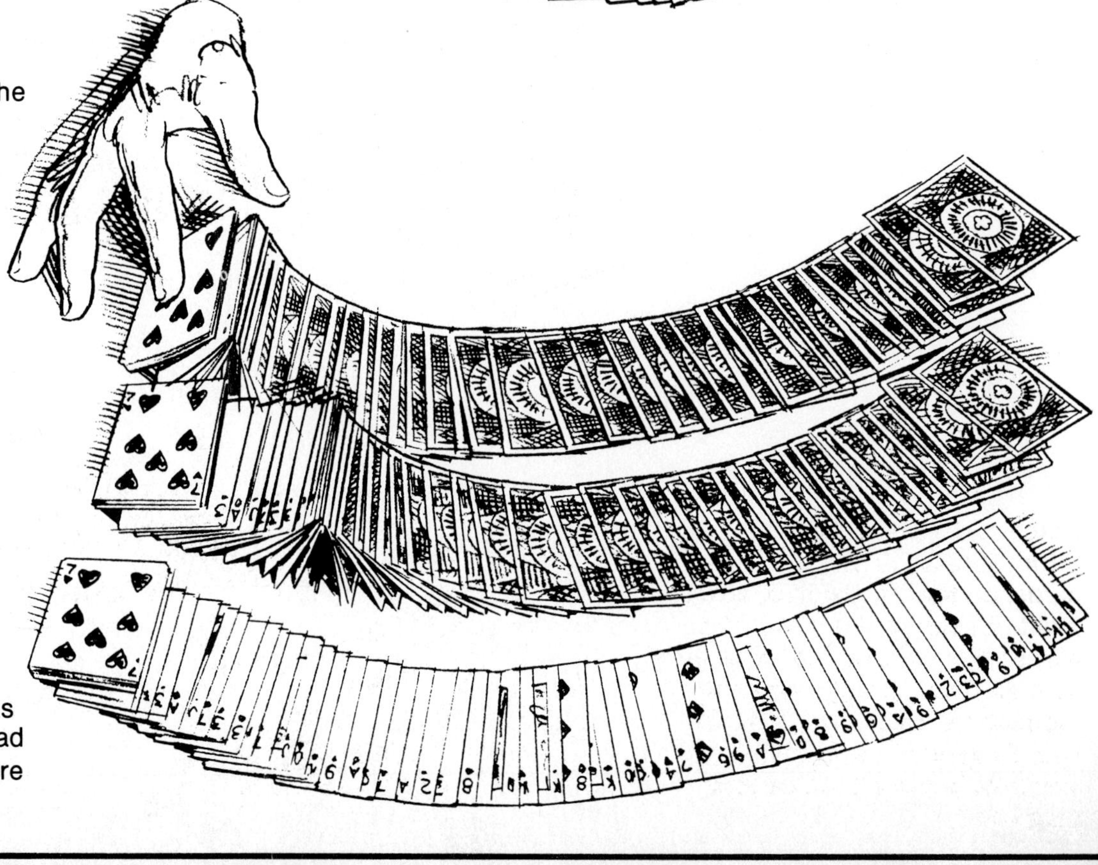

If you are doing card tricks
near a table, use the spread
to demonstrate that you are
using an ordinary deck.

When you spread the cards on your arm keep your wrist as straight as possible.

Do the turnover with your fingers.

Catching the cards isn't as difficult as it looks. Spread the cards, do the turnover and then position your thumb under the last card. Throw the cards clear of your arm with a slight upward motion, and then quickly shoot your R. hand forward and catch the deck in the crotch of your thumb.

back and front palm ★★★

the old-time classic, rarely used and not very practical
but a great move in the hands of an expert

first try this . . .

Card held between R. thumb and fingertips of R. 1 and 2.

R. I moves forward as R. 2 moves back toward wrist, thus pivoting card to this position.

R. 1 and 4 take positions at top and bottom of card

and thumb releases hold.

R. 1 and 4 move toward each other as fingers straighten out and

card pivots to back of hand, where it is clipped

between R. 1 and 4 and adjacent fingers;

now try that again, but this time . . .

execute a throwing motion . . . Bring hand about three inches down and about ten-twelve inches up as you do the above moves.

You have just made the card disappear, and quite effectively, from a few feet away. Now you can reach down behind your knee, recover the card, take your bows and quit while you are ahead, or you can leave the card behind your hand and continue with the back and front palm which goes like this . . .

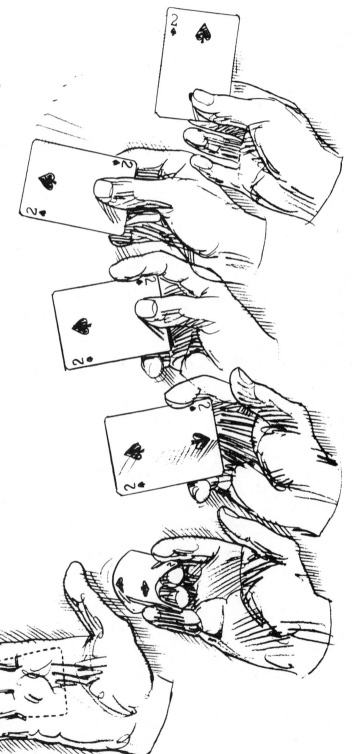

Fingers bend toward base of hand almost as though making a fist and thumb starts forward and

reaches well up on the card, and pulls it back into palm

as the four fingers uncurl and straighten out.

As these moves take place, hand slowly turns, to show empty back to audience.

Card is now clipped between R. 1 and 4 and adjacent fingers.

Once again hand turns over to show palm to audience. As it does so, fingers bend forward and

card slides to the back of the fingers, forced there by pressing against the heel of the hand.

Card is once again clipped on the back of the hand.

Work slowly and carefully observe all of your moves in a mirror. At first the card will be visible every time you turn your hand, but as you become more skilled, you will be able to make the adjustments in position and timing that will make the move quite invisible.

The telltale corners which may protrude between your fingers are difficult if not impossible to eliminate, which is one reason ("talking" is another) why you can't do the back and front palm too close to your audience.

Stage and club performers usually wear thin white cotton gloves when they do card manipulations. A skilled performer can work with fifteen or twenty cards and produce them from behind his hand singly or in fans, discard a portion of a fan while back-palming the balance, and perform other impossible machinations based on the back palm.

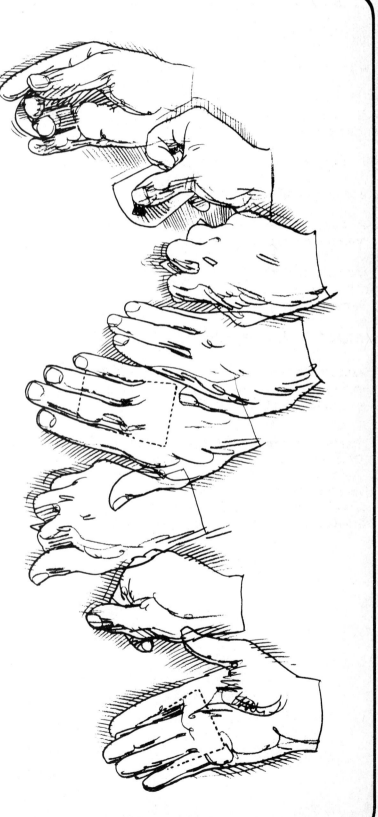

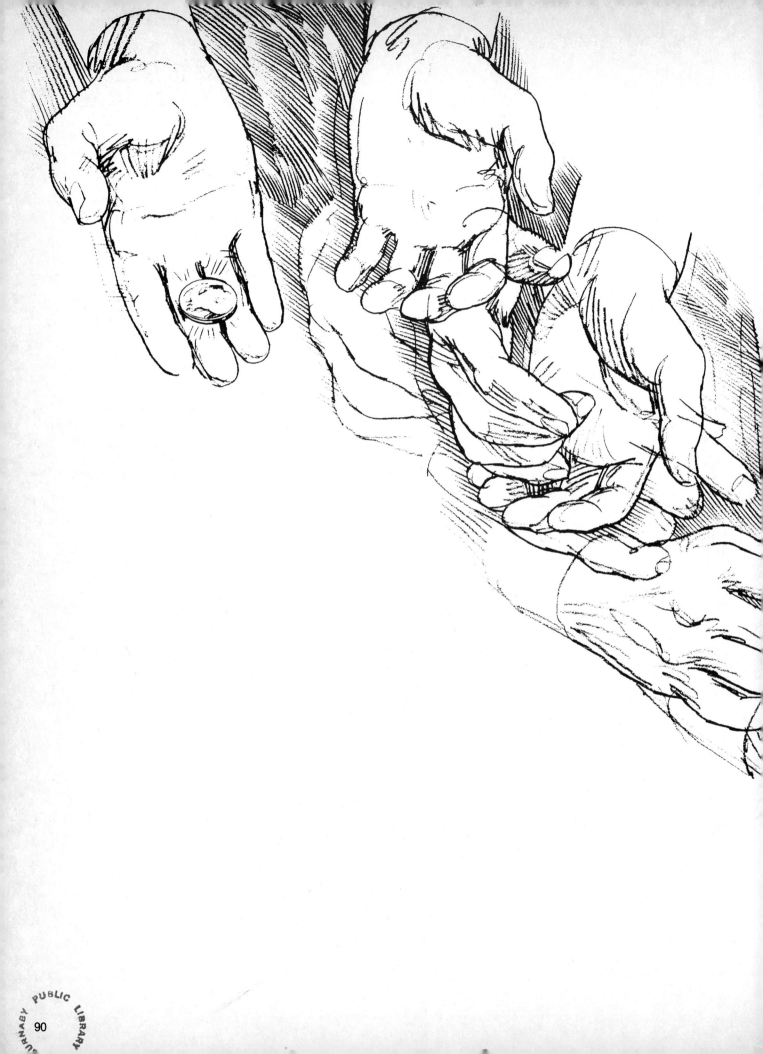

coins

Because they are commonplace—and hence innocent—objects, coins are the ideal medium for sleight of hand.

They are small, varied, immediately available, and they lend themselves to a wide variety of interesting effects, from simple vanishes and transpositions to the incredibly difficult back and front palming routines of the great King of Coins, the late T. Nelson Downs.

As long as he—or somebody close by—has a few pennies in his pockets, the good sleight-of-hand man will always have the props he needs to entertain and mystify.

palming ★★

finger-palm

The old reliable, and in most instances still the best, way to palm small objects.

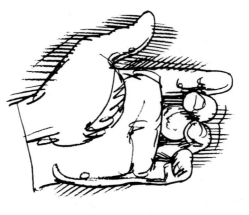

classic palm

Difficult to do well, but it does give you the freedom to use your fingers while palming a coin.
Sharply milled coins work best.

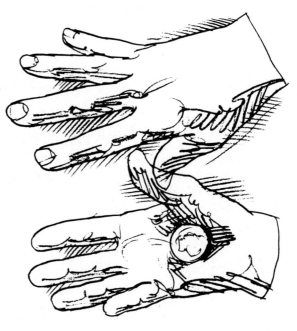

thumb-palm

Another old reliable that is particularly suited to a great many coin moves.

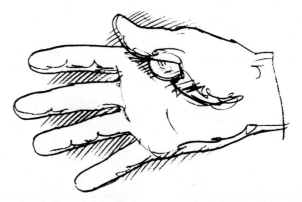

back and front palm

Not really practical and hardly worth the time and effort to perfect, but you should be familiar with it.

coin pivots on this axis

Use coins that are as large as possible, consistent with your hand-size. Half dollars have always been the most popular coins for manipulation, although there has been a recent trend toward silver dollars. Foreign coins are frequently used as well.

The English penny is the same size as a half dollar and traditionally used with it in "Silver to Copper" transpositions. The Mexican peso is a bit larger than our half dollar, the Canadian silver dollar is a bit smaller than our dollar, and there are innumerable foreign coins of every size and hue in between.

It really doesn't matter which coins you use, so long as you use them well.

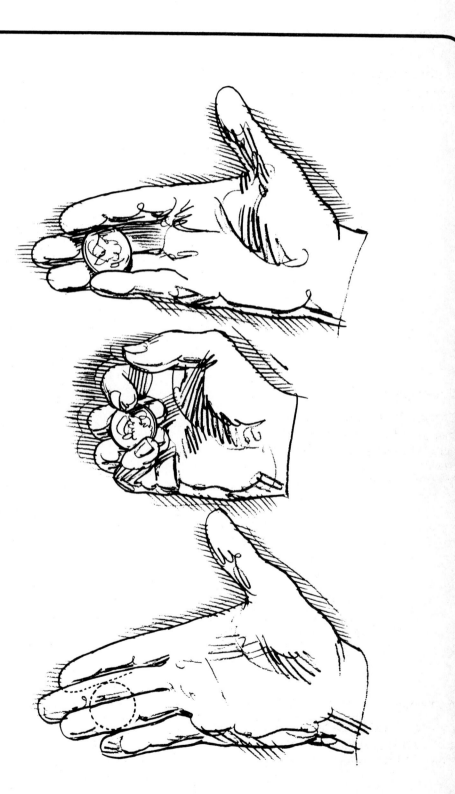

coin gimmicks

Although this book is primarily devoted to pure sleight of hand, there are gimmicks of various types which are widely used by adept sleight-of-hand men, particularly in the realm of coin magic. Following are some of the more popular gimmicked coins with which you should be familiar. Don't be deluded by the fact that because they are mechanical in operation, the need for skill is obviated. On the contrary. Anyone who has ever tried to slip an English penny into a shell half dollar silently can attest to the degree of skill (and practice) required.

hooked coin

A coin to which has been soldered a small hook by which it may be secretly attached to various parts of the clothing during sleight-of-hand routines.

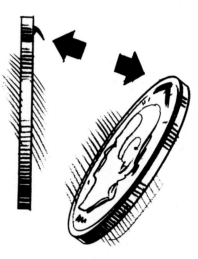

shell coins

Made from real pennies, nickels, quarters and half dollars, and used in vanishes, penetrations, the transformation of copper coins to silver, and so on.

double-faced coins

Two coins—most frequently an English penny and a half dollar—are turned down, soldered together and used in copper-to-silver transformations.

$1.35 trick

A vanish that occurs when a shaved-down dime
and quarter nest between two shell half dollars.

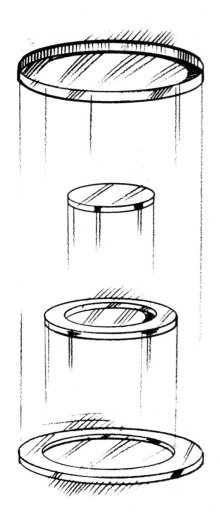

coin wands

A wand at the tip of which the magician can make
a coin appear at will. Used in the Miser's Dream.

dropper for single coin

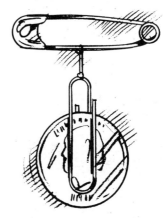

**Before you become involved in the use of
gimmicked coins you should master the basic
sleights with coins and other small objects.**

If you are really into coins, read *Modern Coin
Magic*, **358 pages of dynamite coin effects written
with love and dedication by J. B. Bobo, one of
America's really great coin workers.**

toss vanish ★★

probably the most natural and therefore one of the most deceptive moves for small objects

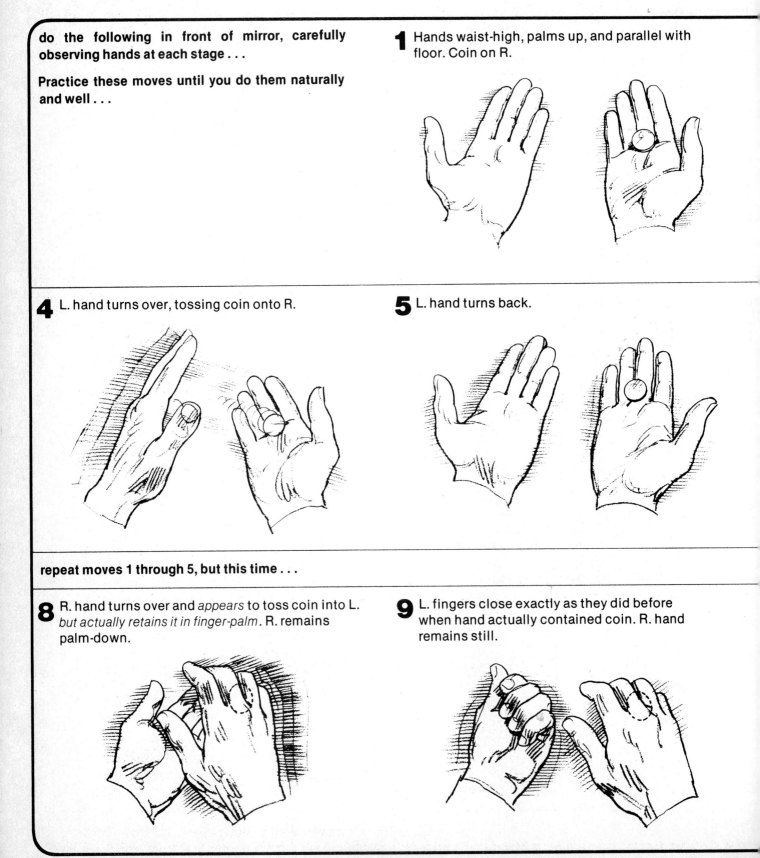

do the following in front of mirror, carefully observing hands at each stage . . .

Practice these moves until you do them naturally and well . . .

1 Hands waist-high, palms up, and parallel with floor. Coin on R.

4 L. hand turns over, tossing coin onto R.

5 L. hand turns back.

repeat moves 1 through 5, but this time . . .

8 R. hand turns over and *appears* to toss coin into L. *but actually retains it in finger-palm*. R. remains palm-down.

9 L. fingers close exactly as they did before when hand actually contained coin. R. hand remains still.

2 R. hand turns over, tossing coin onto L.

3 R. hand turns back.

6 R. hand turns over, tossing coin onto L. palm.

7 L. hand closes over coin.

10 L. fingers slowly rub together as though grinding coin away. At same time R. arm remains where it is or drops to side, depending on which is more natural for you.

11 L. hand opens to show that coin has vanished.

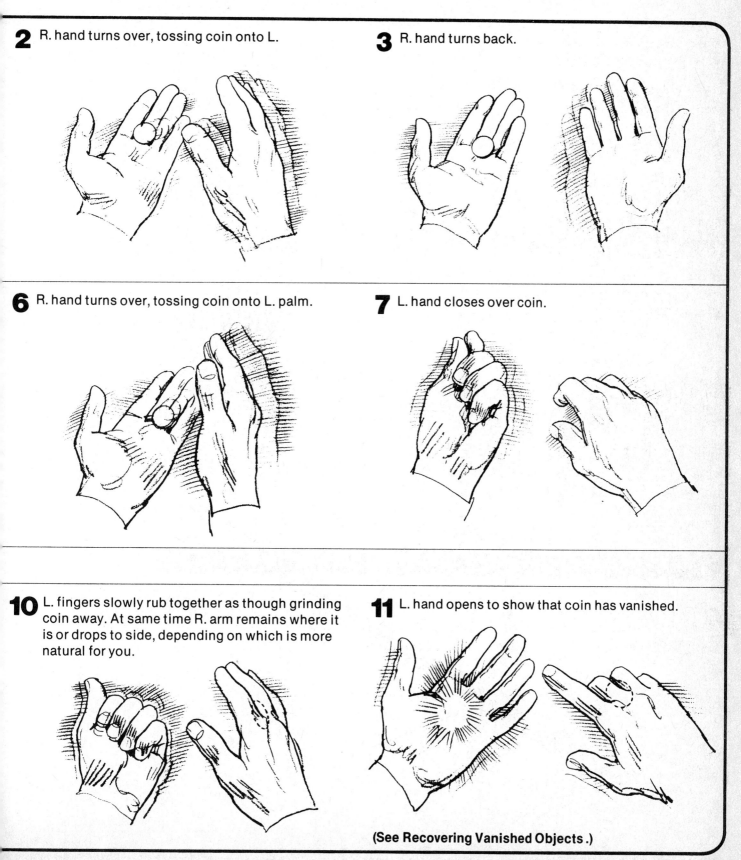

(See Recovering Vanished Objects .)

flick vanish ★★

a beautiful vanish, highly recommended by great coin manipulator Bobo, author of the classic Modern Coin Magic

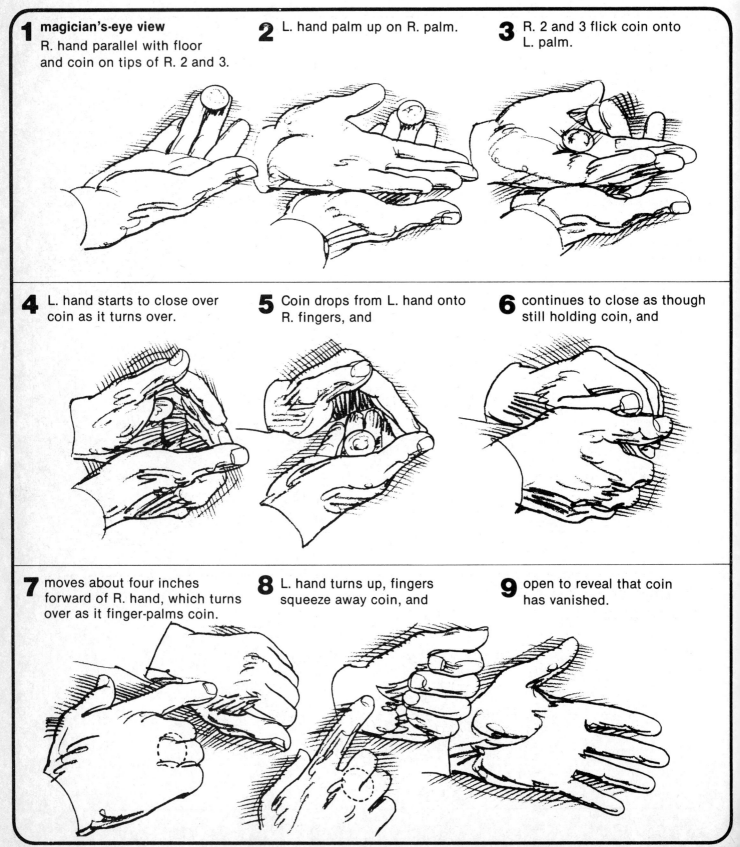

1 **magician's-eye view** R. hand parallel with floor and coin on tips of R. 2 and 3.

2 L. hand palm up on R. palm.

3 R. 2 and 3 flick coin onto L. palm.

4 L. hand starts to close over coin as it turns over.

5 Coin drops from L. hand onto R. fingers, and

6 continues to close as though still holding coin, and

7 moves about four inches forward of R. hand, which turns over as it finger-palms coin.

8 L. hand turns up, fingers squeeze away coin, and

9 open to reveal that coin has vanished.

multiple coin vanish ★★

*a super-convincing sleight for
vanishing several coins at once . . .*

Show several coins on R. palm. L.
hand is at right angles to and about
an inch below R.

R. turns over as in the Toss Vanish
(page 96) and throws coins in
direction of L. hand.

R. 3 and 4 catch coins *with a loud
clink* before they land in L. hand.

L. fingers close as though coins
have actually landed.

L. fingers rub coins away and
hand opens to reveal that they
have vanished.

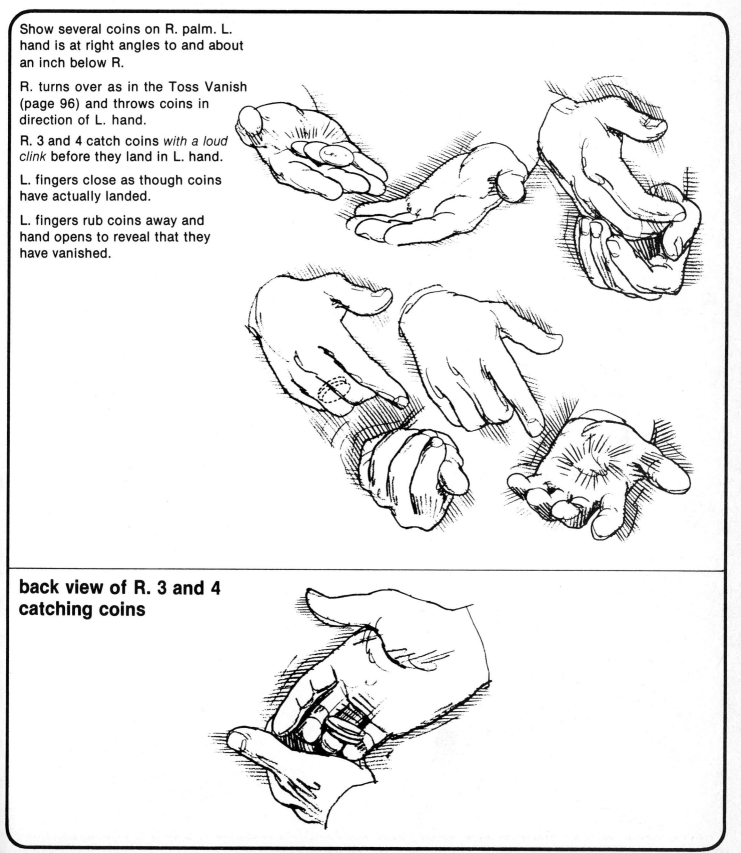

**back view of R. 3 and 4
catching coins**

coin switch ★★

*a basic and indispensable move
for anyone who works with coins*

Quarter is finger-palmed in R. hand. Half dollar is visible between R. thumb and R. 1 and 2.

Half dollar is tossed into open L. palm.

L. closes over half dollar, L. opens, and half dollar is removed.

Above sequence is repeated three times but on third throw quarter is released and half dollar is pulled into a finger-palm by R. 1 and 2.

L. hand closes over quarter, fingers rub together magically, and hand is opened to reveal that half dollar has changed into quarter.

When properly executed, this move is indetectable. It may even be done in the spectator's hand. Simply instruct spectator to close hand the instant he feels coin hit. Repeat the move twice and switch on the third toss.

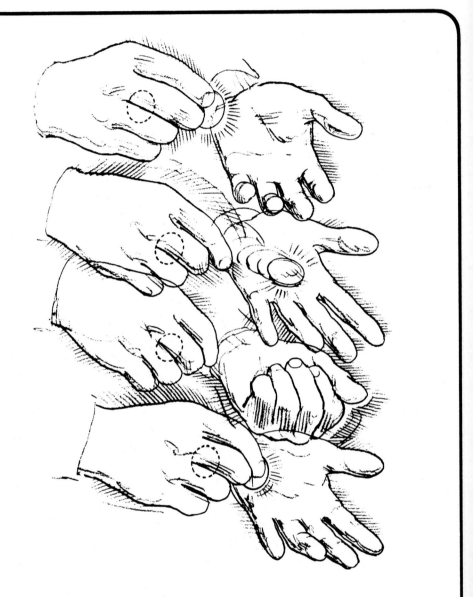

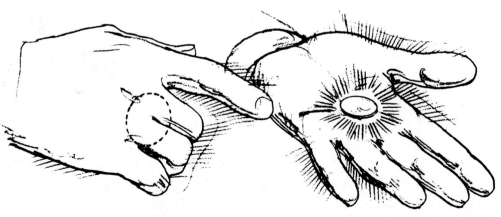

pocket vanish ★

*a simple, surprising, and virtually
indetectable vanish for a single coin ...*

Coin is held between tips of L.
thumb and L. 2.

R. hand passes a handkerchief
over coin.

Pass is repeated.

On third pass R. thumb and R. 2
secretly remove coin and
continue on as before without
hesitation.

At top of pass, R. fingers drop
coin into left breast pocket and
coin has vanished!

thumb-palmvanish ★★

*a neat, totally deceptive vanish that allows for a
great deal of digital freedom while the coin is palmed . . .*

1 Hands are waist height parallel to floor.

2 R. 1 and 2 start to fold in under cover of L. hand,

3 thumb-palm coin and quickly straighten out as

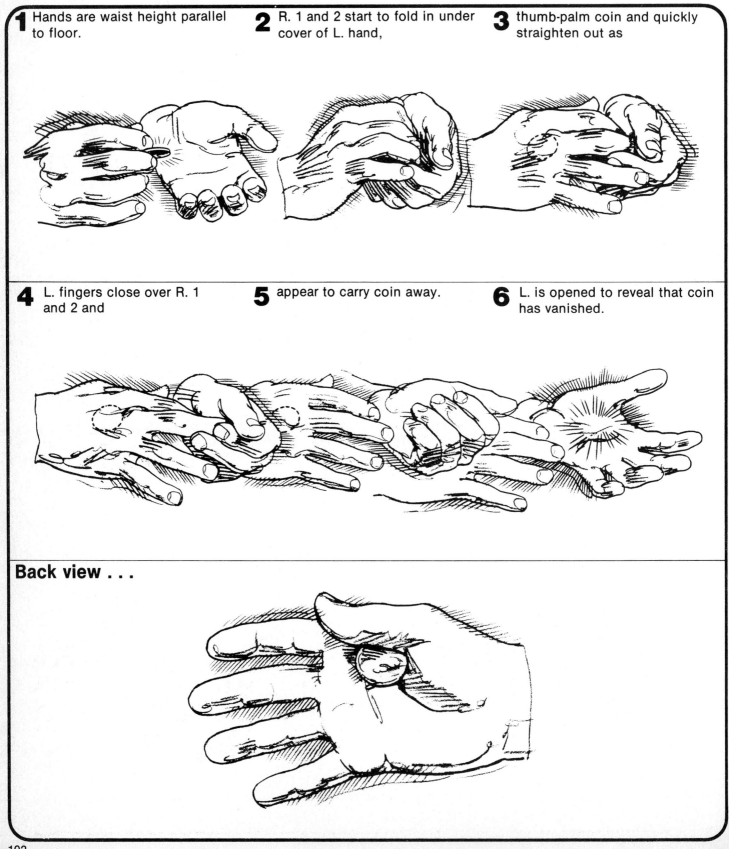

4 L. fingers close over R. 1 and 2 and

5 appear to carry coin away.

6 L. is opened to reveal that coin has vanished.

Back view . . .

thumb-palm switch ★★

*a neat and original way to switch
a coin*

This move is identical to the Thumb-Palm Vanish except that in this instance you leave a different coin in its place.

1 Coin B on open L. palm, and coin A finger-palmed by R. 3 and 4.

2 R. hand picks up B at tips of R. 1 and 2.

3 R. approaches L. and under cover of L. fingers thumb-palms coin B, and

4 at the same time R. 3 and 4 allow A to drop into L. fingers which are in the process of closing over what appears to be coin B.

5 L. hand opens to reveal coin A.

how it looks from behind

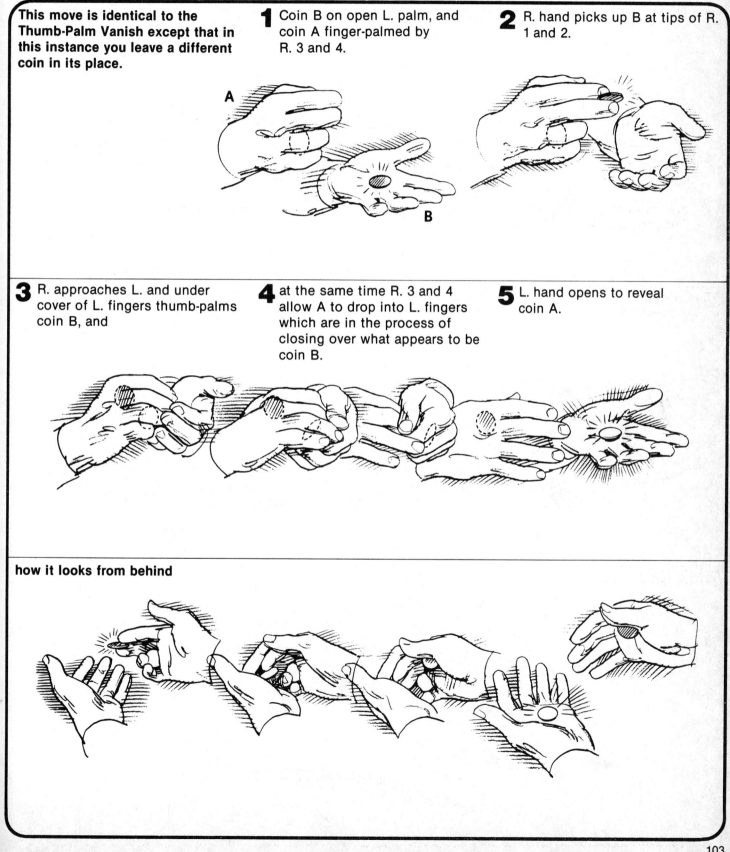

sleeving ★★

*contrary to popular belief, magicians
rarely use their sleeves, but there are moments . . .*

If you wear a conventional jacket
unobstructed by French cuffs,
you should have no trouble
sleeving coins, and eventually
perhaps larger objects as well.
Try the two methods below a
number of times, observe the
results in your mirror and
choose the one you can do
most easily and naturally.

first method

Coin on L. palm.

L. hand travels in direction of R.
and stops short.

R. hand travels toward L. at
same time and coin shoots into
R. sleeve.

L. hand closes and turns over.

R. fingers tap back of
L. hand.

L. hand turns up and opens to
reveal that coin has vanished.

second method

Coin on L. palm.

L. hand tosses coin about an
inch
or so above surface of palm and

R. hand travels towards L. and
scoops up coin in R. sleeve.

L. hand closes and turns over.

R. fingers tap back of L. hand.

L. hand turns up and opens to
reveal coin has vanished.

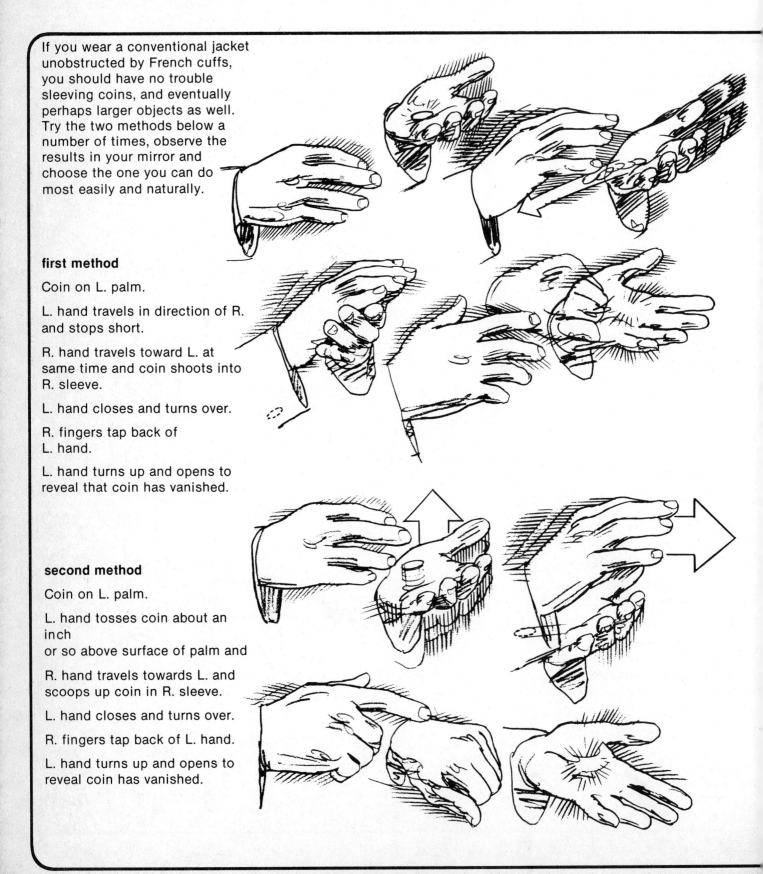

sleeve coin switch

Half dollar is finger-palmed in R. hand. As soon as quarter in L. palm is sleeved, R. drops half dollar in its place. Move continues as above, but instead of having vanished, quarter has changed to half dollar.

after the French Drop

after you can do the French Drop well, try this version . . .

After R. hand apparently takes coin, L. fingers, in process of turning over, drop coin down R. sleeve.

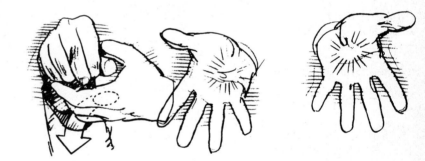

squeeze vanish

a small coin—preferably a penny because it has a smooth edge, although any coin will work—is held parallel to the floor between R. thumb and R. 1.

L. hand approaches, palm down, as though to remove coin.

Under cover of L. hand, R. thumb and R. 1 squeeze together and squirt coin into L. sleeve just as though it were a watermelon seed.

L. hand closes as though it has coin, turns over and rubs coin away.

L. hand is opened to reveal that coin has vanished.

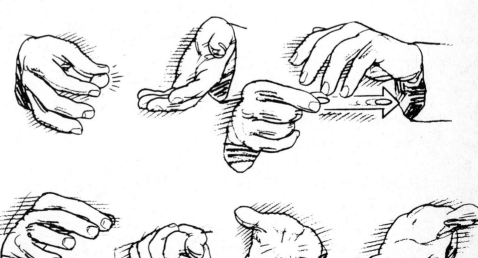

rising coin trick ★★

*a fantastic dinner-table trick that your audience
will long remember—and talk about*

the effect

Magician drops a quarter into a
glass of water and upon
command the coin slowly rises up
out of the glass.

required

A strand of black hair
approximately twenty inches long
and a bit of *magicians wax.

to prepare

Make a knot at both ends of the
hair and affix a small pellet of
wax to each. Press one pellet to
the top button of your jacket and
the other end to a half dollar
which you drop in the change
partition of your R. jacket pocket.

to perform

At the appropriate moment reach
into your pocket for the half
dollar, display it at your
fingertips, and slowly and
deliberately drop it into a full
glass of water which sits about
six inches from the table edge.

Without touching the glass, make
several mysterious passes over it,
your left thumb pressing down on
the taut hair, making the coin
slowly rise to the surface.

When the coin reaches the top, grasp it with your R. hand, scraping the pellet loose with your R. thumbnail and transferring the coin to your fingertips.

As the L. hand comes forward to show the coin—which may be examined provided no trace of wax remains on it—the pellet is dropped to the table and pulled back into your lap as the R. hand raises the glass of water.

note This effect, like many tricks, should be worked out to your own specifications. Some magicians affix one end of the hair to their cuff button, wrap the hair around their sleeve, and then affix the second end alongside the first. The hair is then ready whenever they need it. Others attach one end to a top vest button and the other to the bottom one, secure one pellet to their thumbnail during dinner, and then transfer it to the coin when they are ready to perform the trick.

Your personal preference, the clothes you are wearing and the degree of skill—and experience—you have aquired are all factors.

*Magician's wax always remains soft. It is available at magic supply houses or you can make your own by carefully melting a small quantity of beeswax over the stove and adding a few drops of turpentine (this is highly flammable, so beware) to it. Venice turpentine, available at art supply stores, is better. To make it black, add a few drops of India ink, or better still, melt in a bit of black crayon or black candle-coloring.

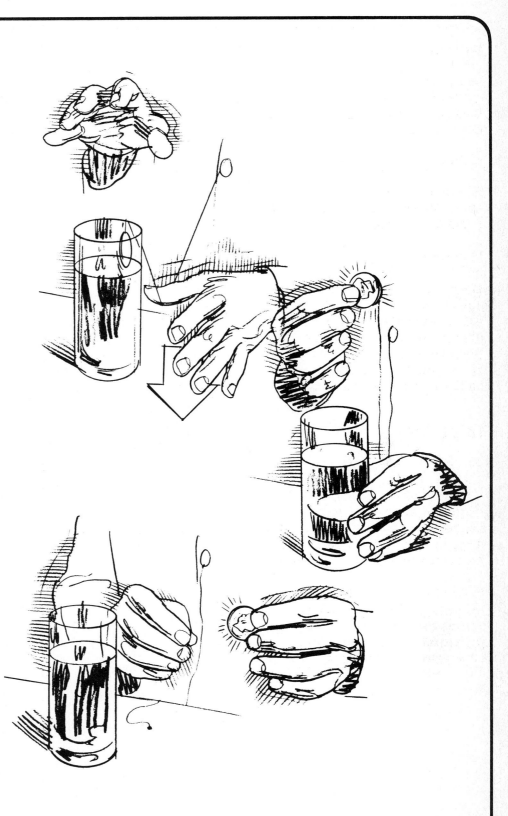

coin roll ★★★

*a neat, popular flourish, but like most good
moves, it takes a great deal of practice to do well . . .*

Coin is held against the inside of the hand by the tip of the thumb, which slides it up to the top of the hand and over the first finger near the knuckle, where it rests on the ledge formed by the first and second fingers.

The first finger pushes out slightly as the second finger pulls in, and the coin, momentarily gripped at the bottom edge by the first and second fingers, is half flipped, half pulled to the next ledge formed by the second and third fingers.

The second finger pushes out as the third pulls in, and the coin flips over to the ledge formed by the third and fourth fingers.

The gap between the third and fourth fingers opens and the coin is worked into it. The tip of the thumb pushes the coin up against the side of the hand and over the top of the first finger, where the sequence is repeated for as long as desired.

Work as closely to the knuckles as you can and keep your hand as fistlike in shape as possible.

If you have a small hand, a quarter will probably work best for you. If your hand is the size of the average adult's, however, a half dollar will be closer to your size.

Good coin manipulators can keep a coin rolling around each hand simultaneously, and some can keep several going at once.

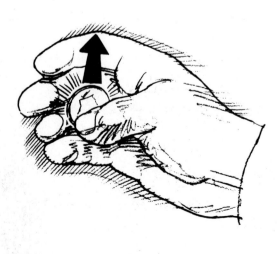

coin production move ★★

for producing a single coin at the fingertips, particularly during the Miser's Dream . . .

Coin is thumb-palmed in either hand.

First and second fingers bend back and grasp coin between them, and

quickly straighten out.

The first finger drops slightly behind second, shifting coin into a position more visible to your audience.

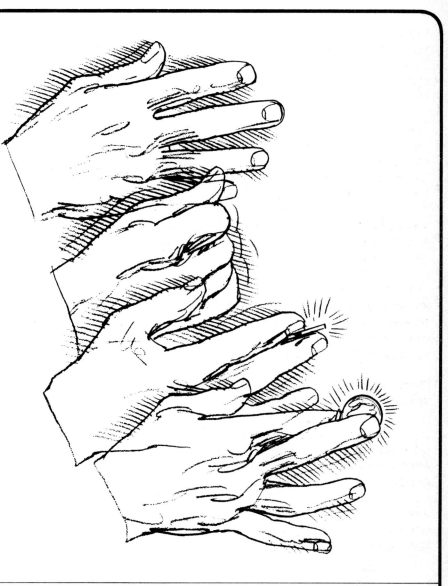

back view

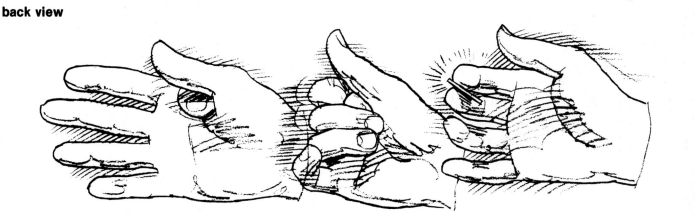

an impromptu coin routine ★★★

just one of an infinite number of combinations to give you an idea of the enormous range of possibilities

required

one half-dollar and one English penny or any other combination of coins you prefer

handkerchief

holder for a single coin

to prepare

Place the English penny in holder attached under upper left portion of jacket (or improvise your own method for readily securing a coin).

to perform

Show half-dollar and do the French Drop,

Rub the coin into your forehead and recover from your nose,

Do thumb-palm and recover from under L. hand.

Flip coin in air to show your audience you have nothing concealed.

Do Toss Vanish and reach under jacket to recover coin. Immediately steal English penny in finger-palm and come out with half-dollar visible between R. thumb and R. 2.

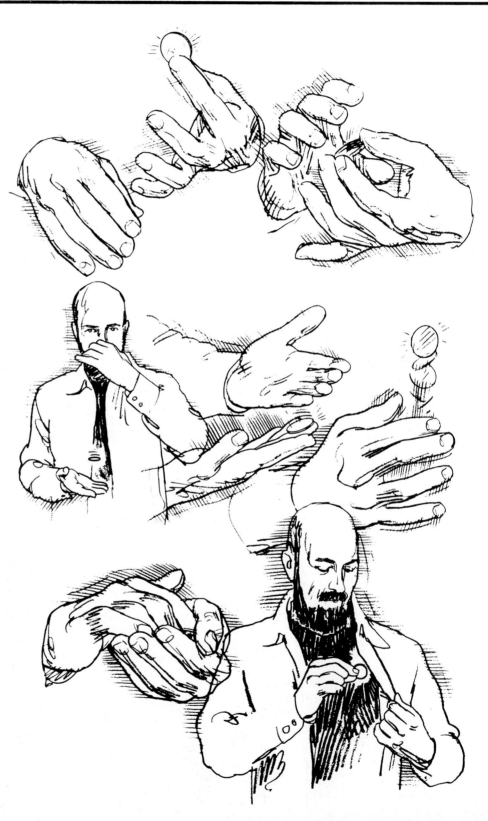

Do Coin Switch,
English penny in L., half-dollar
finger-palmed in R.

Do French Drop Switch,
but instead of showing that coin
in right hand has changed, keep
R. hand closed and place coin
(half-dollar) into right jacket or
trouser pocket and leave it there.
(Audience thinks you have placed
English penny in your pocket).

Show R. empty and produce
English penny from under back of
R. hand.

Hold English penny between L.
thumb and L. 2.

Flick handkerchief out of left
breast pocket and do
Handkerchief Vanish.

Show hands empty and replace
handkerchief.

the come back coins ★★★

a superb after dinner coin trick

the effect

Two half-dollars are placed in L. hand. Magician places third half-dollar in his pocket from which it disappears to rejoin the other two. The effect is repeated once more. On the third repeat the three half-dollars vanish completely!

to prepare

Place four half-dollars in your R. jacket pocket.

to perform

Reach into R. jacket pocket and visibly remove three half-dollars and finger-palm the fourth.

Throw the three-halves on the table in front of you.

Pick up one half-dollar with R. hand and throw on open L. palm.

Pick up second half-dollar with R. and throw on open L. palm secretly tossing the finger-palmed half-dollar along with it.

Close L. fingers over what appears to be two but are really three half-dollars.

Pick up remaining half-dollar with R., appear to place it in jacket pocket, but actually finger-palm it and quietly rest hand on edge of table.

Open L. to reveal that third coin has rejoined other two.

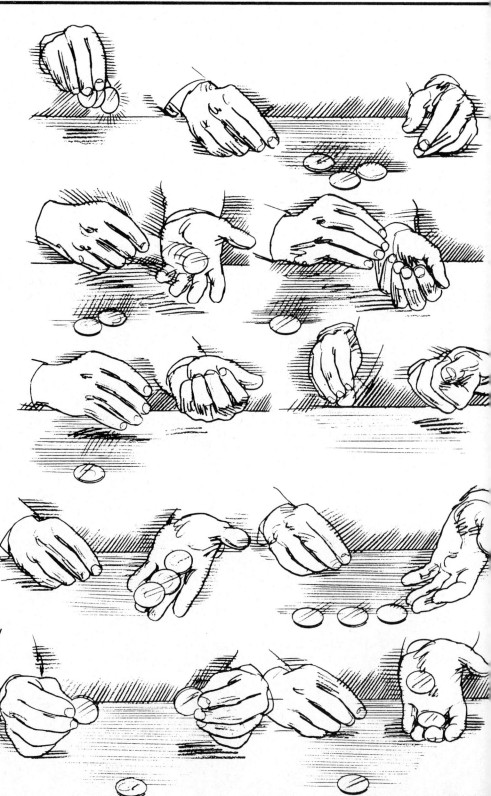

Throw three coins on table.

Pick up one half-dollar with L. hand and second half-dollar with R.

Throw second half-dollar onto open L. hand in position from which it can be finger-palmed.

Toss coins from L. (actually only toss one and finger-palm the other) onto R. hand.

Openly show two half-dollars on R. palm.

Make L. fist and openly place the two coins on top.

Allow coins to sink into fist visibly.

Drop third half-dollar in right jacket pocket.

Quietly rest empty R. hand on edge of table and open L. to reveal that coin has again rejoined the other two.

Toss coins on table.

Pick up two coins in R. hand and execute the Multiple Coin Vanish.

Pick up third coin with R. hand and silently drop it and the two finger-palmed coins in jacket pocket.

Open L. hand to reveal that all three coins have vanished!

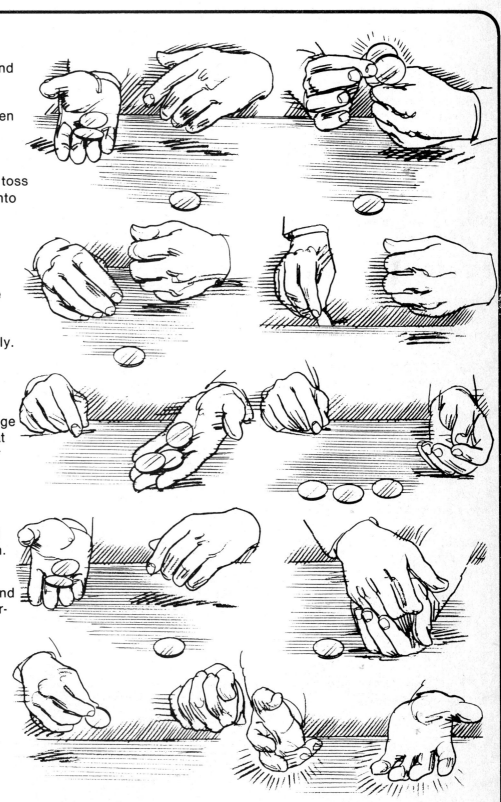

coins through table ★★★

one of the better versions of the
classic coins-through-table trick . . .

This effect is performed at the dinner table, and ideally, with a napkin accross your lap.

Place four half dollars, yours or borrowed, on the table. (If your hands are small, use quarters.)

Place coins, one at a time, onto L. palm, last coin at edge of hand, as illustrated, counting "One, two, three, four" as you do so.

Close L. fingers over coins and bringing hand back toward edge of table, point R. 1 and say "Four coins here."

Turn L. hand over and point L. 1 at empty R and say, "Nothing here." At this instant release grip on fourth coin and allow it to fall into your lap.

Immediately raise your L. fist over the table and place your R. hand under table, quickly picking up the coin from your lap on the way.

Say, "Watch closely," and slap L. hand onto table. A split second later, snap coin against underside of table with R. fingers.

Raise L. hand and say, "Three coins here." Bring R. out from under table, throw coin to right of other three and say, "And one coin right through the table."

Scoop up three coins with L. and drop them into R. hand placing first coin in position for finger-palm and next two more or less on palm, counting "One, two, three" as you do so.

Turn R. over, tossing two coins into L. and secretly retaining third in finger-palm in R.

Hold L. fist over table as before, immediately pick up coin on table with R., and place hand under table.

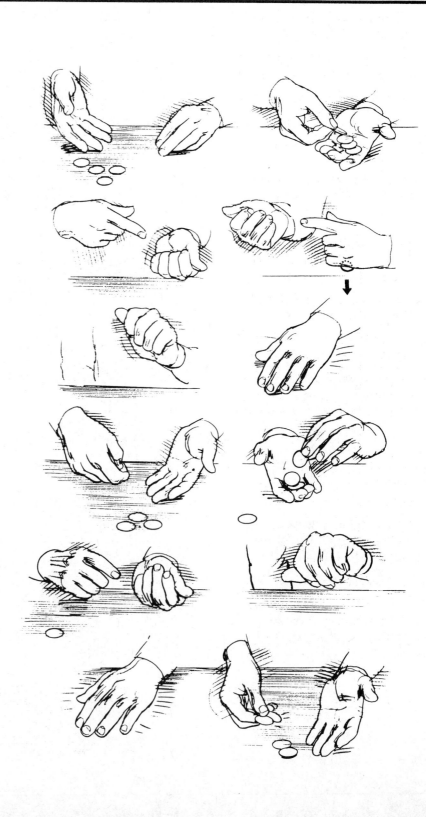

114

Slap L. on tabletop, raise hand and say, "Two coins here."

Bring R. hand out from under table and say, "And two coins here."

Place four coins on edge of table.

Pick up one coin with R. and say, "One." Place it on top of coin to left and say, "Two."

Pick up farthest left coin with L. hand and say, "One." Place it on top of remaining coin and say, "Two," but in process of drawing both coins up and into hand, let bottom coin slide off table into your lap.

Slap L. on tabletop, raise it and say, "One coin here."

Bring R. out from under table and say, "And three coins here."

Pick up last coin with R., do Toss Vanish, apparently tossing coin into L. hand but actually retaining it in R. finger-palm.

Hold empty L. fist over tabletop. Pick up three coins with R. and along with finger-palmed fourth, head under table.

Slap left hand down on tabletop and loudly snap one coin against underside of table with R.

Raise L. hand and show nothing underneath it.

Bring R. from under table and throw all four coins down on tabletop.

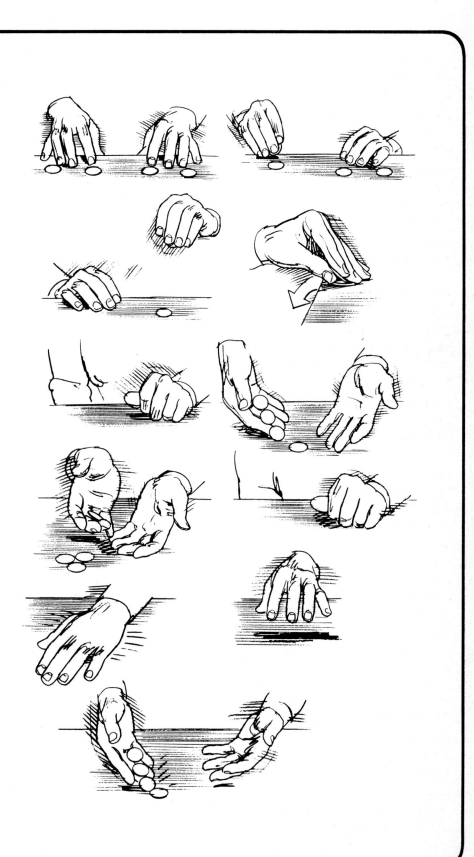

the miser's dream ★★

*the classic coin trick, and still going
strong after 140 years or more*

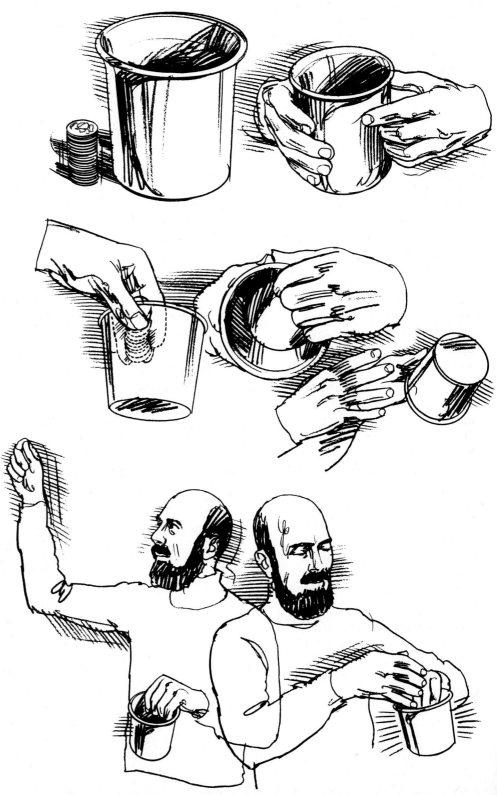

the effect

Magician rolls back his sleeves,
displays an empty bucket, and
produces dozens of coins at his
fingertips, which he tosses into
the bucket with resounding
"clangs."

required

About fifteen roughly half-dollar-
sized coins and a receptacle to
throw them in. A wine bucket, or
anything similar, preferably of
metal, will do.

preparation

Bucket on table and stack of
coins behind it.

basic routine

Magician removes bucket from
table and in process steals stack
of coins in L. hand. He displays
inside of bucket, and grasping it
by rim with L. hand, sets stack of
coins against inside edge, and
displays outside.

He spots something in the air,
reaches up with his R. hand,
catches the object and tosses it
into the bucket with a clang.

(Actually, he only appeared to
catch something. In reality he
allowed one coin from the stack
in the bucket to drop to the
bottom at the same instant he
tossed his "catch" into it.)

He reaches into bucket and
retrieves coin, which he displays.
He then appears to toss it back in
the bucket but actually thumb-
palms it, allowing a second coin
from the stack to drop, thus
making it sound as though he
tossed in the coin.

He reaches behind his elbow for another, in the air for a third, and so on, appearing to toss each into the bucket but actually thumb-palming the same coin and allowing another to fall from the stack at the precise moment.

He continues in this fashion until all the coins are gone.

Note In actual practice the routine is usually enlivened considerably. For example, the magician might call a young assistant from the audience and produce coins from his—or her—elbows, ears, etc. He might have his young assistant reach into the air for a coin and toss it into the bucket. (He releases a coin into the bucket at the appropriate moment completing the illusion.)

He could steal a stack of coins from a dropper under his coat jacket, and holding his hand up to his assistant's nose, could allow the whole stream of coins to cascade noisily into the bucket.

From time to time he could reach into the bucket to stir up the coins, stealing several in the process, which he could then produce at his fingertips and visually toss into the bucket, singly or as a group.

Frequently the magician appears to toss a coin high into the air, only to have it clank into his bucket in a delayed reaction some seconds later, to his apparent surprise.

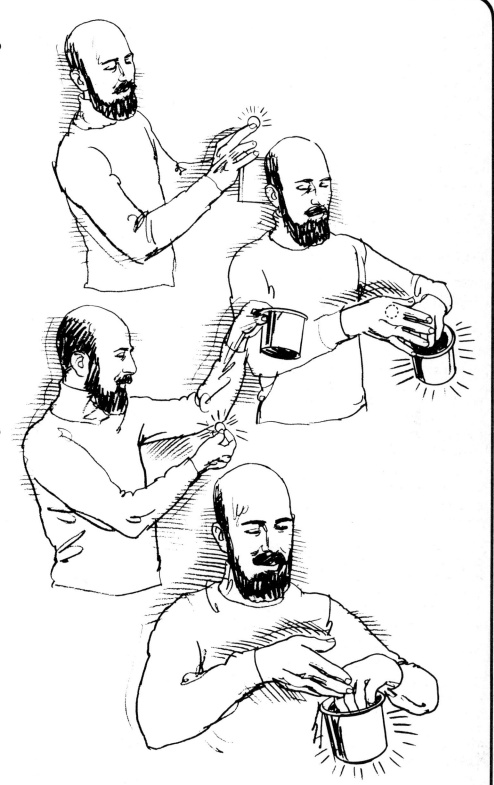

balls

Big, little, soft, hard . . . from the Cups and Balls of prehistory to Cardini's beautiful Billiard Ball routine, from the elusive pea tucked away under the shell to the giant cannonball the magician of old used to produce from a hat, sleight-of-hand men have always been partial to balls, and here, to maintain that tradition, are a number of sleights and routines to get you started.

balls and ball gimmicks

wooden balls

The balls generally used for the Multiplying Billiard Ball trick and other effects are turned wood, brightly enameled (red is the most popular and also the most visible color), and are made in 1¼", 1½", 1¾" and 2" diameters. They look and sound much more convincing than plastic, but they frequently chip when dropped, so put some padding over the floor when practicing.

foil balls

For practice or for show, crumple an 8"x12" sheet of aluminum kitchen foil into a ball about 1" in diameter. You can increase the size as you grow more skillful . . . and more daring. Foil balls are light, cheap, easy to handle, look well, and you have an inexhaustible supply on the kitchen shelf right now.

sponge balls

Sponge balls, used for close-up effects (and sometimes the Cups and Balls), are made of coarse sponge rubber or plastic. You can make your own with a pair of scissors. Snip carefully, make them as round as possible, and all the same size.

cork balls

White-painted cork balls approximately ⅞" in diameter are frequently used for the Cups and Balls. They are lightweight and easy to work with, but unless handled carefully, they have a tendency to talk.

droppers

Magicians "steal" balls from "droppers" of various types. They are secreted under the jacket in various convenient locations, either pinned or sewed in, and can be homemade or purchased from any good magical supply house. Cloth types are better because after balls are stolen, the dropper lies flat and is therefore less conspicuous.

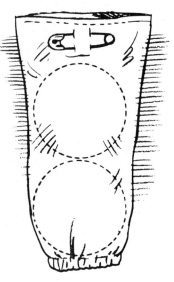

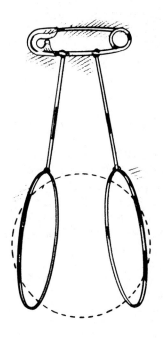

shell

This is the gimmick that makes the Multiplying Billiard Ball trick the amazing effect that it is. Generally stamped out of metal but sometimes turned out of wood, the shell fits over a ball, is painted the same color, and from the front, can't be distinguished from a solid ball.

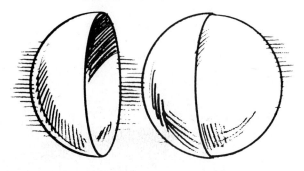

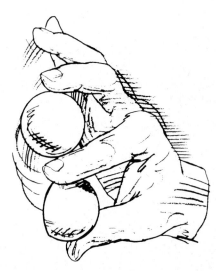

palming balls ★★

The essence of all sleight of hand is the ability to secrete (palm) an object in your hand unseen by your audience. In order to do that successfully, your hands have to look just as natural when they are palming an object as when they are not. Learn to hold—and use—your hands pretty much the same way in either case, and it will never occur to your audience that you are concealing something from their view.

Once you get the hang of it, you will be able to palm fairly large objects with confidence and ease.

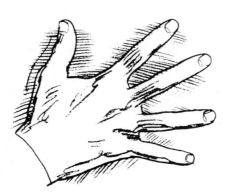

not this

or this

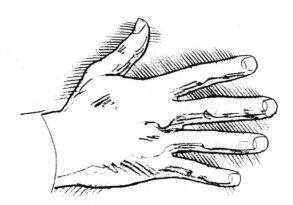

but naturally, like this

classic palm

The ball is held in palm of either hand, where slight pressure from the fleshy pad of the thumb holds it in place. This palm is used during certain effects where the fingers must be free to manipulate while the object is palmed.
If your hands are especially dry, you will find it difficult to grip smooth objects. A few dabs of glycerine will frequently lubricate and soften the skin sufficiently.

Relax, don't hold your arms stiffly, don't sneak glances at your hands, and don't distort your fingers!

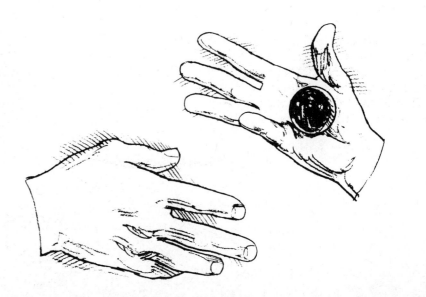

finger-palm

Hold the ball at the base of your fingers and always keep the back of your hand toward the audience. Bear in mind that the effect you are in the process of performing is worthless if anyone catches a glimpse of the palmed object.

Learn to finger-palm with both hands and practice wherever you are. Get in the habit of keeping an object finger-palmed and soon you will be able to use your hands naturally and *unselfconsciously* while you keep an object concealed.

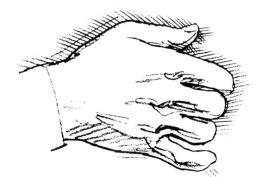

touch-palm

This is an easy and perfectly natural palm if you are working with a fairly large ball or other object. Simply fold back your third finger and hold the ball against your palm with the tip.

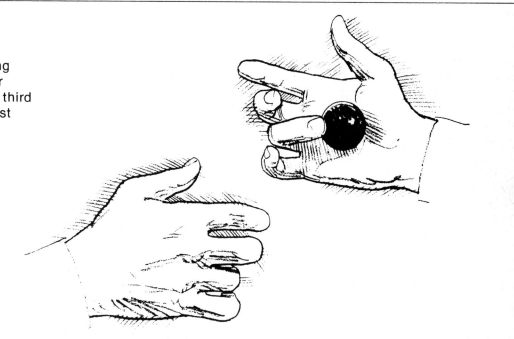

french drop ★★

*for any small object, one of the most popular
and deceptive vanishes ever*

**Slowly repeat moves
1 to 5 in front
of mirror until
you can do them
smoothly and well**

1 L. hand waist-high in front of body. Object between L. thumb and L. 2.

2 R. hand approaches L., thumb down, fingers on top. . . .

3 closes over object, and in same motion, . . .

4 carries object forward and to right, and slowly turns over.

5 R. fingers slowly open to reveal object.

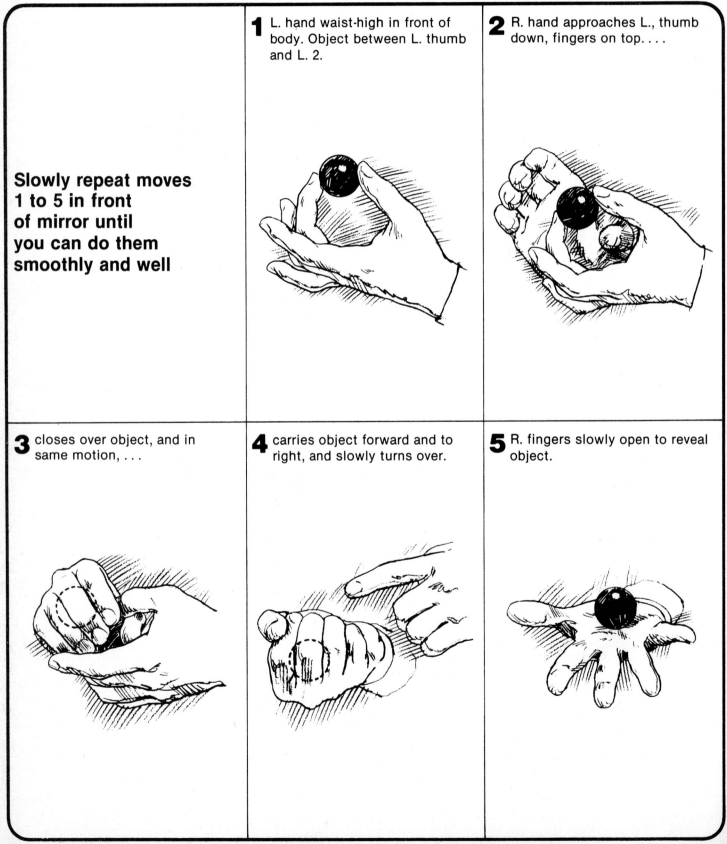

now repeat exactly, but this time . . .

Bring R. hand over to L. as in (2), previous page. Close R. hand around object . . . thumb under, fingers on top.

Under cover of R. fingers, drop ball into L. palm but continue to close R. hand exactly as before when object was actually taken . . .

Hold R. hand with fingers puffed out, as though it actually contained object, and bring hand forward and to right.

Turn over, gently grind fingers together, and slowly open hand to reveal object has vanished!

top-of-fist-vanish ★★

a classic vanish for balls over an inch or so in diameter

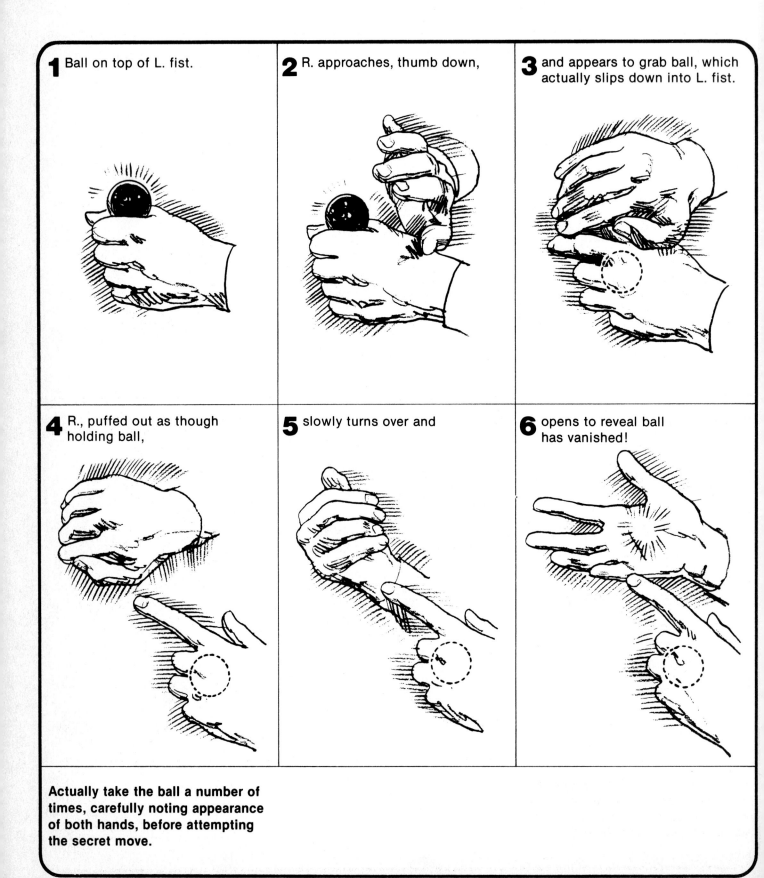

1 Ball on top of L. fist.

2 R. approaches, thumb down,

3 and appears to grab ball, which actually slips down into L. fist.

4 R., puffed out as though holding ball,

5 slowly turns over and

6 opens to reveal ball has vanished!

Actually take the ball a number of times, carefully noting appearance of both hands, before attempting the secret move.

bottom-of-fist-vanish ★★

*a useful variation of the Top-of-Fist Vanish
although not as widely used*

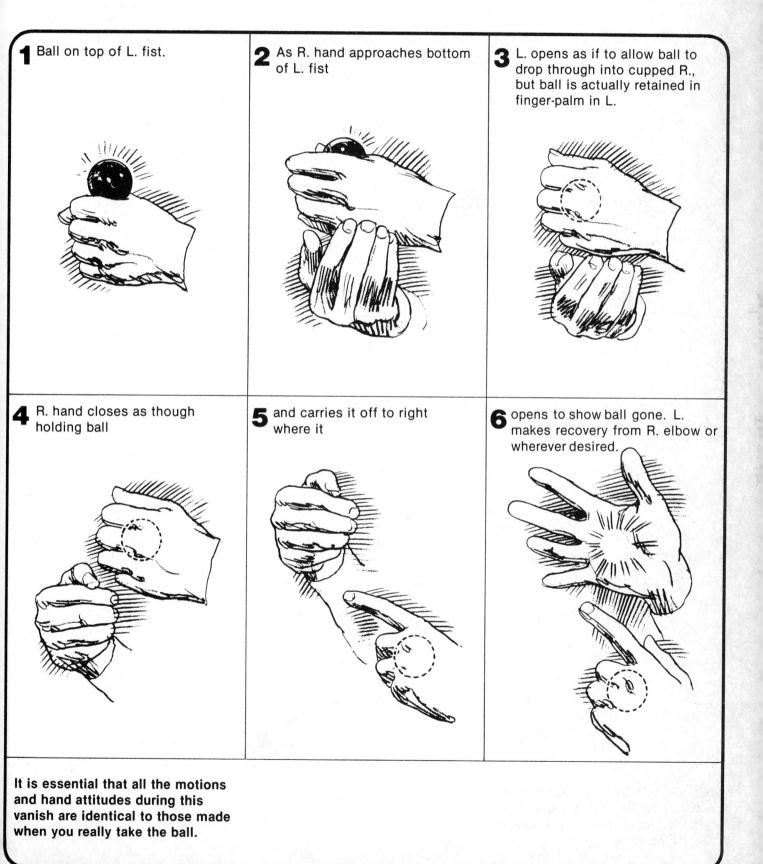

1 Ball on top of L. fist.

2 As R. hand approaches bottom of L. fist

3 L. opens as if to allow ball to drop through into cupped R., but ball is actually retained in finger-palm in L.

4 R. hand closes as though holding ball

5 and carries it off to right where it

6 opens to show ball gone. L. makes recovery from R. elbow or wherever desired.

It is essential that all the motions and hand attitudes during this vanish are identical to those made when you really take the ball.

palm vanish ★★

an extremely natural and therefore highly deceptive move for any chunky object

do these moves first, observe carefully in mirror, and watch your angles!

Ball rests on L. palm.

R. hand approaches, and

removes ball (note the way fingers of L. hand come up, thus shielding ball from view), and carries it about 6 inches to right, slowly turning over as it does so.

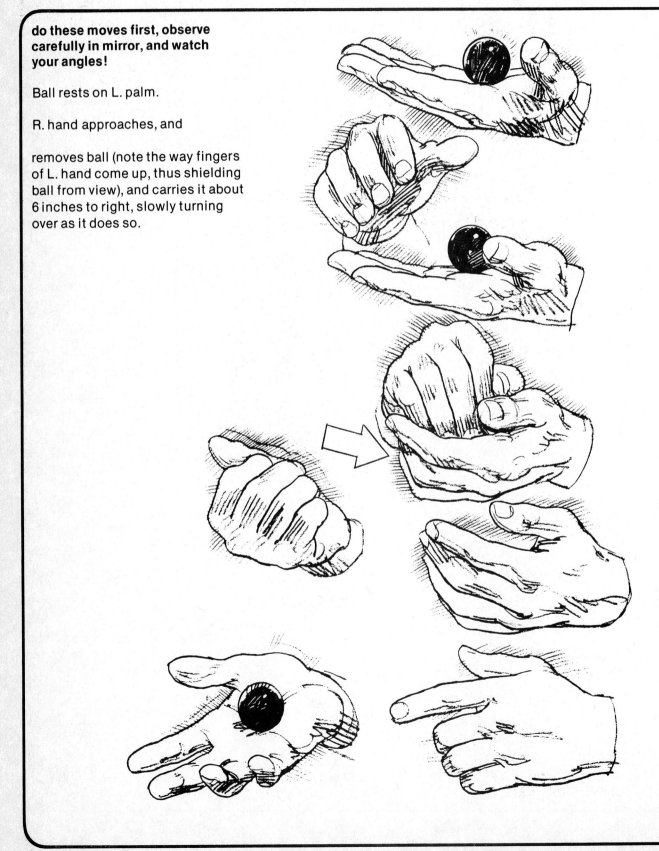

when you can do these moves smoothly and naturally, try this . . .

R. hand approaches L.

When R. fingers cover ball, L. fingers close, gripping ball in finger-palm

and left hand pivots down, but this time ball remains palmed in L. hand, and

R., puffed out as though holding ball,

moves to the right, turns over, and reveals that ball has vanished!

fingertip production ★★

*used in recoveries or in a billiard ball routine,
particularly when no shell is used*

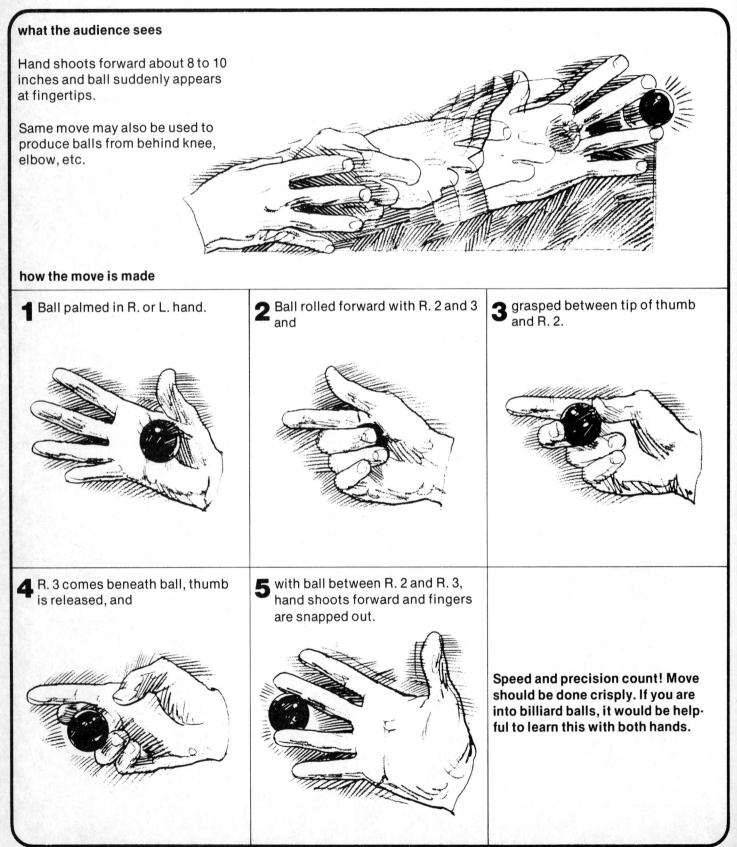

what the audience sees

Hand shoots forward about 8 to 10 inches and ball suddenly appears at fingertips.

Same move may also be used to produce balls from behind knee, elbow, etc.

how the move is made

1 Ball palmed in R. or L. hand.

2 Ball rolled forward with R. 2 and 3 and

3 grasped between tip of thumb and R. 2.

4 R. 3 comes beneath ball, thumb is released, and

5 with ball between R. 2 and R. 3, hand shoots forward and fingers are snapped out.

Speed and precision count! Move should be done crisply. If you are into billiard balls, it would be helpful to learn this with both hands.

palm roll vanish ★★

*not really a natural-looking vanish
but a good one nevertheless . . .*

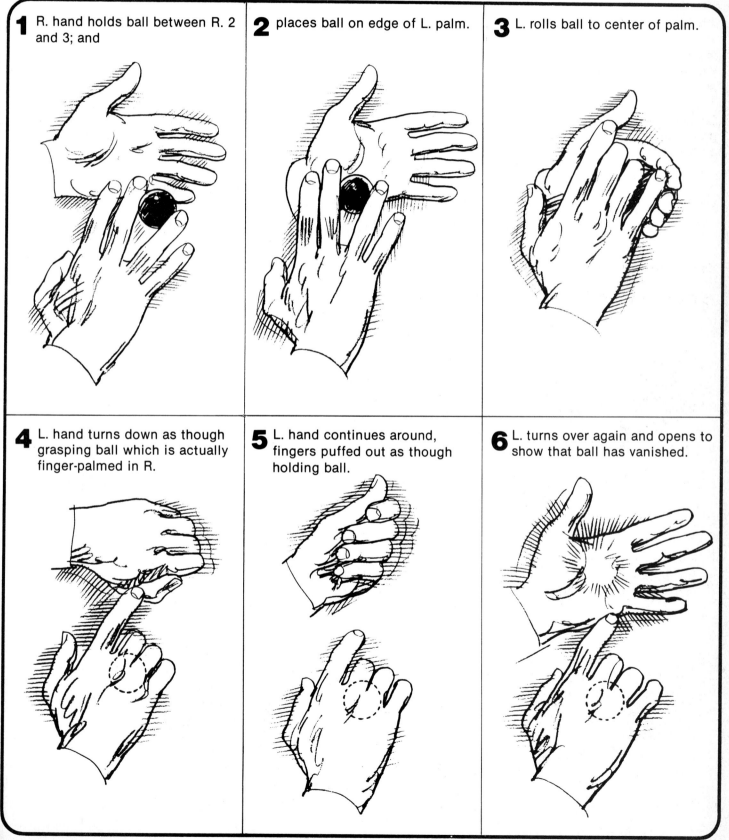

1 R. hand holds ball between R. 2 and 3; and

2 places ball on edge of L. palm.

3 L. rolls ball to center of palm.

4 L. hand turns down as though grasping ball which is actually finger-palmed in R.

5 L. hand continues around, fingers puffed out as though holding ball.

6 L. turns over again and opens to show that ball has vanished.

recoveries

Vanished objects may be recovered from behind elbows, knees, or spectator's ear, nose, etc. Make sure the object really appears to come from the elbow however, and not from your hand, which is merely in the vicinity of your elbow.

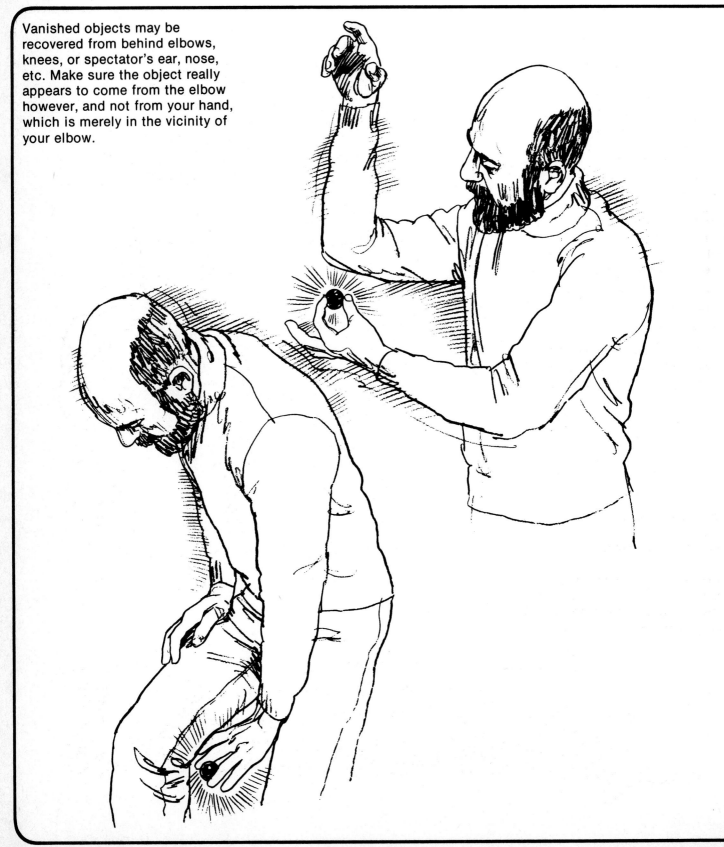

From your nose

This is a good move in conjunction
with the French Drop.
Appear to take object in R. hand
and rub it into your forehead.
Distinctly show your R. hand
empty and immediately bring your
L. hand up to your face. Grasp the
tip of your nose between L. thumb
and L. 1 and allow object to fall
from L. into R. hand, which is held
open at waist-height.

Variation: Instead of rubbing
object into your forehead, pretend
to swallow it.

Note: Don't pretend to place
objects in mouth, nose, or ears in
the presence of young children.

From under hand

Object just vanished.

Move R. hand under L. and turn over.
Move L. hand away to reveal object
lying on R. palm.

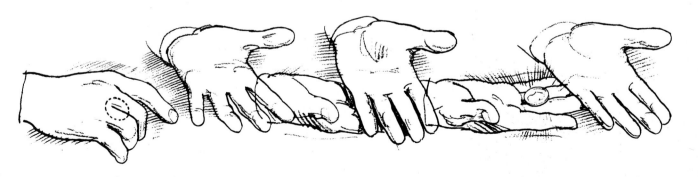

ball acquitment ★★★

a smooth, graceful method for showing both hands empty when they actually contain an object

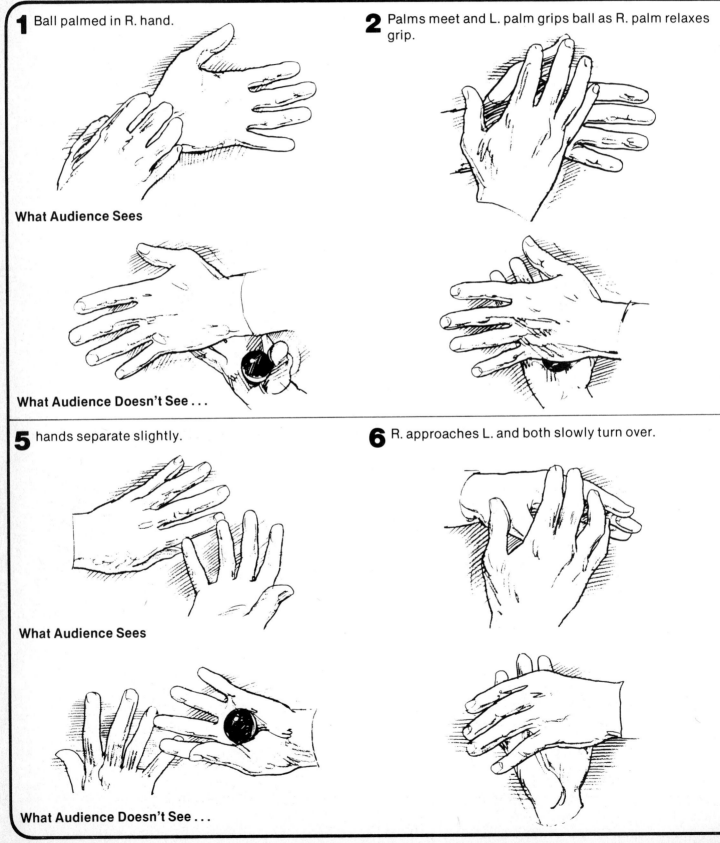

1 Ball palmed in R. hand.

What Audience Sees

What Audience Doesn't See . . .

2 Palms meet and L. palm grips ball as R. palm relaxes grip.

5 hands separate slightly.

What Audience Sees

What Audience Doesn't See . . .

6 R. approaches L. and both slowly turn over.

3 L. slowly turns over under cover of R.

4 R. turns over and

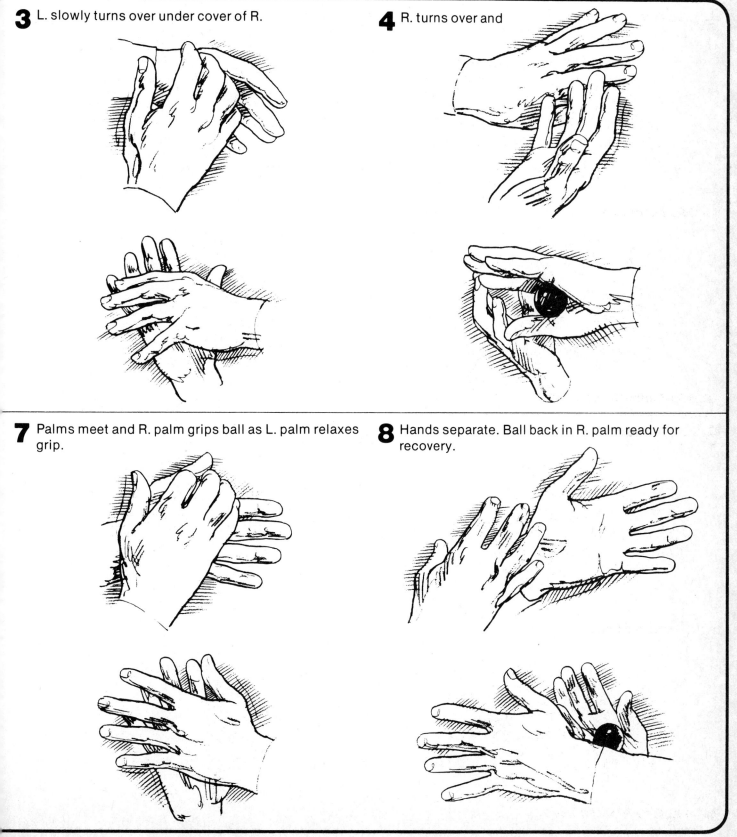

7 Palms meet and R. palm grips ball as L. palm relaxes grip.

8 Hands separate. Ball back in R. palm ready for recovery.

color change ★★★

this beautiful color change is based on the same move as the ball acquitment

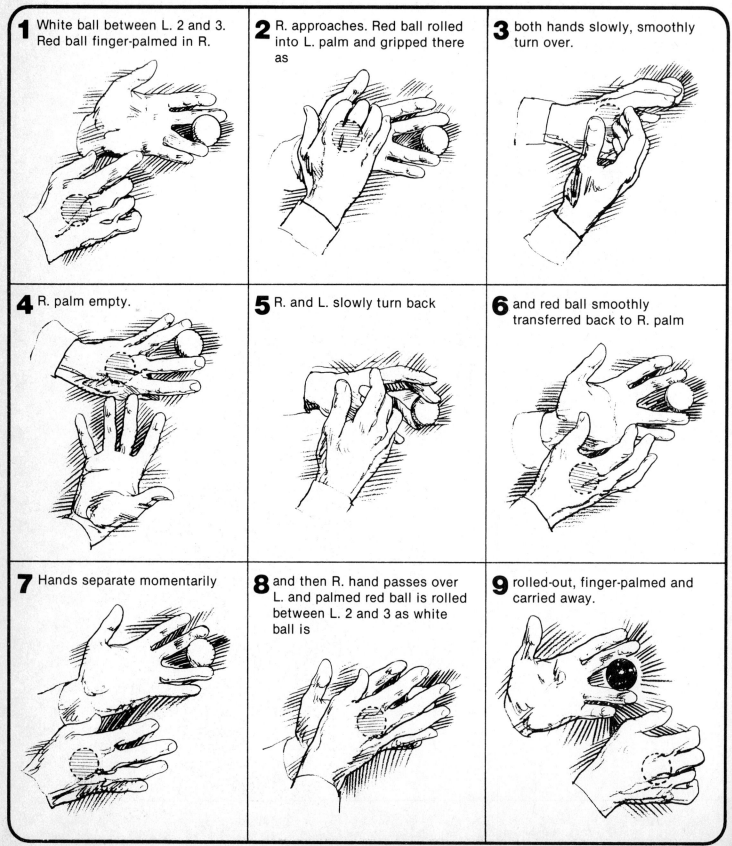

1 White ball between L. 2 and 3. Red ball finger-palmed in R.

2 R. approaches. Red ball rolled into L. palm and gripped there as

3 both hands slowly, smoothly turn over.

4 R. palm empty.

5 R. and L. slowly turn back

6 and red ball smoothly transferred back to R. palm

7 Hands separate momentarily

8 and then R. hand passes over L. and palmed red ball is rolled between L. 2 and 3 as white ball is

9 rolled-out, finger-palmed and carried away.

this move should be one smooth, flowing motion from start to finish

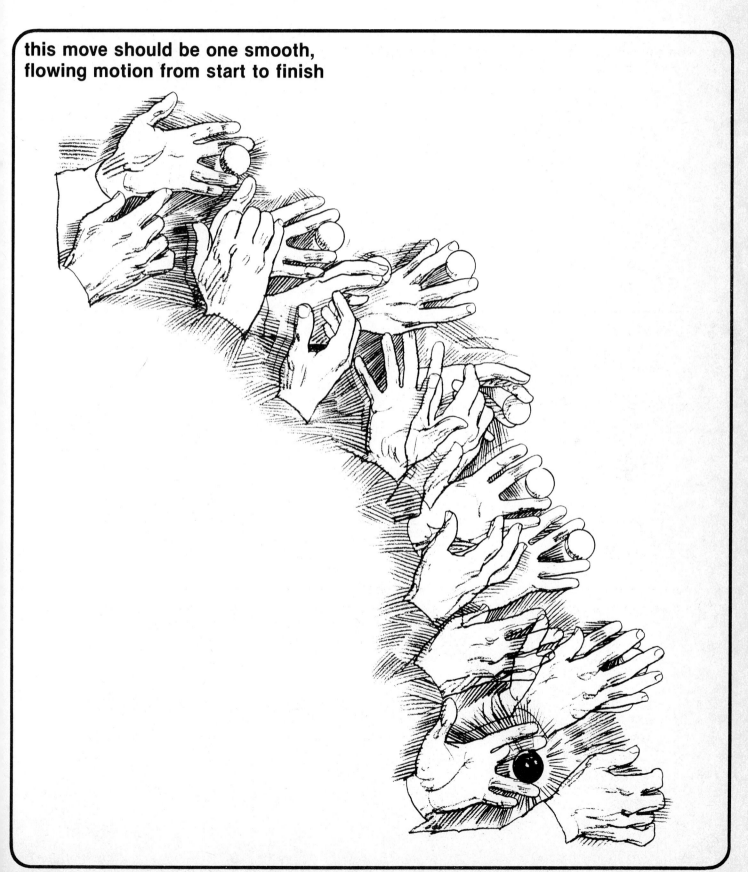

the bill tarr continuous ball production ★★★

a surprising production for use in a routine, but don't repeat more than three times!

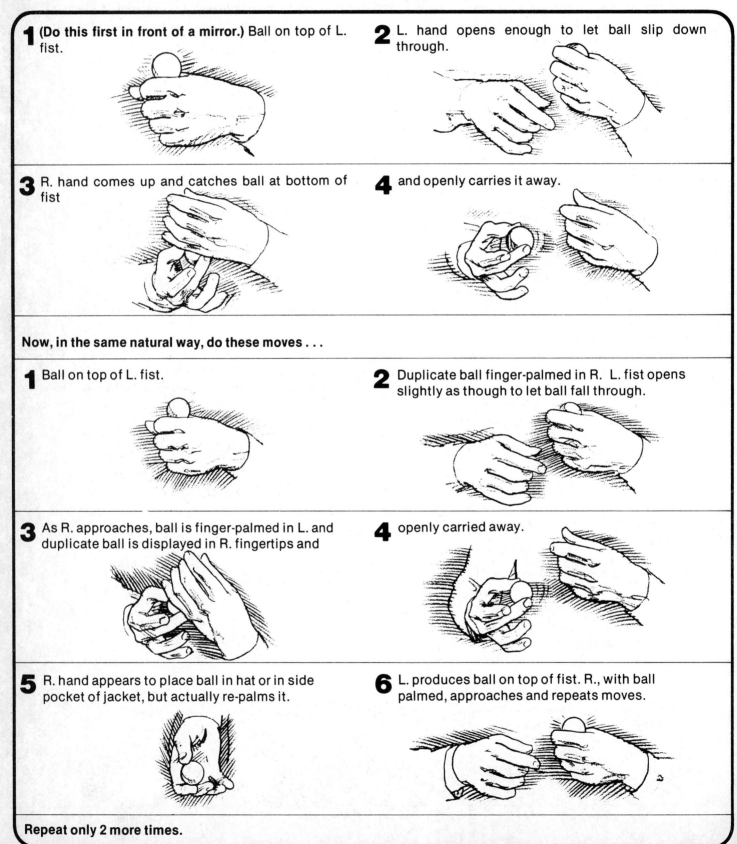

1 (Do this first in front of a mirror.) Ball on top of L. fist.

2 L. hand opens enough to let ball slip down through.

3 R. hand comes up and catches ball at bottom of fist

4 and openly carries it away.

Now, in the same natural way, do these moves . . .

1 Ball on top of L. fist.

2 Duplicate ball finger-palmed in R. L. fist opens slightly as though to let ball fall through.

3 As R. approaches, ball is finger-palmed in L. and duplicate ball is displayed in R. fingertips and

4 openly carried away.

5 R. hand appears to place ball in hat or in side pocket of jacket, but actually re-palms it.

6 L. produces ball on top of fist. R., with ball palmed, approaches and repeats moves.

Repeat only 2 more times.

What the audience doesn't see . . .

1 Ball on L. fist. Duplicate finger-palmed in R.

2 As R. approaches, ball in L. slips down into hand.

3 R. appears to take ball but actually

4 shows duplicate at fingertips, and carries it off.

how the ball is produced

1 Ball in finger-palm.

2 Hand moves up and forward about 8 to 10 inches, opening slightly to give ball freedom to roll.

3 Thumb gets under ball, and combination of thumb and momentum

4 brings ball to top of fist.

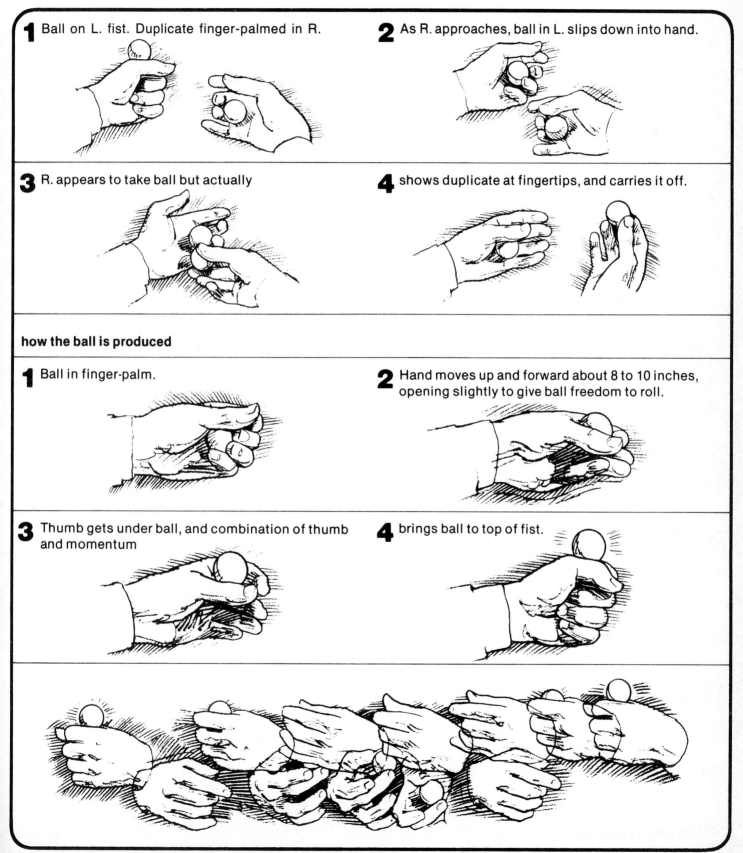

ball roll ★★

*a neat little flourish, the difficulty of which is
directly proportional to the
smoothness of the ball and the dryness of your hands*

Start with ball between R. 1
and R. 2.

R. 3 comes up behind ball and rolls
it down between R. 2 and R. 3.

R. 4. repeats action, rolling ball
between R. 3 and R. 4.

R. 2 comes down in front of ball
and rolls it up between R. 3 and
R. 2. R. 1 repeats action, rolling ball
between R. 2 and R. 1.

Repeat sequence, causing ball to
roll rapidly around hand.

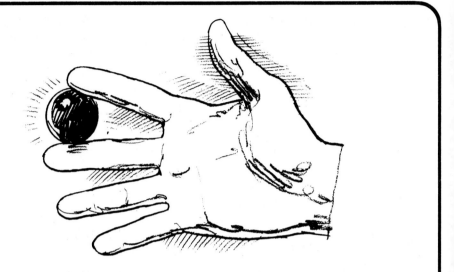

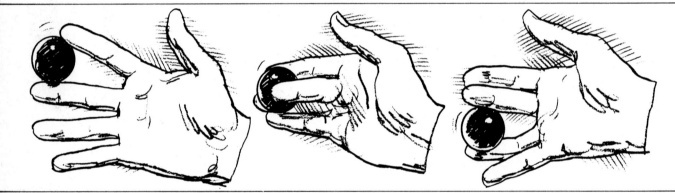

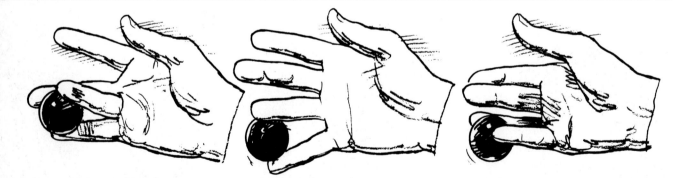

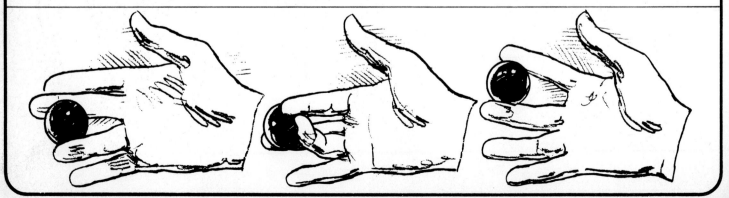

elevator ★★

a momentary interlude during a billiard ball routine, and happily, a lot easier than it looks

Start with one ball on each palm, bring hands together, and applying gentle, easy pressure, make balls roll from heels of hands up to the fingertips and down again.

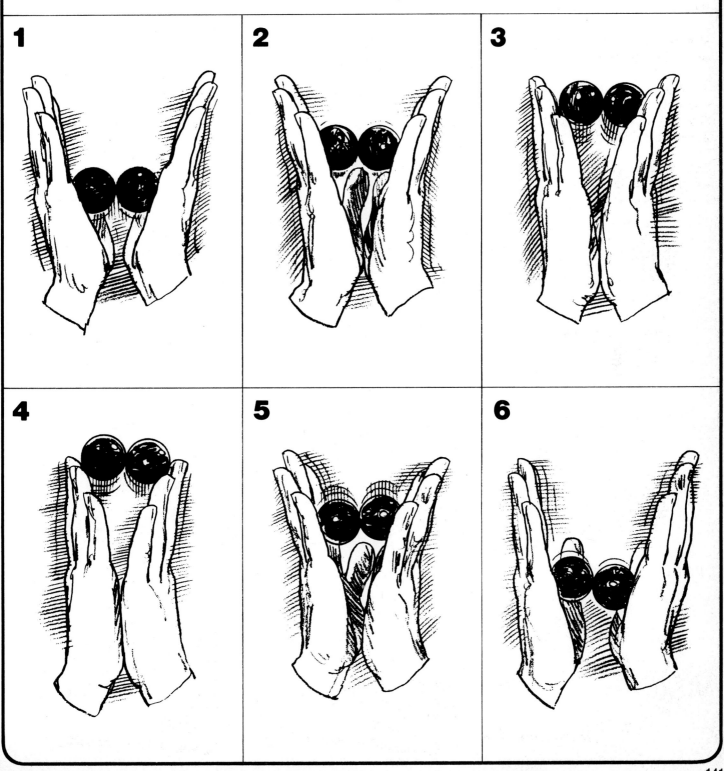

basic multiplying ball moves ★★

*these are basic moves to learn before you can
do a Multiplying Billiard Ball routine*

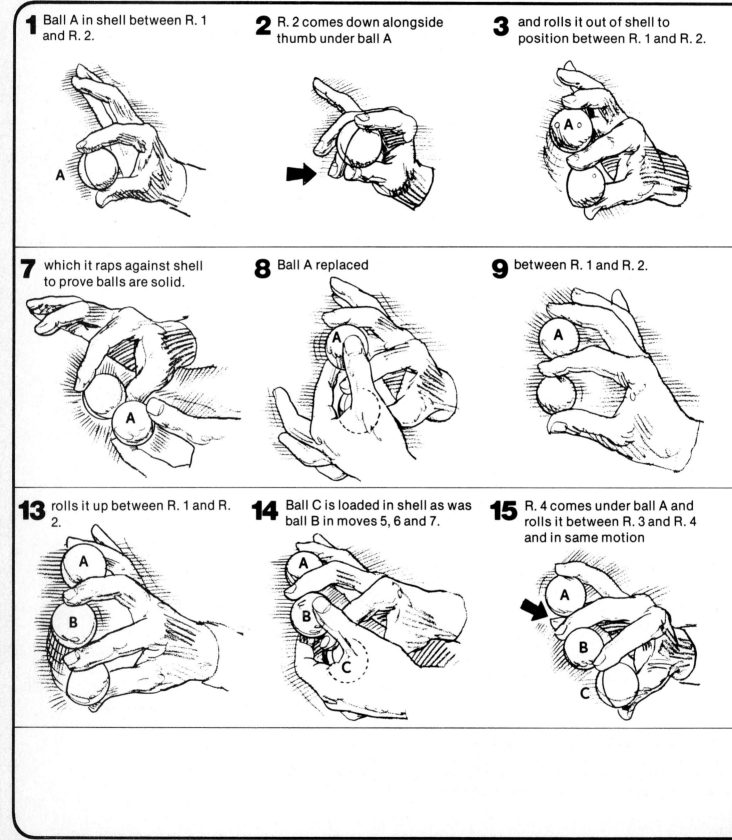

1 Ball A in shell between R. 1
and R. 2.

2 R. 2 comes down alongside
thumb under ball A

3 and rolls it out of shell to
position between R. 1 and R. 2.

7 which it raps against shell
to prove balls are solid.

8 Ball A replaced

9 between R. 1 and R. 2.

13 rolls it up between R. 1 and R.
2.

14 Ball C is loaded in shell as was
ball B in moves 5, 6 and 7.

15 R. 4 comes under ball A and
rolls it between R. 3 and R. 4
and in same motion

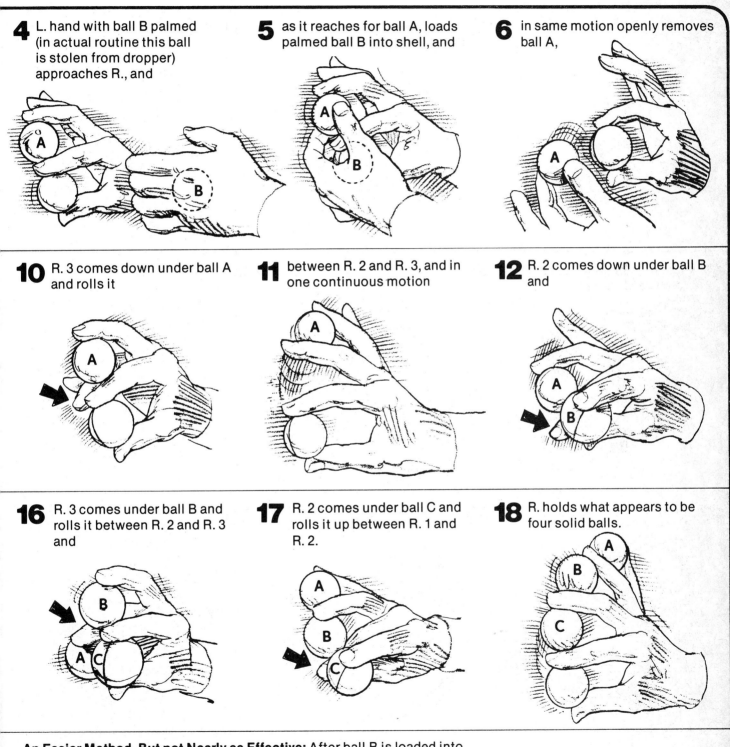

4 L. hand with ball B palmed (in actual routine this ball is stolen from dropper) approaches R., and

5 as it reaches for ball A, loads palmed ball B into shell, and

6 in same motion openly removes ball A,

10 R. 3 comes down under ball A and rolls it

11 between R. 2 and R. 3, and in one continuous motion

12 R. 2 comes down under ball B and

16 R. 3 comes under ball B and rolls it between R. 2 and R. 3 and

17 R. 2 comes under ball C and rolls it up between R. 1 and R. 2.

18 R. holds what appears to be four solid balls.

An Easier Method, But not Nearly as Effective: After ball B is loaded into shell, L. hand replaces ball A between R. 2 and R. 3, thus eliminating moves 10 and 11. After ball 3 is loaded into shell, L. hand replaces ball B between R. 3 and R. 4, thus eliminating moves 15 and 16.

basic billiard ball routine ★★★

this basic routine requires no droppers or props and can be done fairly close up, provided your audience is in front of you

Start with one ball in upper-left jacket pocket and ball in shell in upper-right jacket pocket. If you have only one pocket, place ball and shell on top of single ball in upper left pocket. Show one ball in hand.

Billiard Ball routines are generally—but not necessarily—done in pantomime. Work very slowly and distinctly and pause sufficiently between moves to give your audience a chance to see what has happened after each move.

Do Top-of-Fist Vanish but instead of making ball disappear,

rub ball through right knee.

Recover ball from under R. knee with L. hand.

Do French Drop.

but instead of making ball disappear, appear to place ball in mouth.

Pretend to swallow ball.

Find ball and shell in pocket and remove as single ball, which you hold between R. thumb and R. 1.

Produce ball 2.

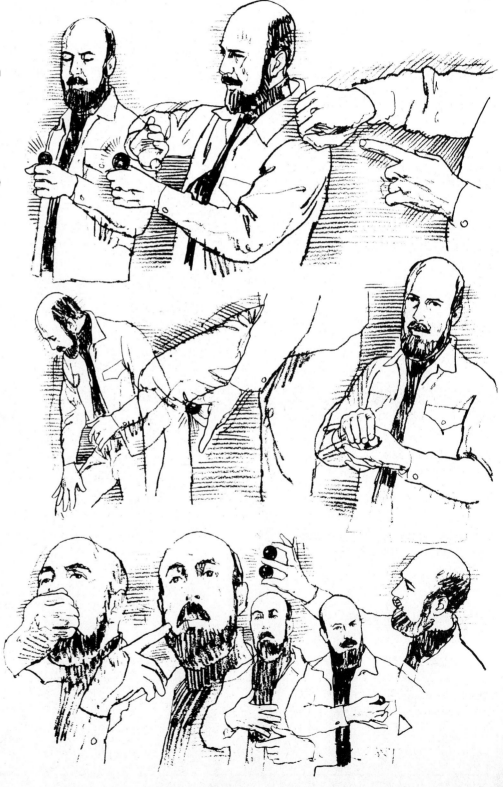

Lightly strike ball against R. knee 2 times.

As hand swings against R. knee for third time, quickly roll ball into shell and

at same instant make ball palmed in L. visible.

Place that ball between R. 1 and R. 2

and produce ball 3.

Do Shell Vanish and

make ball disappear by apparently tossing in air

and squeeze it out of upper-left jacket pocket with L. hand.

Remove and place between R. 2 and R. 3.

Produce ball 4. Display, bow and drop balls in hat or place in pocket.

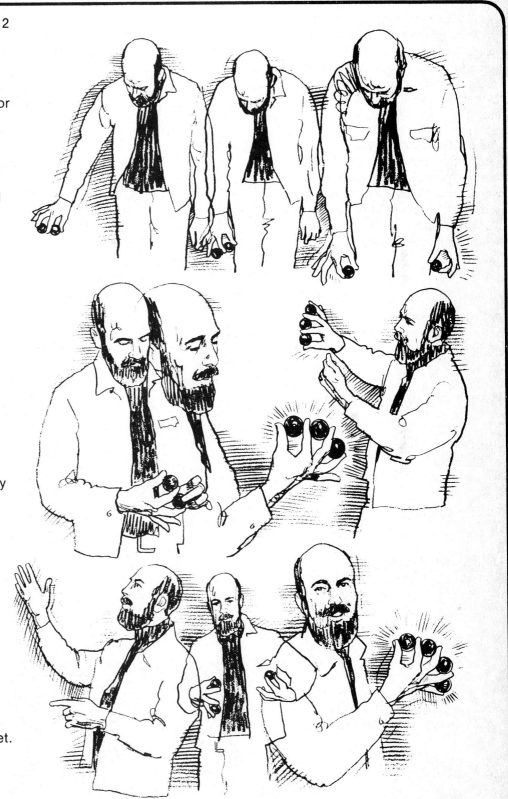

shell color change ★★

an effective and relatively easy way to color-change a ball

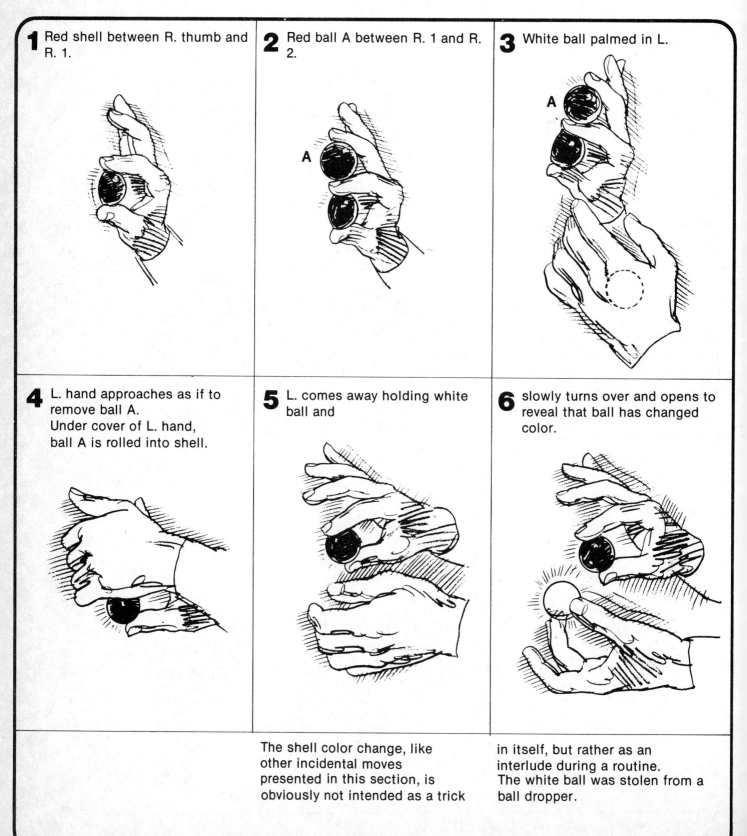

1 Red shell between R. thumb and R. 1.

2 Red ball A between R. 1 and R. 2.

3 White ball palmed in L.

4 L. hand approaches as if to remove ball A. Under cover of L. hand, ball A is rolled into shell.

5 L. comes away holding white ball and

6 slowly turns over and opens to reveal that ball has changed color.

The shell color change, like other incidental moves presented in this section, is obviously not intended as a trick in itself, but rather as an interlude during a routine. The white ball was stolen from a ball dropper.

shell vanish ★★

a logical vanish for use during
a billiard ball routine . . .

R. hand holds empty shell and one, two or three balls.

L. hand approaches, apparently to take ball A.

Under cover of L. hand ball A. is slipped into shell.

L. closes as though holding ball and appears to carry it away.

Ball is vanished as desired.

Recovery is made in air or from behind knee by snapping ball out of shell and back between R. 1 and 2.

The Shell Vanish is sometimes used to end a Billiard Ball routine. The magician apparently holds ball A in his L. hand. He drops shell and remaining balls in his hat or in pocket, makes ball A dissappear, and takes his bows.

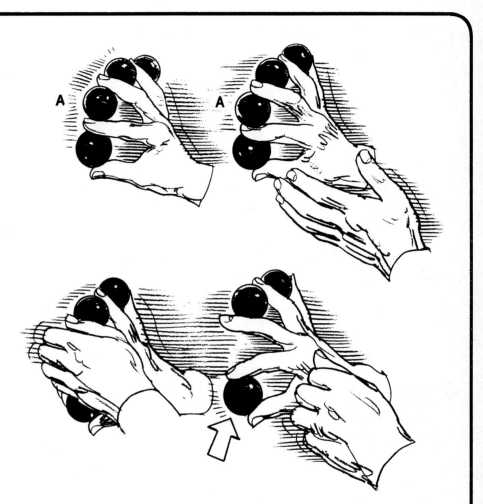

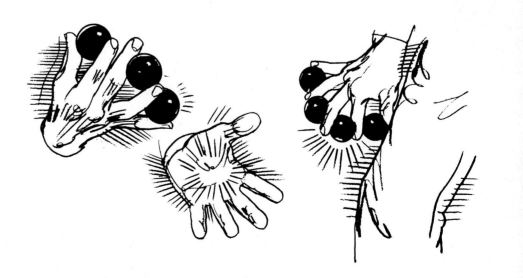

basic sponge ball vanish ★★

a very easy, very deceptive move, but be sure to get your angles right . . .

Ball pinched at edge by R. thumb and R. 2

is placed in L. palm.

L. fingers close over ball but R. retains its grip and merely pulls ball out of L.'s grasp.

L. fingers continue to close without pause and L. hand is puffed out as though holding ball.

L. opens and ball has vanished.

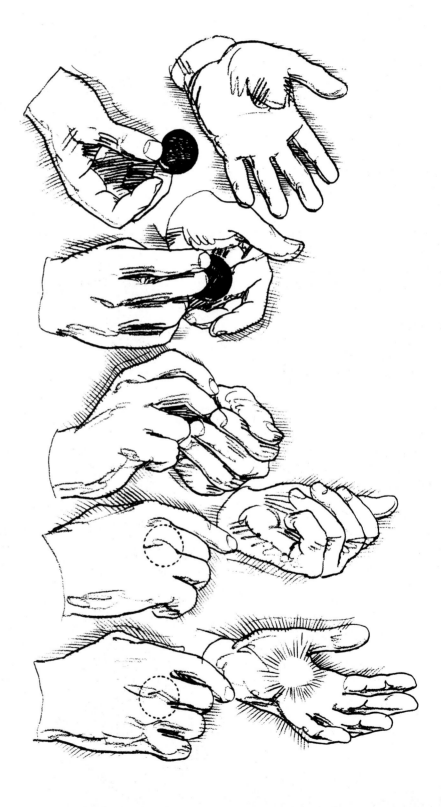

fist vanish ★★★

a handy, different and very deceptive
sponge ball move for use during a routine . . .

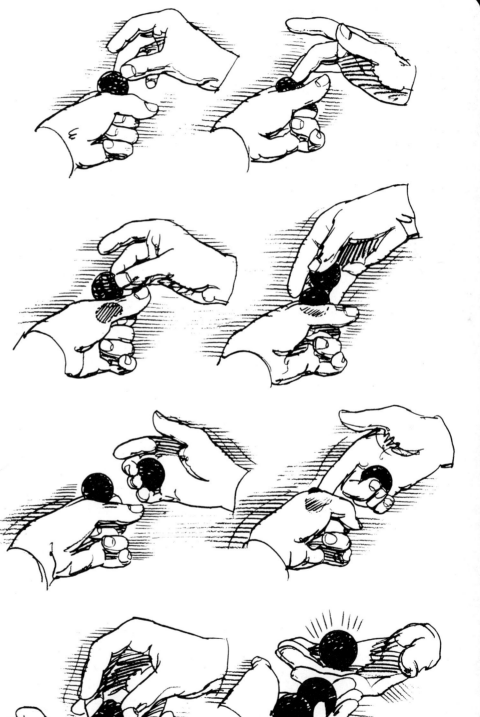

as the magician sees it

Place sponge ball on top of L. fist.

Press L. 2 close to palm to act as a stop and use tip of R. 2 to tuck ball into top of fist as far as it will go.

Place second ball on top of L. fist.

Bring R. hand over to tuck second ball into fist. Under cover of R. fingers, finger-palm second ball and let first ball pop up out of fist to take its place.

Tuck second ball back into fist as before.

Pick up third ball, secretly add palmed ball to it, and place it in spectator's hand.

Open your L. hand and ask spectator to open his to reveal that one ball has mysteriously left your hand and joined spectator's.

You can appear to tuck three or four balls into your hand with this move. Tuck in the first, go to pocket and bring same finger-palmed ball out as though it were a new ball, appear to tuck it into fist, and so on.

mini sponge-ball routine ★★★

a long-time, impromptu favorite of magicians everywhere

the effect

Magician removes two sponge balls from his pocket. He places one in his hand and one in spectator's hand. The magician's ball vanishes. Spectator opens his hand and both balls pop out!

Magician reaches into his pocket and removes a third ball. He places two balls in spectator's hand and third ball back in his pocket. Spectator opens his hand and third ball has rejoined the first two!

Magician places two balls back in spectator's hand and again places third ball in his pocket. Spectator opens hand and two balls plus three small balls pop out!

preparation

Sponge balls are available singly or in sets, complete with routines, at magic shops everywhere. To make your own, buy a fairly fine-textured, soft sponge pad and cut four cubes of approximately one-and-one half inches and three cubes of approximately three-quarters of an inch, and with a pair of scissors, trim as close to perfect balls as you can.

Place four sponge balls and three small ones in R. jacket pocket.

doing the trick

Magician reaches into R. jacket pocket and removes two balls, which he places on table or on spectator's open, palm-up hand.

He appears to place one ball on his own L. hand using the sponge-ball vanish or any other method he prefers.

With first ball finger-palmed in his R. hand, he picks up second ball B, and secretly adding ball A to it, holds both as one.

He places both balls as one into spectator's hand and requests that spectator close hand tightly and keep it closed until told to open.

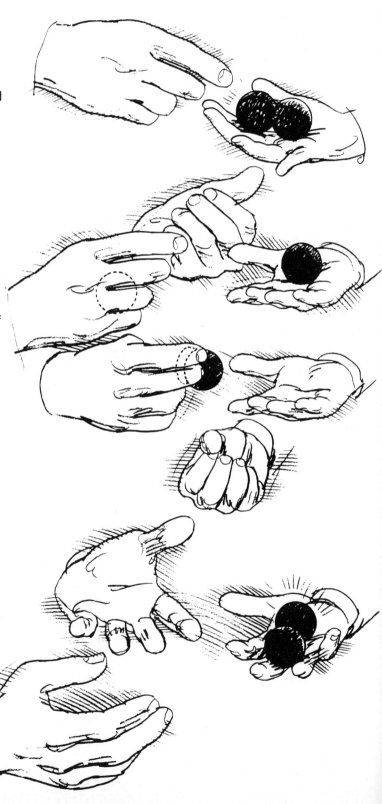

Magician opens his hand to show that his ball has vanished. Spectator opens his hand and both balls pop out.

Magician reaches into his pocket for a third ball and while there quickly finger-palms fourth ball.

He places two balls in spectator's hand, secretly adding the third, finger-palmed ball, and requests that spectator keep hand closed until told to open it.

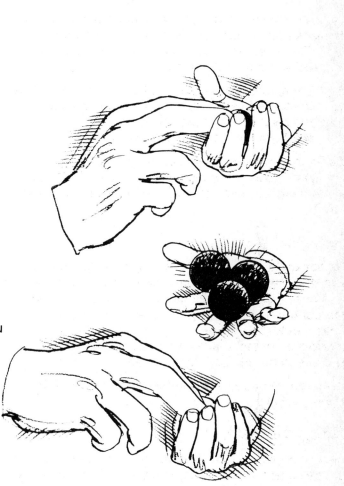

Magician openly places third ball back in his pocket and while there quickly palms off the three small balls.

Spectator opens his hand and three balls pop out.

Magician places two balls back in spectator's hand secretly adding the three small balls.

He openly places third ball back in his pocket. Spectator opens his hand and two balls plus three small ones pop out.

This very elementary routine is merely to acquaint you with the possibilities. As your skills increase, you should create your own more interesting, more elaborate version.

cups and balls ★★★

*the oldest recorded trick and still one of the
greatest exhibitions of pure sleight of hand . . .*

the effect

Magician displays three metal cups and three small
balls, which invisibly pass from cup to cup in a
bewildering series of appearances and
disappearances.

required

Three cups and four balls of cork or cloth or
hard rubber approximately ¾″ to ⅞″
in diameter.

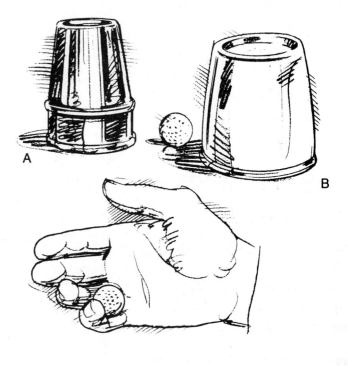

A

B

Standard cups look like A or B, are generally made of
steel or aluminum, and are available at magic supply
houses in various diameters, from mini (not practical)
to standard (approximately three inches in diameter),
which is the best size for learning the basic moves.

Until you get your set you can use stiff paper cups
(the type with recessed top) or, for practicing basic
moves, plastic tumblers.

learn these moves first

palming

Always hold the ball at the base of R. 3 and 4,
and always hold both hands in that same basic
position, whether a ball is palmed there or not.

introducing the ball

Ball palmed at base of R. 1 and 2.

R., holding cup at base between R. thumb and R. 1
and 2, raises it about five or six inches above table,
mouth tilted slightly toward performer.

On descent, bottom portion of hand swings in toward
mouth, bringing ball beneath cup.

Ball is released under cup as it comes to rest on
table.

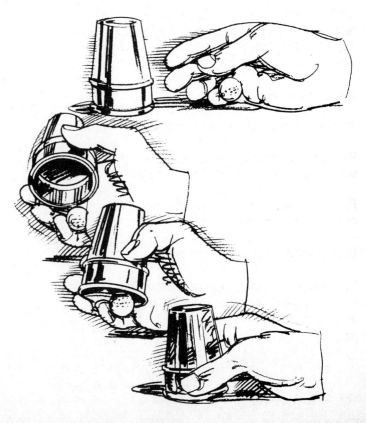

basic cups and balls vanish

Although almost any vanish can be used during a Cups and Balls routine, the following adaptation of the Toss Vanish is probably the most natural.

Ball held between R. thumb and R. 1.

Ball tossed toward L. palm.

R. 4, slightly extended, keeps ball from reaching L. fingers.

L. fingers close as though ball was received.

placing ball under cup

Hold ball between R. thumb and R. 1 and drop ball into L. hand.

Close L. fingers around ball.

Tilt cup to right with R. hand, place fingers under cup and slide fingers out, leaving ball behind.

appearing to place ball under cup

Do the basic Cups and Balls Vanish, actually retaining ball in R. finger-palm. Place L. fingers under cup and slide them out again precisely as you did when you actually placed a ball under the cup.

the penetrating cups

This move only works well with metal cups.

Pick up cup with L. hand and hold lightly, mouth up, about five or six inches from table.

Pick up second cup with R. hand and hold four or five inches above first cup.

Drop second cup into first cup.

The weight of second cup knocks first from your hand. Allow it to fall immediately, grasping second in its place, creating the illusion of one cup passing through another.

You can let the second cup fall through to the table or you can quickly catch it in your R. hand before it does.

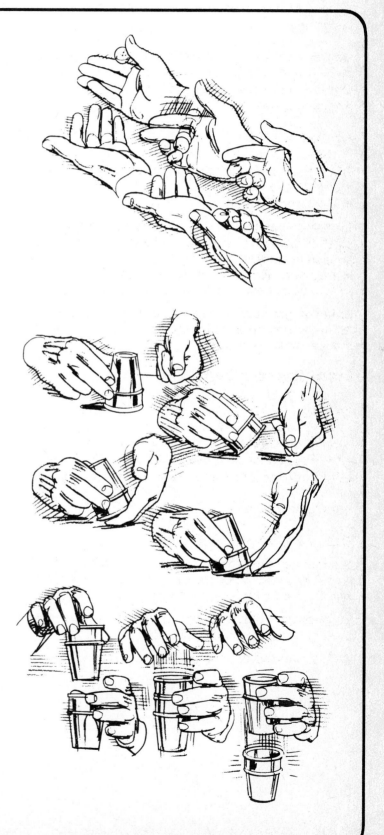

Following is a short routine (with a smashing climax) to acquaint you with the possibilities of the Cups and Balls. Eventually you may want to create your own longer, more elaborate routine. Although only one or two patter suggestions are included, Cups and Balls workers generally point out what they are doing while they are doing it. Work crisply and at a fairly good pace, and when you do your own routine, don't let it go on for too long. Until you are really a master, and probably even then, five or six minutes should be more than ample.

Work sitting down at a sturdy, comfortable table, with your audience in front of you.

preparation

Three cups stacked, mouth up on table, four balls in R. jacket pocket, and three small limes or very small lemons, or comparably-sized pieces of firm fruit approximately two and one quarter inches in diameter in your L. jacket pocket.

to perform

Set cups in line, mouth up. Cup on your left is 1, middle cup is 2 and cup on your right is 3.

Do Penetrating Cups. Cup 3 penetrates cup 2 and cup 2 penetrates cup 1.

Turn cups mouth down about six inches apart.

Remove three balls from R. jacket pocket and palm fourth.

Set one ball on top of each cup with R. hand.

Tilt cup 3 forward with R., dropping ball into L. hand. Load palmed ball into cup as you tilt cup back on table.

Toss ball back into R. and execute basic vanish, palming ball in R.

Make throwing motion in direction of cup 3 with L. hand. Open to show that ball has vanished.

Pick up cup 3 with R., revealing ball back underneath.

Remove ball with L. and load palmed ball back under Cup 3 with R.

Place ball on top of cup 3 with L.

Remove ball from top of cup 2 with L.

Pick up cup 2 with R.

Place ball on table in position just occupied by cup 2.

Bring cup 2 down on top of cup 3.

Raise both cups together with R. to reveal that ball has penetrated through cup to table.

Separate top cup from stack (cup 2) and the ball that is secretly in it and place it over center ball.

Pick up ball from table and place it on top of cup 2 with R.

Place cup 3 on top of cup 2 with L.

Raise cup 3 and cup 2 together with L. to reveal two balls under cup.

Place cup 3 over two center balls with R.

Pick up ball on top of cup 1 and place on top of cup 2 with R.

Place cup 2 over cup 3 with L.

Raise cups 2 and 3 with R. to reveal 3 balls under cup.

Place cup 2 six inches to right of cup 1 with R.

Place cup 3 six inches to right of cup 2.

Place one ball in front of each cup with R. (one ball is secretly under cup 2).

Pick up ball 3 with R., transfer to L. and place under cup 3.

Pick up ball 1 with R., transfer to L. and place under cup 1.

Pick up ball 2 with R., apparently transfer to L. (basic vanish), and say, "I'll place this ball in my pocket," and place hand, apparently containing ball, into L. pocket.

Bring empty L. up and rest on edge of table.

Raise cup 2 with R. to reveal that ball is back under cup.

Pick up ball with L., loading palmed ball under cup 2 with R.

Say, "Let's try that again." Openly place ball in L. pocket and palm small lime.

Lift up cup 2 with R. to reveal ball back again. The instant you lift cup, bring up L. hand with lime palmed and rest on edge of table and pass cup from R. to L.

Load lime into cup with L. and as you pick up ball with R., bring it to the attention of your audience, and set cup 2 (and lime) down with L.

Toss ball to R., fake to L. and appear to place ball in pocket with appropriate remark.

Pick up cup three with R., remove ball with L. and load palmed ball with R.

Openly place in L. pocket and palm second lime.

Pick up cup 3 with R. and reveal that ball is back again.

Left hand, with lime palmed, comes up and rests on edge of table as before, and R. passes cup to L., which loads lime.
Pick up ball with R. and set cup (and lime) in position 3.

Transfer ball to L. and place in pocket.

Raise cup 1 with R., remove ball with L., and place in R.

Fake transfer to L. and appear to place in pocket where you palm third lime.

Raise cup and as you do so, release palmed ball, making it appear as though it was under cup all the time. (A few trials in front of your mirror will make it look convincing.)

Immediately transfer cup to L., load lime, and place cup on table as you pick up ball 3 in R.

Openly transfer ball to L. and place in pocket.

Say, "We finally have these cups empty. Right?" and with that, tilt cups backward onto table, reveal the limes (or whatever you have loaded), and take your bows.

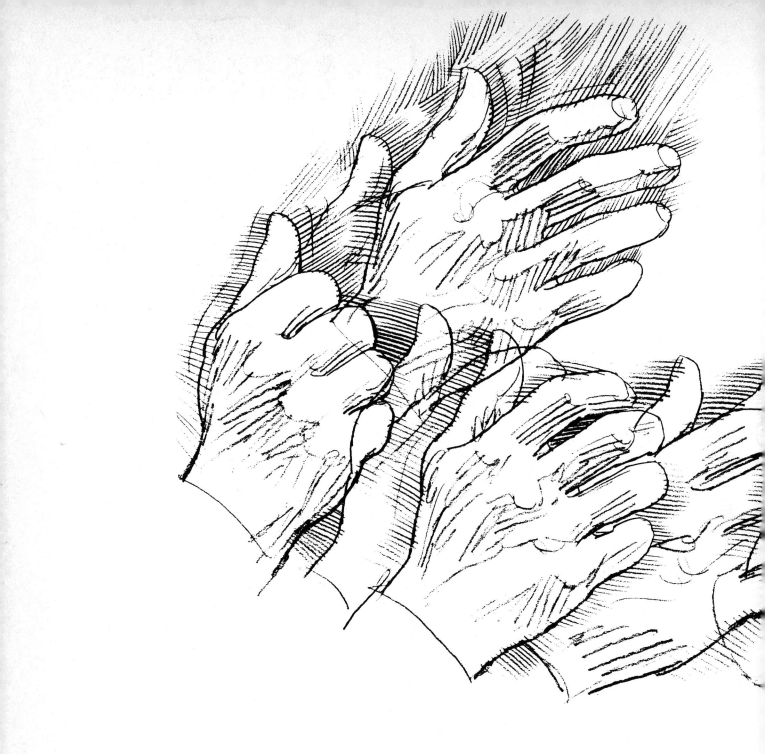

thimbles

Small, bright, colorful and easy to handle! That's what make thimbles so ideal for close-up magic and manipulation. Although they have never really reached the status of cards or coins, there are a great many magicians who specialize in their use. You'll find a number of good, basic sleights in the next few pages to start you on your way.

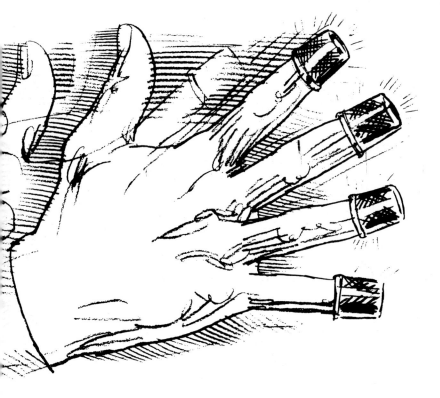

thumb palm ★★

*the basic move upon which most
thimble sleights depend.*

Bring R. 1 back and
deposit thimble in crotch of
thumb.

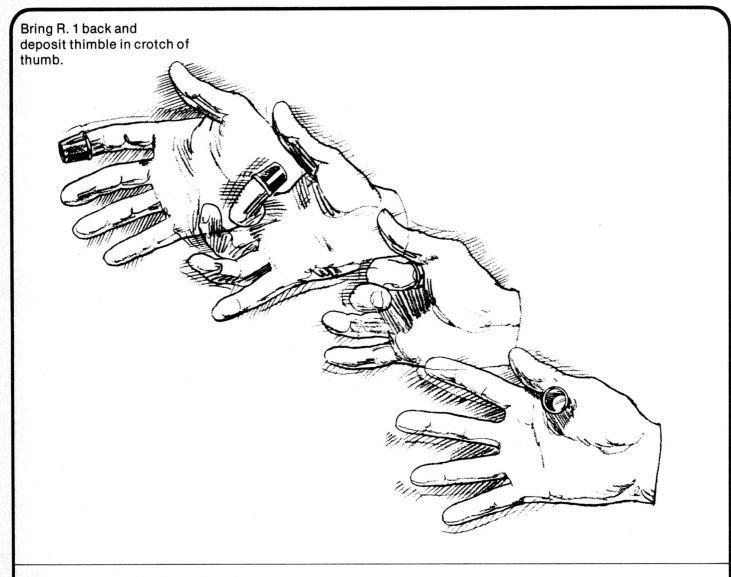

After you can thumb-palm a
thimble from the first finger of
either hand, learn to palm with the
second and third fingers as well.
It's a good idea to practice with
both hands at once, since there are
some effects which require the
ability to thumb-palm with the left
as well as the right, and it is no
more time-consuming to practice
with both hands than it is with one.

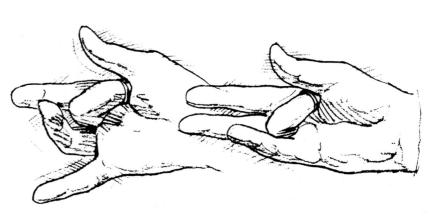

thimble gimmicks

giant thimbles

oversized thimbles in various colors, frequently made of wood and rhinestone-studded, used to assure better visibility from stage

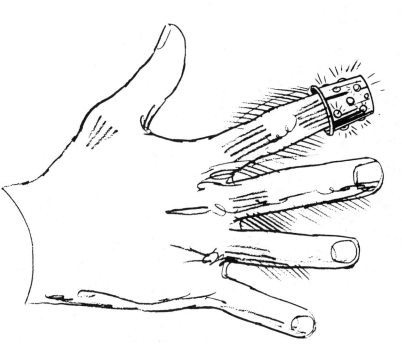

holders

devices, usually of stiff fiberboard or metal to which are affixed elastic loops designed to hold thimbles in readiness for stealing during a multiplying thimble routine

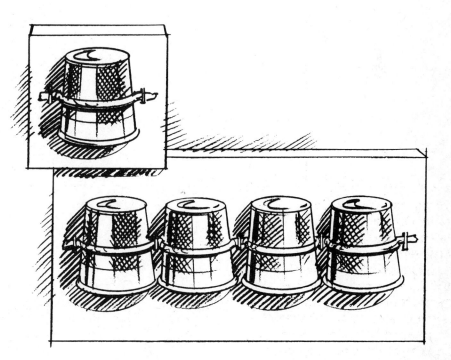

Most metal thimbles are too slippery to be used effectively. Plastic thimbles are obviously more colorful and grip better, provided you can find your size. If you are fortunate enough to locate good thimbles, stock up, because once they are gone, you may never find them again.

basic thimble vanish ★★

the basic thimble sleight . . . a must for every sleight-of-hand artist . . .

1 Thimble rests on L. palm.

2 L. hand slowly turns over.

3 Under cover of L., which remains still, thimble is immediately thumb-palmed.

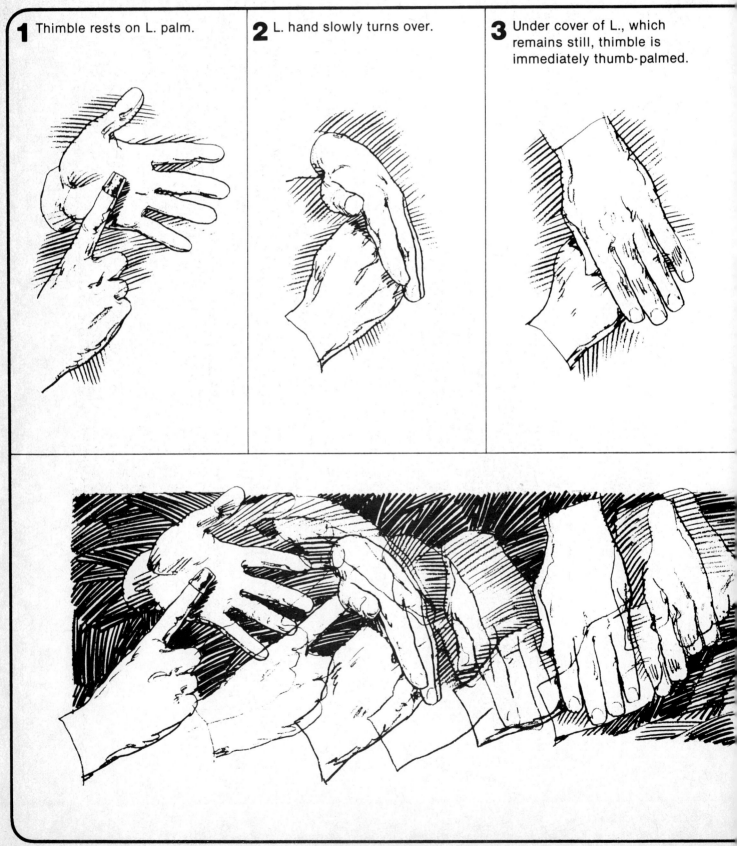

4 R.1 quickly straightens out again and L. hand closes around it and

5 slides off finger as though carrying thimble away. (R. hand remains still throughout entire effect.) L. hand turns over and

6 opens to reveal that thimble has vanished.

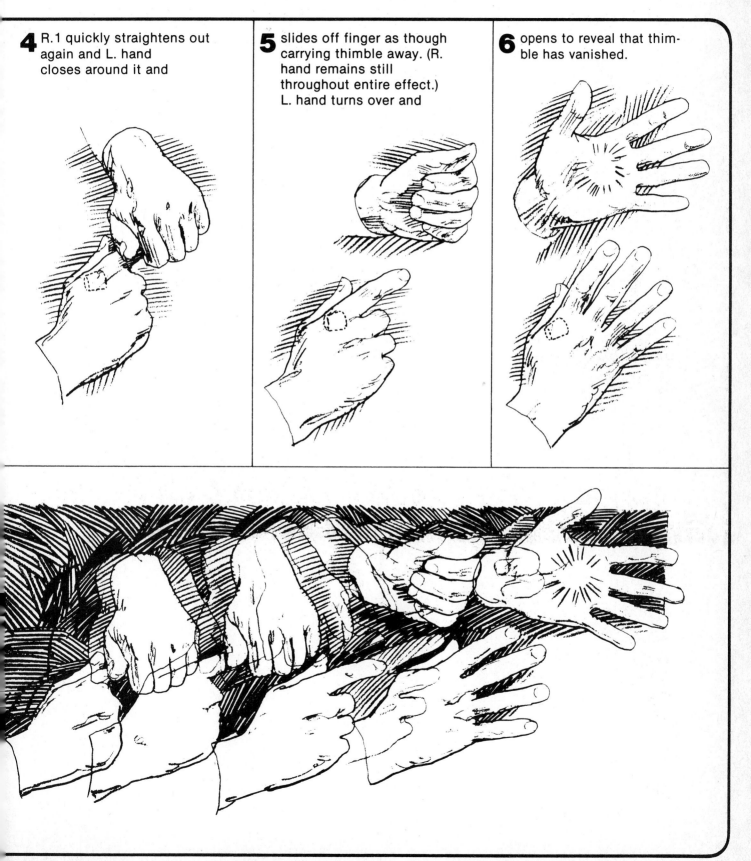

see-through vanish ★★

a simple, beautiful, very deceptive move

do these moves in front of mirror

R. hand remains motionless throughout move

1 Thimble at base of L. 2.

2 Close L. firmly over finger.

3 Open L. 2 to show thimble.

4 Close hand over L. 2.

5 Pull thimble off finger with rapid movement to left.

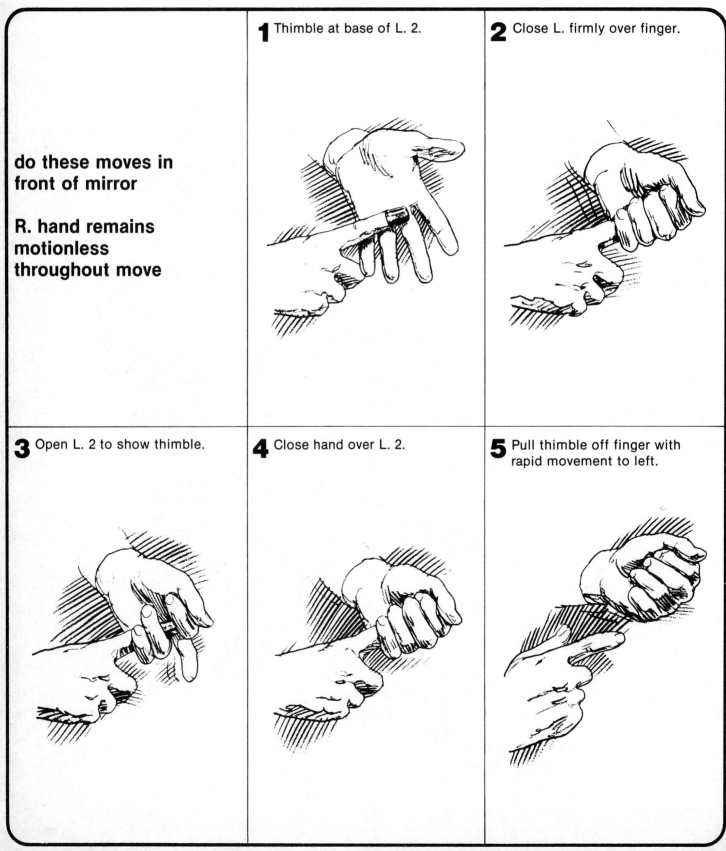

when you can do moves 1 to 5 smoothly, try this . . .

Repeat moves 1 to 4.

Move L. fist sharply to left but do *not* take thimble with it.

The instant L. fist starts to move, quickly thumb-palm thimble and then

immediately straighten out.

Squeeze away thimble, and open L. hand to reveal it has vanished.

Even though thumb-palm is done without cover, the speed of execution coupled with the motion of the left hand makes the move invisible!

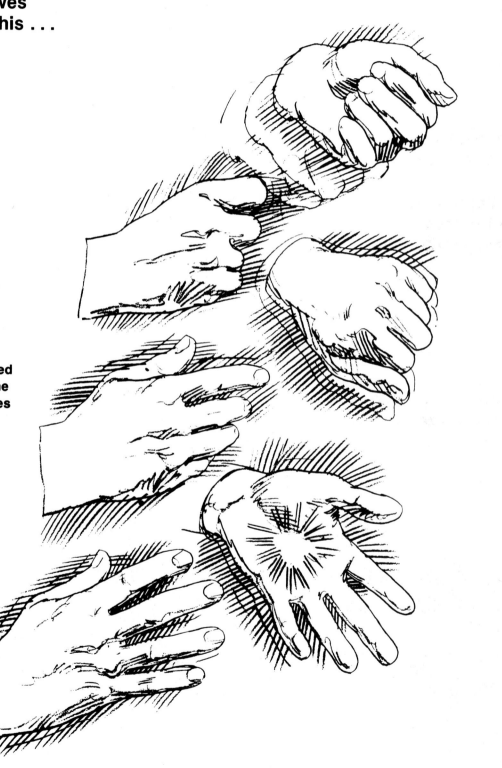

push vanish ★

a very simple, very natural, very casual vanish, but totally deceptive

what audience sees

Thimble on R. 1. L. hand closed into a loose fist.

R. I thrusts into L., and

pulls out without thimble.

L. hand opens to reveal thimble vanished.

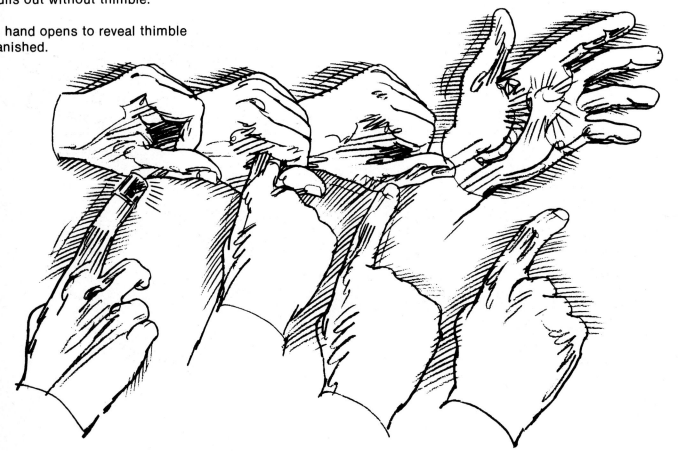

what they don't see

As soon as R. 1 enters L. fist it bends back toward R. palm and

thimble is taken by R. thumb and R. 2.

R. 1 straightens out and pulls out of L. fist.

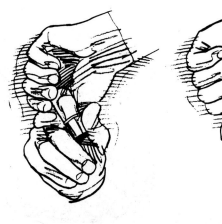

thumb vanish ★

similar to the push vanish, but even easier . . .

what audience sees.

L. forms loose fist.

R. thumb, wearing thimble, thrusts into L. fist and

emerges empty.

L. hand turns over and opens to reveal thimble has vanished.

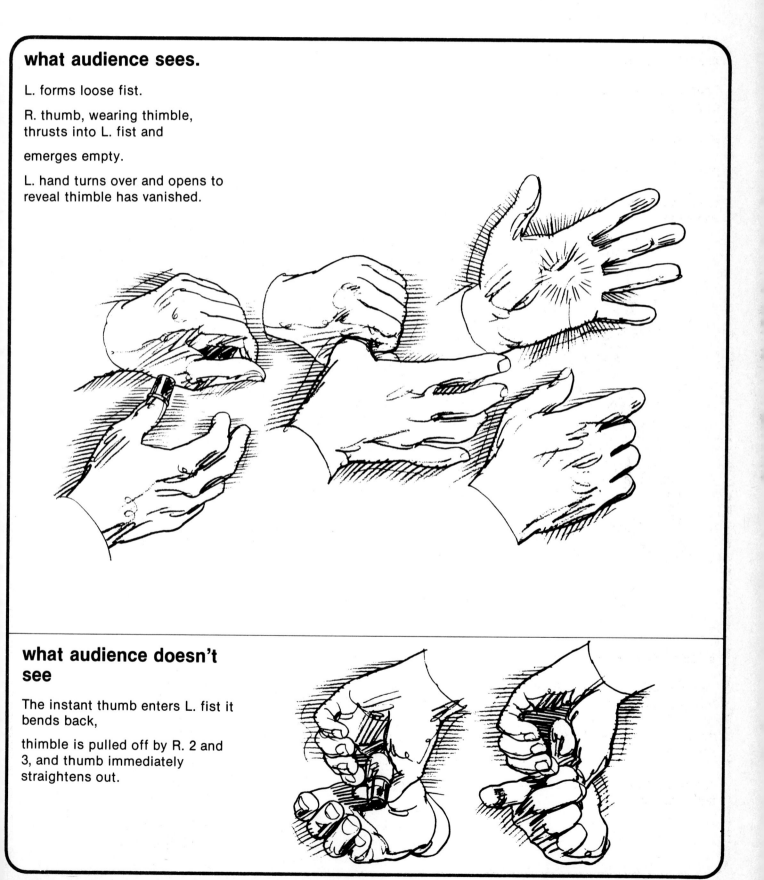

what audience doesn't see

The instant thumb enters L. fist it bends back,

thimble is pulled off by R. 2 and 3, and thumb immediately straightens out.

thimble hop ★

*a cute little flourish you may be able
to use in a close-up routine*

Thimble hops back and forth
between the first and second
fingers of either hand, or better
still, both hands simultaneously.

Start with thimble on first finger.
Bend fingers inward, grasp thimble
between thumb and third finger,
slip out first finger, slip in second,
and straighten fingers out. Repeat
several times.

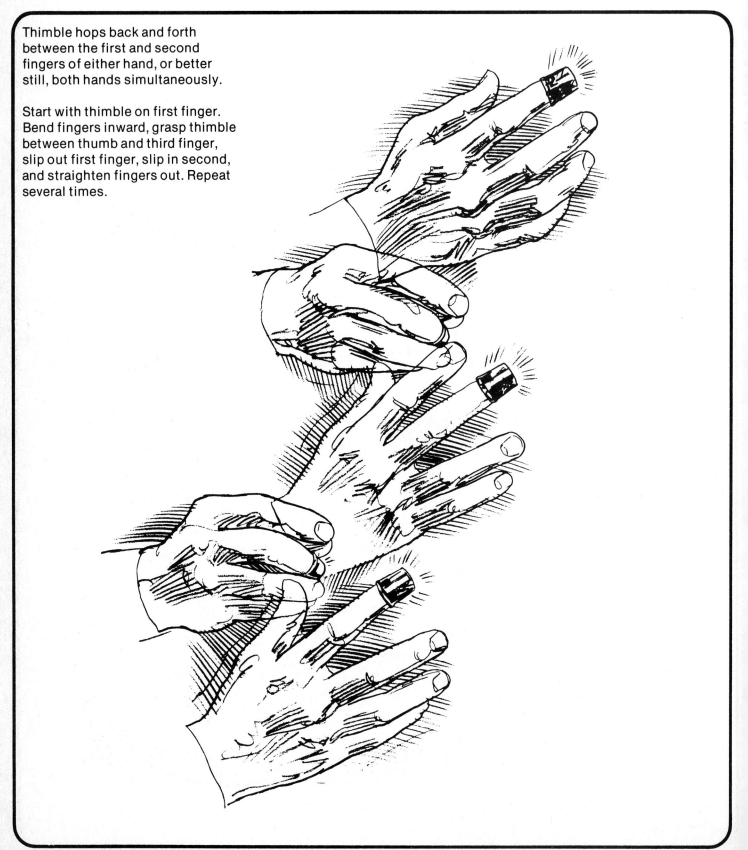

pop thimble recovery ★

a cute way to reveal the vanished thimble . . .

Place thimble on R. or L.2 and snap off with thumb making as loud a "pop" as you can.

Try different thimbles—and fingers—until you get a loud, sharp "pop."

Appear to place thimble into right hand, pretend to swallow, and recover with a loud "pop" from behind elbow, knee, etc.

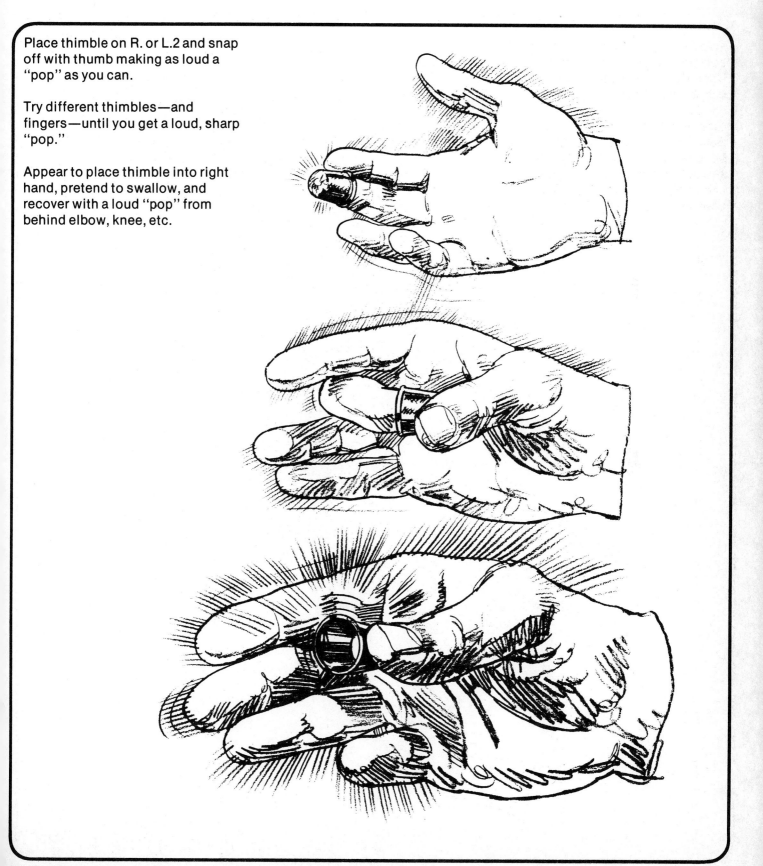

the jumping thimble ★★

*a cute little flourish for
use in a thimble routine*

what your audience sees . . .

(Do this move with a beat: 1, 2, 3, 4 . . . 1, 2, 3, 4.)

How to do it

Start with thimble thumb-palmed in L. hand, duplicate thimble on R. forefinger, and hands in front of body at waist-level, first fingers pointing toward right.

Hold arms stationary and pivot hands from wrist.

Shift hands to left, quickly thumb-palm R. thimble and at same time recover L. thimble.

Shift to right. Thumb-palm L. thimble and recover R. thimble.

Pause and repeat sequence again.

cigarettes and silks

Lighted cigarettes plucked out of thin air . . . that's the trick we most associate with cigarettes, but there are countless other intriguing effects. Following are a number of them to get you started, including, of course, the lit production of cigarettes!

Silks . . . the bright and colorful squares of silk or nylon that magicians so blithely produce and vanish right before your eyes, are surprisingly well adapted to sleights and flourishes of various types. Following are a few effects to introduce you to this colorful world.

palming cigarettes ★★

thumb-palm

The basic method for palming cigarettes, lit or unlit. If palmed lit, the hand should be kept in motion to avoid tell-tale traces of smoke.

The same basic move can be used to produce up to four or five cigarettes. If used in this fashion, however, the trick must be done as an opener. Produce, puff, discard, and repeat until hand is empty

finger-palming

cigarettes can be finger-palmed like this   or like this

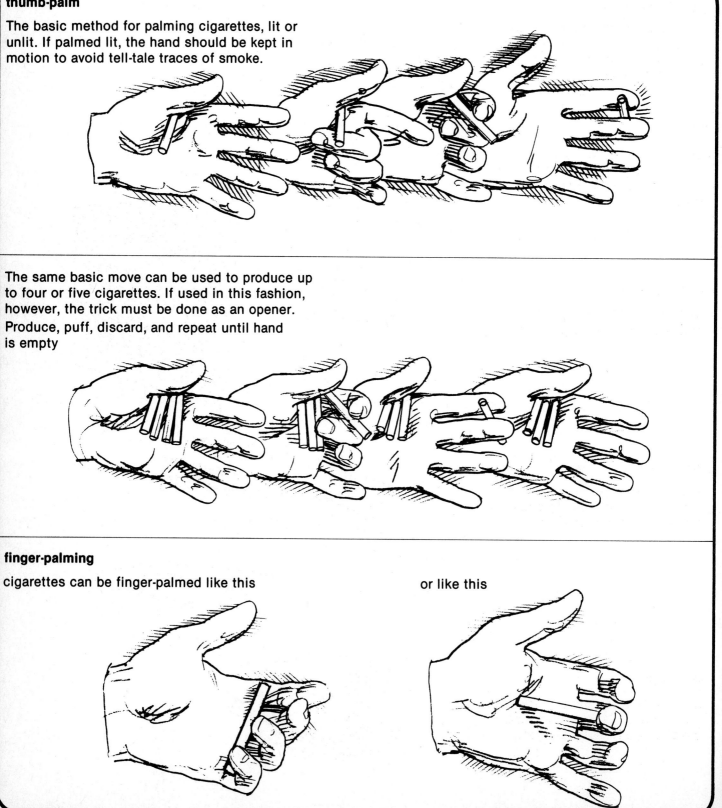

gimmicks

cigarette dropper

A small black sheet-metal case which drops ten or twelve standard or three-quarter-length unlit cigarettes, one at a time, into your fingers when pressure from the heel of your hand is applied against it.

Droppers are worn under your jacket on either or both sides, with openings approximately level with the bottom edge.

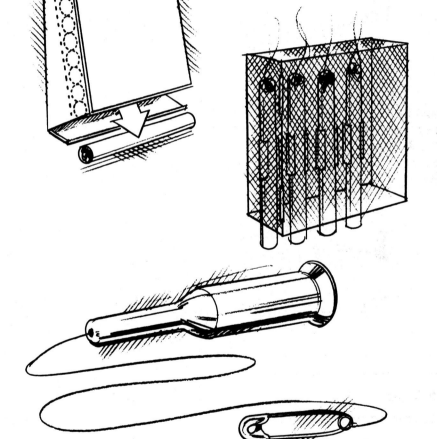

cigarette tank

Device to hold from one to four lit cigarettes. Not really practical.

cigarette pull

A device which vanishes a lit or unlit cigarette by pulling it up your sleeve or under your jacket.

thumb tip

a utility device, generally stamped out of metal, flesh-colored, and used to vanish various objects

basic cigarette vanish ★★

the standard, and most effective vanish
for a lit or an unlit cigarette . . .

1 Cigarette between R. 1 and R. 2.

2 L. hand slowly passes over front of R.

3 Under cover of L. fingers, R. thumb-palms cigarette and R. 1 and 2 quickly straighten out.

4 L. closes over R. 1 and 2 as if removing cigarette.

5 L. turns over and

6 opens to reveal that cigarette has vanished.

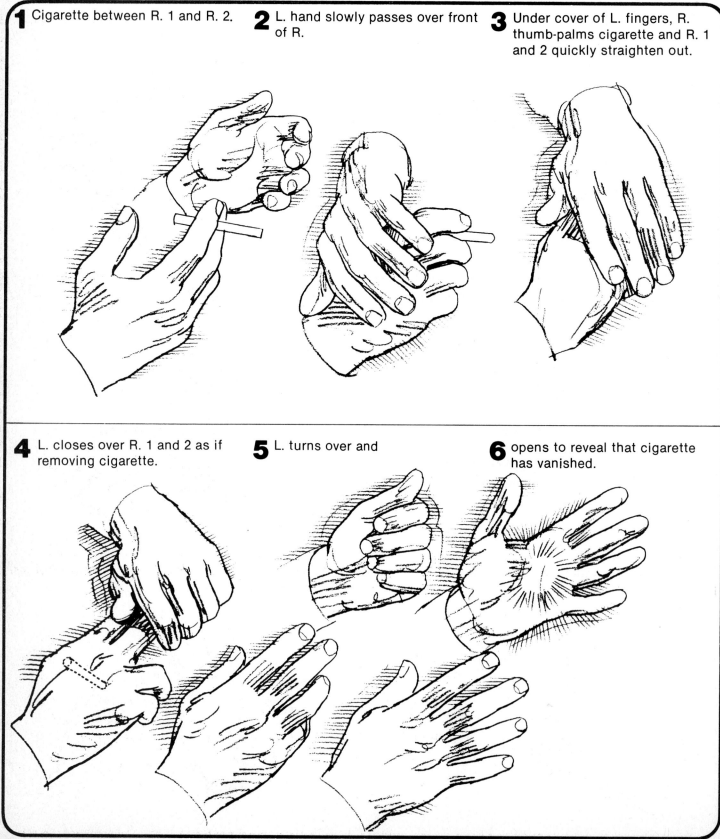

cigarette palm vanish ★★

a pretty little move for impromptu work

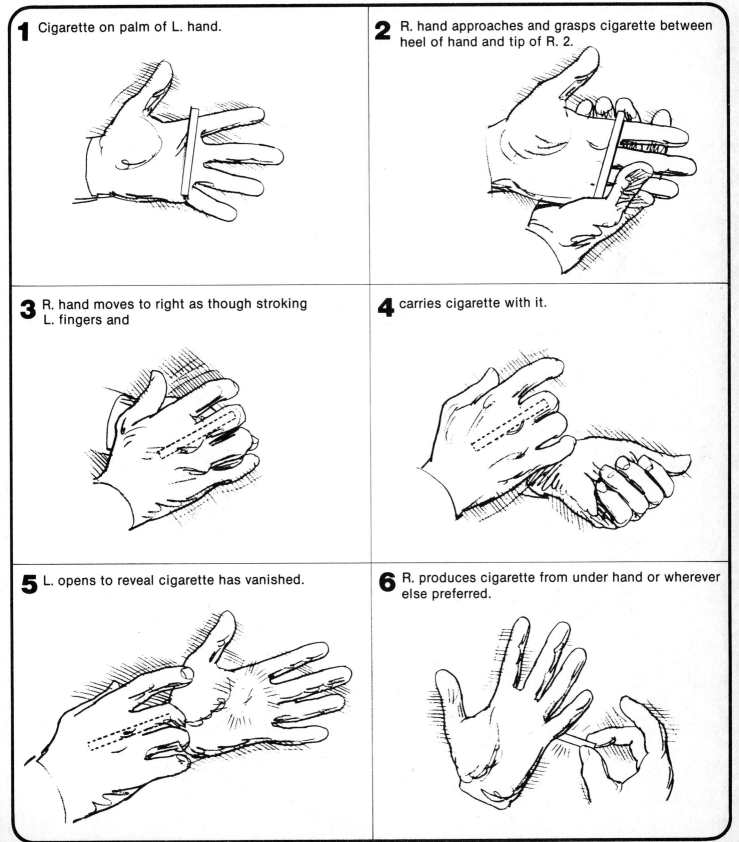

1 Cigarette on palm of L. hand.

2 R. hand approaches and grasps cigarette between heel of hand and tip of R. 2.

3 R. hand moves to right as though stroking L. fingers and

4 carries cigarette with it.

5 L. opens to reveal cigarette has vanished.

6 R. produces cigarette from under hand or wherever else preferred.

thumb tip vanish ★★

*with sleeves rolled up to the elbows you vanish
a cigarette right before their eyes . . .*

required

one thumb tip available
at a good magic supply house

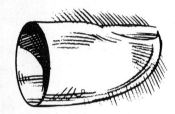

to prepare

Place thumb tip on R. thumb.

to perform

Show L. hand empty.

Turn L. hand over and as right
fingers tap back of hand, steal
thumb tip in L. palm.

Turn L. fist over again

Remove cigarette from lips with R.
hand, allowing audience to see that
R. hand is otherwise empty.

Drop cigarette into fist (actually
thumb tip) and

push cigarette into fist with thumb,
extinguishing it.

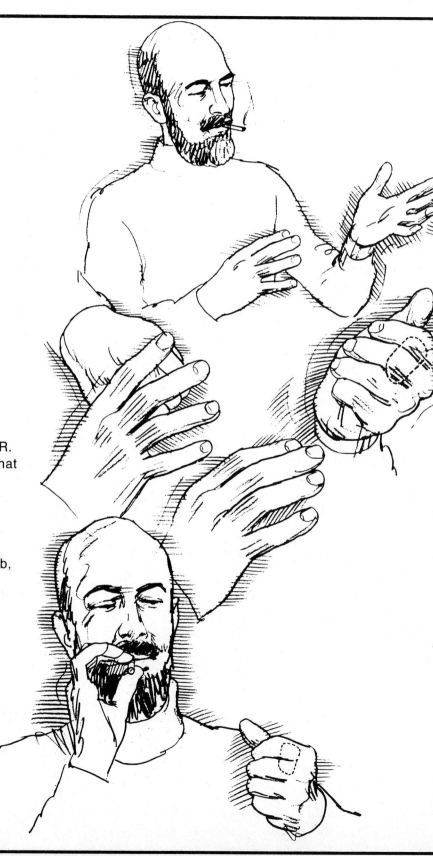

Remove thumb (with tip) and rub cigarette away.

Open hand to show that cigarette has vanished.

This is a classic method of vanishing a cigarette, and a masterpiece when well presented, but it is not as simple as it appears. Your first problem is to obtain your thumb tip. How and when you do it depends on circumstances. If you are doing tricks, you can get it from your pocket or table at the end of your previous effect. If you are sitting with friends, you might slip it on well in advance, perhaps when you go to your pocket for matches or a handkerchief.

You can get rid of it by reaching into your pocket or onto your table for props for your next trick, but be sure the cigarette is out! A bit of wet sponge or cloth in the bottom of your thumb tip will help.

Like every trick you do, think it out well in advance, practice your moves, and rehearse all of the details. Careful planning and clean presentation can turn a good trick into a miracle!

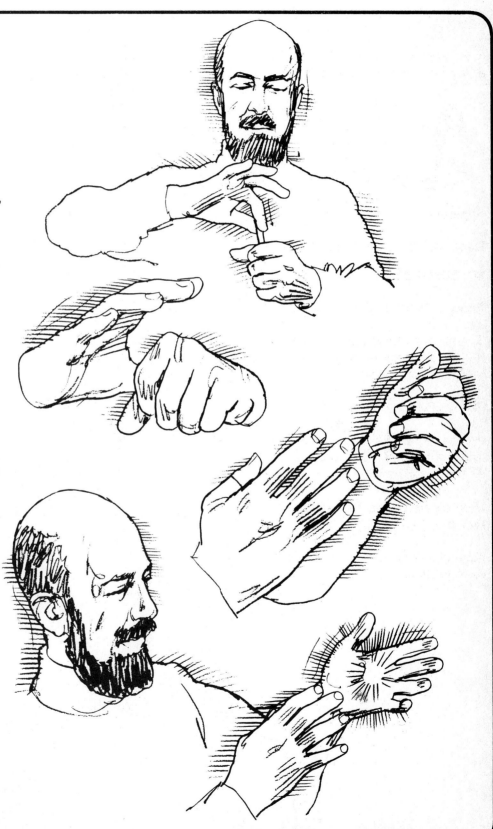

impromptu production ★★

*a good close-up effect, not terribly difficult, and a
fitting climax to a series of cigarette sleights . . .*

the effect

After having performed a number of sleights with an unlit cigarette, the magician places it in his pocket. Another cigarette immediately pops up. This, too, is placed into pocket, another appears, and so on until seven or eight cigarettes have been produced.

magician's-eye view

Cigarette A exhibited in L. hand. Cigarette B palmed in R.

During process of removing A, R. hand positions B behind L. 2, where it is

gripped between L. 1 and L. 3.

Under cover of R. fingers L. 2 immediately pivots B around the axis formed by L. 1 and L. 3 and into the L. hand.

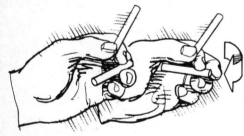

R. simultaneously removes A between R. thumb and R. 1 and visibly carries it toward right jacket pocket, where it appears to leave it.

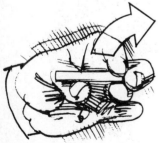

L. thumb snaps B into position between L. thumb and L. 1, from which point entire sequence is repeated several more times.

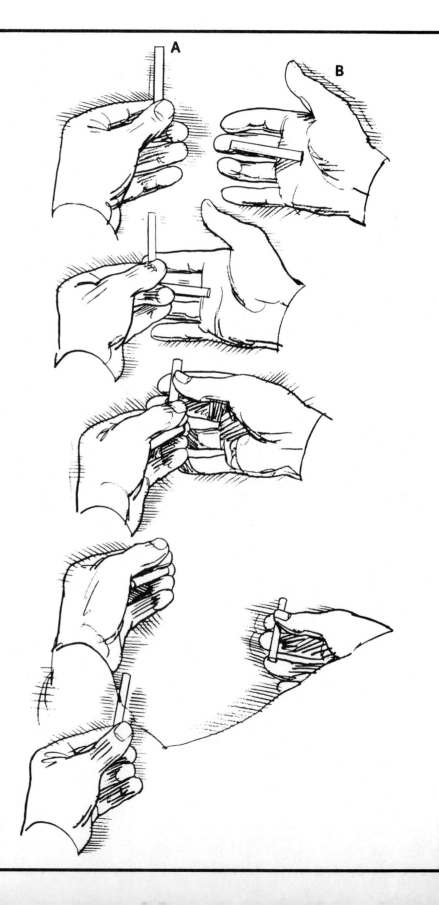

method two

Cigarette A is held between L. thumb and L. 1 and 2. Cigarette B is held in R. thumb-palm.

R. hand approaches and tip of B is placed alongside A and top of A is grasped between R. thumb and tip of R. 1.

Retain B in L. hand and remove A with R.

As R. proceeds toward pocket, use R. 2 to pivot B between R. thumb and R. 1 so that it can be seen by audience.

Pretend to place B in pocket, but with it actually thumb-palmed, come up and remove A and repeat move several more times.

Start your routine by doing method one three times and then switch to method two for three of four more times. On last move, leave cigarette in pocket, produce next one and light up.

Timing is important. Gaze, and keep gazing, intently at cigarette as R. hand carries it off to your pocket. As soon as R. begins to enter pocket avert your glance to L. hand, simultaneously produce cigarette and keep gazing at it as R. comes up to take it away. Don't look at R. as it approaches L!

Incidentally, this routine may be done with small cigars as well. Realistic dummies will hold up substantially better than brittle cigars.

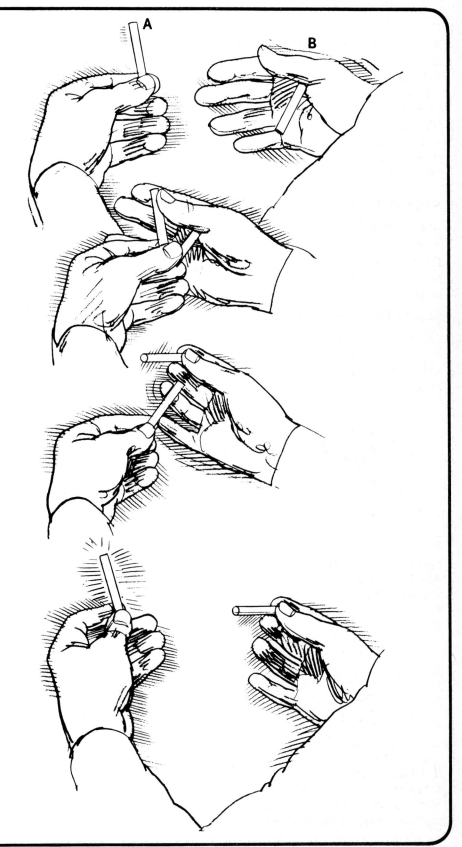

179

mini-routine ★★★

*a neat vanish, acquitment and recovery
with a lit, or unlit, cigarette*

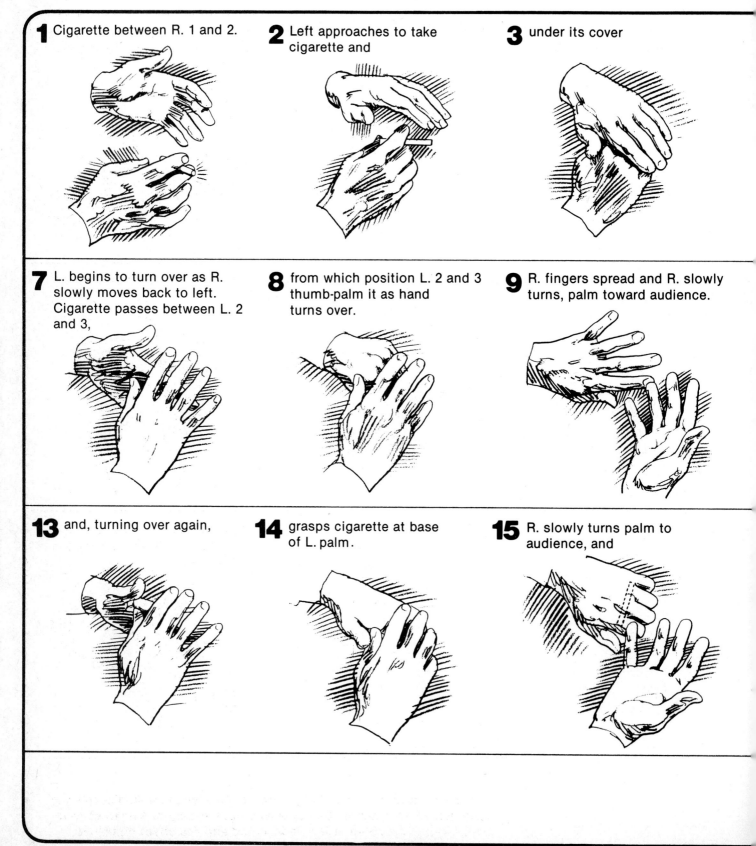

1 Cigarette between R. 1 and 2.

2 Left approaches to take cigarette and

3 under its cover

7 L. begins to turn over as R. slowly moves back to left. Cigarette passes between L. 2 and 3,

8 from which position L. 2 and 3 thumb-palm it as hand turns over.

9 R. fingers spread and R. slowly turns, palm toward audience.

13 and, turning over again,

14 grasps cigarette at base of L. palm.

15 R. slowly turns palm to audience, and

4 R. thumb palms cigarette as L. goes through motion of taking cigarette and carrying it off.

5 L., apparently holding cigarette, turns over and,

6 as R. moves several inches to right, opens to reveal cigarette has vanished.

10 L. hands drops slightly so that R. fingertips come under edge of L. palm, where

11 R. 2 and 3 grasp cigarette. L. continues down, as R. slowly turns and thumb-palms cigarette.

12 L. turns palm toward audience

16 then back again.

17 R. fingertips gently rub back of left hand, and cigarette,

18 pushed up by L. thumb, slowly rises, is removed by R. and smoked.

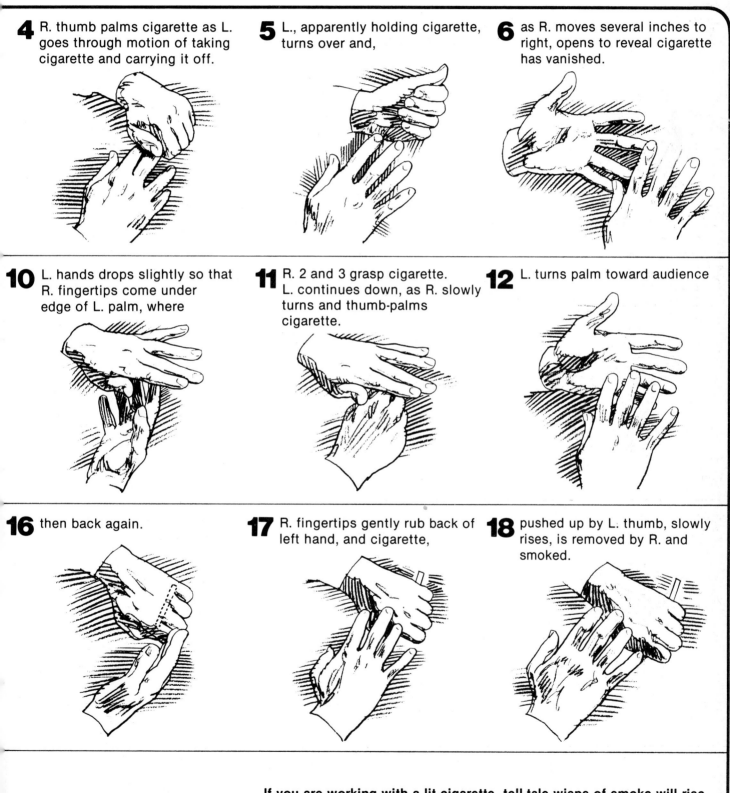

If you are working with a lit cigarette, tell-tale wisps of smoke will rise from behind your hands. Gently blow a light stream of smoke at your hands and the problem will be eliminated and the effect enhanced.

tap vanish ★★

a clean, deceptive vanish when done well . . .

Cigarette held in L. hand, as illustrated. R. fingertips tap cigarette several times, driving it into L. palm.

Cigarette, held between L. thumb and L. 2 is pivoted (snapped) back to fingertips by pushing down with tip of L. 1.

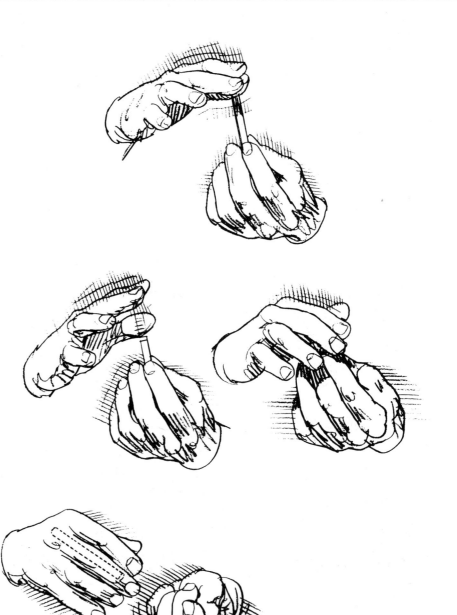

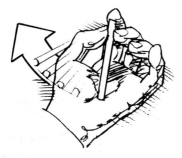

Repeat the above series once more.

The third time, when the cigarette is almost down into the L. hand for its full length, make the last tap with a somewhat forward motion and the cigarette will pop up into the R. palm.

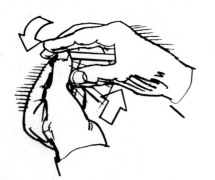

Close L. hand as though it contained the cigarette, slowly squeeze the cigarette away, open to reveal that it has vanished and recover the cigarette from the L. elbow, or wherever you prefer.

cigarette roll ★★

*a neat flourish but it's not
worth smoking just to use it*

Roll cigarette—lit or unlit—from
finger to finger. When it arrives
between 3 and 4, thumb-palm it
and begin all over.

Work precisely and rapidly for best
effect.

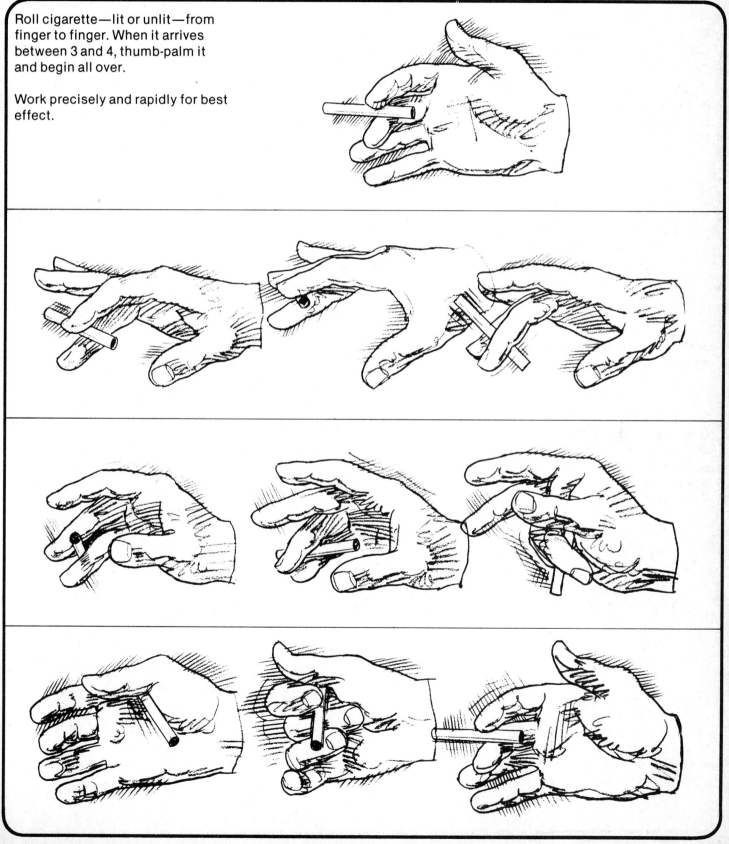

lit cigarette production ★★★

for many years, one of the most exciting—and puzzling—tricks

the effect

The magician reaches up and plucks a lit cigarette out of the air. He puffs on it once or twice, discards it, spots another, reaches up and produces it, and continues in this fashion until he has produced anywhere from ten to twelve cigarettes.

required

Two cigarette droppers each of which contains six or seven unlit three-quarter-length cigarettes. One dropper is pinned to the lining of each side of your jacket, with opening adjacent to bottom edge of jacket.

the basic moves

the production

Cigarette thumb-palmed in either hand.

R. or L. 2 goes under cigarette and R. or L. 1 goes on top.

Fingers straighten out and cigarette is produced.

the switch

Dummy is finger-palmed in either hand.

Cigarette is held between R. or L. 1 and 2. Hand flicks downward and dummy is discarded at same instant lit cigarette is thumb-palmed.

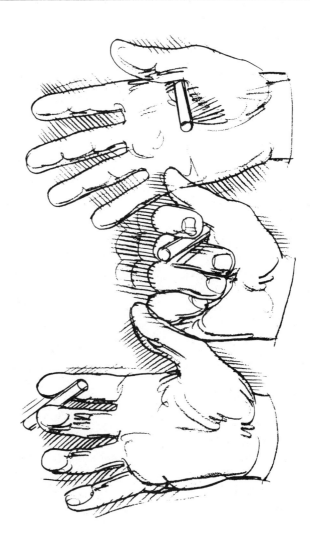

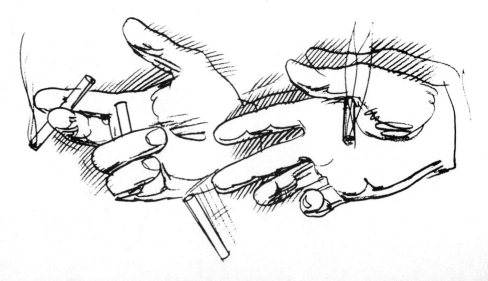

the basic routine

Magician lights cigarette, and standing with right shoulder toward audience, puffs on it several times.

At same time L. hand steals dummy from left dropper.

Turning so left shoulder is toward audience, L. removes lit cigarette from mouth, switches for and discards dummy.

Magician produces lit cigarette with L. hand. At same time R. steals dummy from dropper, and moves are repeated until supply is exhausted.

In actual practice, embellishments are added. Vanishes and recoveries are included in the routine, an acquitment such as the Mini Routine might be
worked in, and the act might end with the production of a lit cigar and/or a pipe (not actually lit but made to appear so by exhaling a large volume of smoke, from the previously produced lit cigarette, through it).

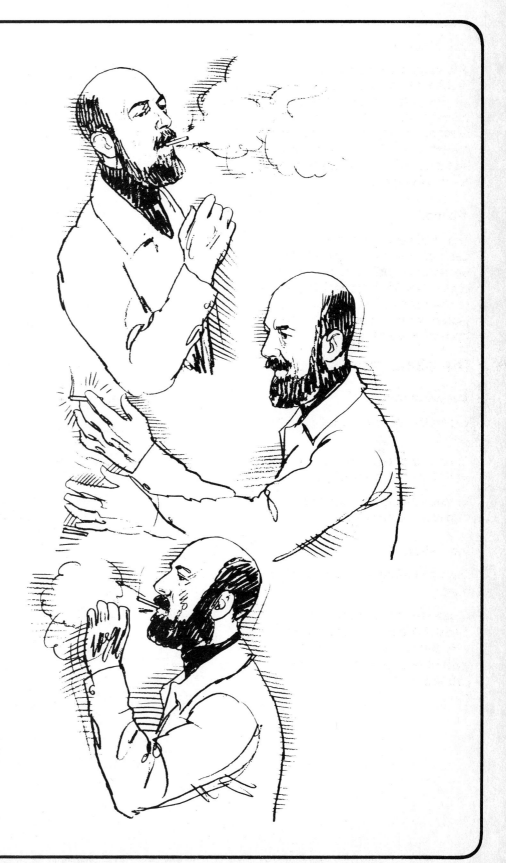

silks

Magician's silks are very thin, compressible squares of fine silk made in a wide range of colors, sizes, shapes and designs. They are used in a great variety of tricks and are especially effective as production items from empty hats, paper tubes, boxes and so on.

flags

streamers (generally 6″ wide and anywhere from 10′ to 50′ long)

rainbows

card silks

specialty silks

silk gimmicks

handkerchief ball
Device used for the bare-hand production of silks.
Comes with or without an attached thumb-loop.

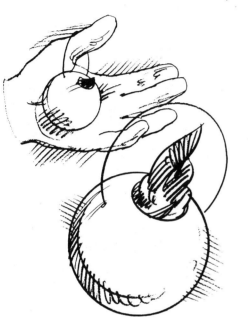

hollow billiard ball for the silk to ball effect

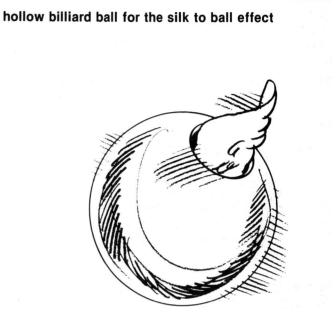

die tube

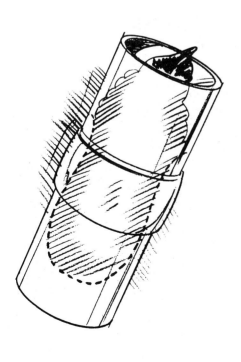

another gimmick for the bare-hand production of a silk

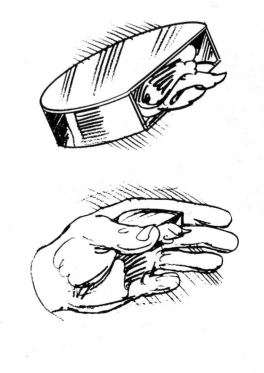

vanishing knot ★

a standard vanishing knot flourish for use in a silk routine . . .

Twirl silk into a loose rope.

Grasp end A between L. 1 and 2 about six inches from left end.

Grasp B between R. 1 and 2 about six inches from right end.

Toss end B over L. hand and grasp between L. thumb and L. 1.

Reach through loop with R. 1 and 2, and grasp A.

Place L. 2 under end A and over end B and pull A through loop with R. 1 and 2.

Keep L. 2 over B, draw loop fairly tight, and then remove L. 2.

Hold knotted silk with L. hand.

Grasp knot with R., sweep hand down length of silk and apparently pull knot off silk and disolve away.

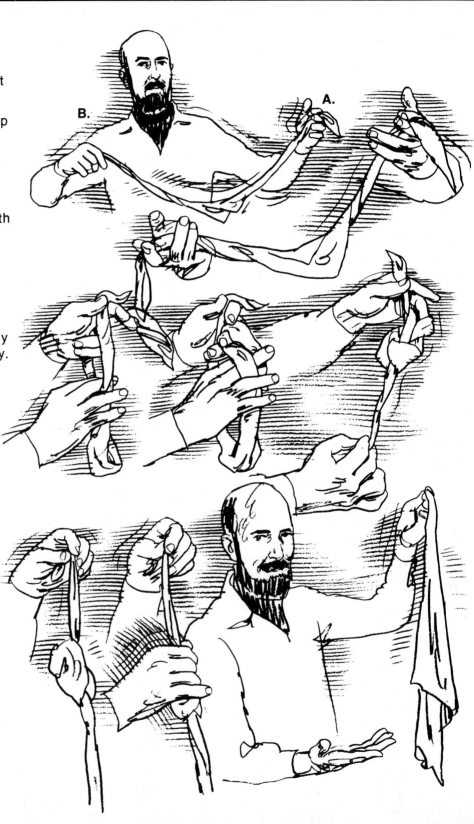

instant knot ★★

a little flourish to use when handling silks

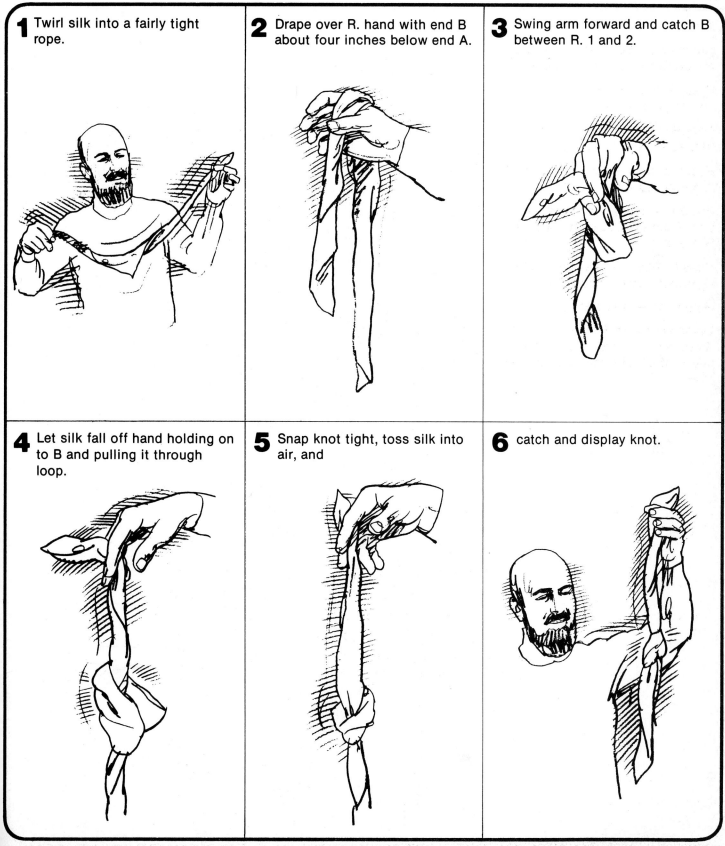

1 Twirl silk into a fairly tight rope.

2 Drape over R. hand with end B about four inches below end A.

3 Swing arm forward and catch B between R. 1 and 2.

4 Let silk fall off hand holding on to B and pulling it through loop.

5 Snap knot tight, toss silk into air, and

6 catch and display knot.

the untying silk ★★

a superb, professional stage effect that blends in with almost any type of program, but don't try it close up . . .

the effect

Magician removes silk from breast pocket, twirls it into a loose rope and ties a simple knot in it. As he holds it, the silk mysteriously rises and unties itself.

to prepare

Sew a twenty-two-inch length of strong, fine black thread into the corner of an eighteen-inch silk. Tie the free end of the thread to a small safety pin and affix it under the left side of your jacket about three inches below your shoulder. Place your silk in your upper left breast pocket with the unthreaded corner easily accessible.

to perform

Grasp the corner diagonally opposite the threaded corner and remove silk from pocket with R. hand.

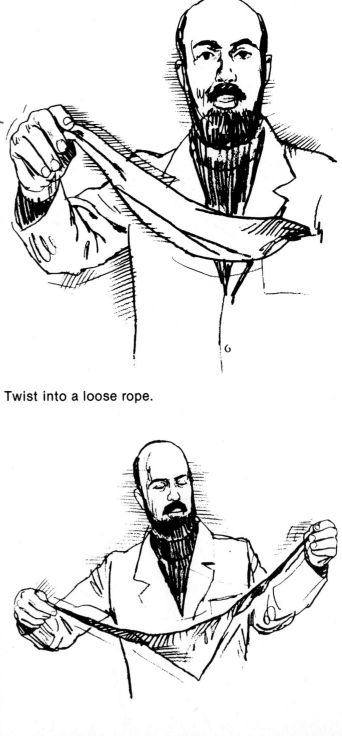

Twist into a loose rope.

Tie a simple knot.

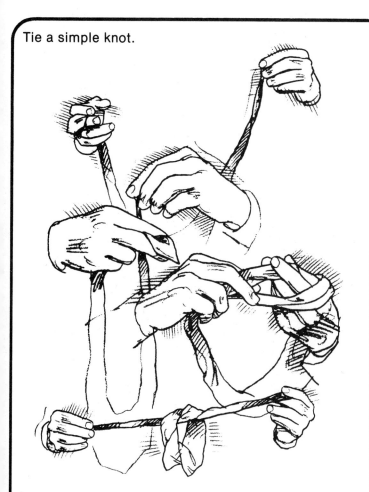

Hold silk by the corner and hook L. thumb over the thread.

Raise R. hand slightly as you pull down on thread with L. thumb and the silk mysteriously unties!

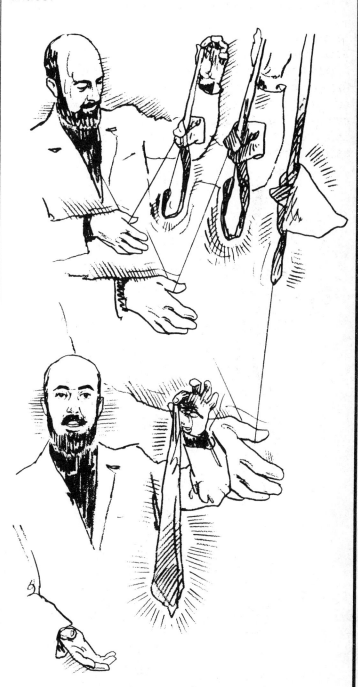

If an eighteen-inch silk requires too long a pull to get it to untie, try a fifteen-incher and a shorter length of thread. Experiment, try the pin in various places and use different lengths of thread until you find the perfect combination for you.

color-changing silk ★★★

a beautiful effect, but it requires two silks,
a color-changing gimmick and a lot of practice . . .

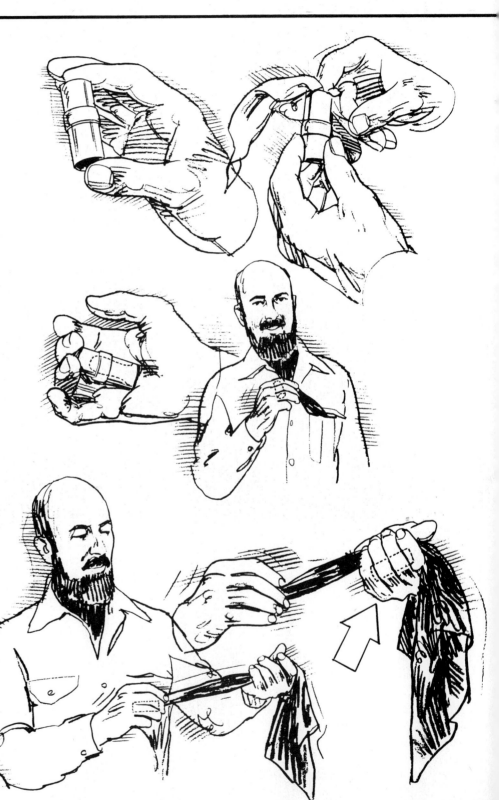

required

Two fourteen-inch silks of sharply contrasting colors and a color-changing tube which you can buy at a magic shop or make out of brass, plastic or cardboard.

to prepare

Start at one corner and stuff red silk into tube. Place green silk in left breast pocket or on your table, depending on how and where you are working.

to perform

R. hand secures gimmick in finger-palm, tape end toward fingers, and removes silk from pocket.

Run silk through R. hand two times.

On third pass drop gimmick onto L. palm and, without hesitation, continue to run silk through palm, but don't pull all the way through.

Alternately poke green silk into top of L. fist and help red silk to emerge from bottom until

red silk is clear of fist, held only by pressure of L. 4 against palm.

Display silk

on both sides.

Crumple up and place back in pocket or on table along with gimmick.

pocket vanish ★★

*a neat, no-gimmick vanish, but it won't work
in dungarees . . .*

**This is an old but very mystifying
vanish, particularly effective if
you have a close rapport with your
audience.**

Show silk between L. thumb and
L. 1.

Turn hand over.

Rub palms together in a circular
motion, causing silk to ball up
between hands.

L. hand, containing silk, turns
over and

R., puffed out as though holding
silk, reaches into R. trouser pocket.

Noticing reaction of audience, who
think they have caught you in act
of sneaking silk to pocket, smile
and say, "I wouldn't fool you . . ."
as you flick silk out of L. hand,
retaining corner between L. thumb
and palm.

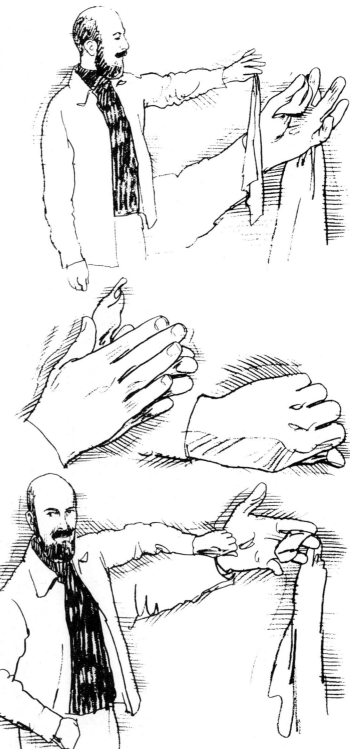

Roll up silk again, but this time turn L. over empty,

finger-palm silk in R., and go to pocket and

thrust silk into upper portion.

As if aware of audience suspicions, show R. hand distinctly empty and turning pocket inside out, say, "The pocket is empty."

Turn hand over, slowly rub silk away and open hand to reveal that silk has vanished.

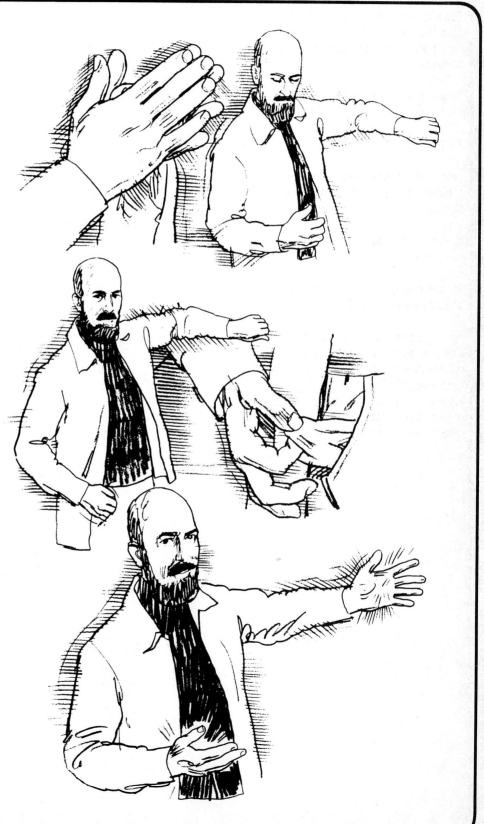

barehand silk production ★★★

the prettiest of all silk productions and a nice opener for a billard-ball routine

required

One handkerchief ball into which an eighteen-inch silk has been stuffed, finger-palmed in R. hand.

a ping-pong ball will hold a fifteen-inch silk

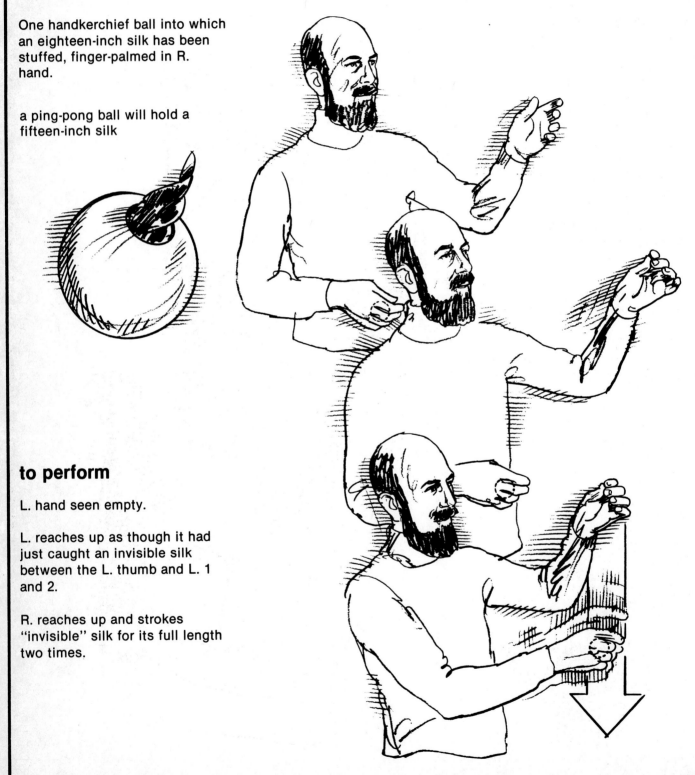

to perform

L. hand seen empty.

L. reaches up as though it had just caught an invisible silk between the L. thumb and L. 1 and 2.

R. reaches up and strokes "invisible" silk for its full length two times.

At beginning of third stroke L. thumb and L. 1 and 2 grasp corner of silk. R. hand strokes down as before and silk is magically produced.

Three thin fifteen-inch silks will fit into an aluminum handkerchief ball. Produce the first silk as above, stroke it once, and on the second stroke, produce the second silk alongside the first. Stroke them, and produce the third.

When stuffing several silks, twist ends together as illustrated.

Use a hollow billiard ball instead of a handkerchief ball (available at magic supply houses), stuff the produced silk into your fist, turning it into a billiard ball, and use it to start your routine.

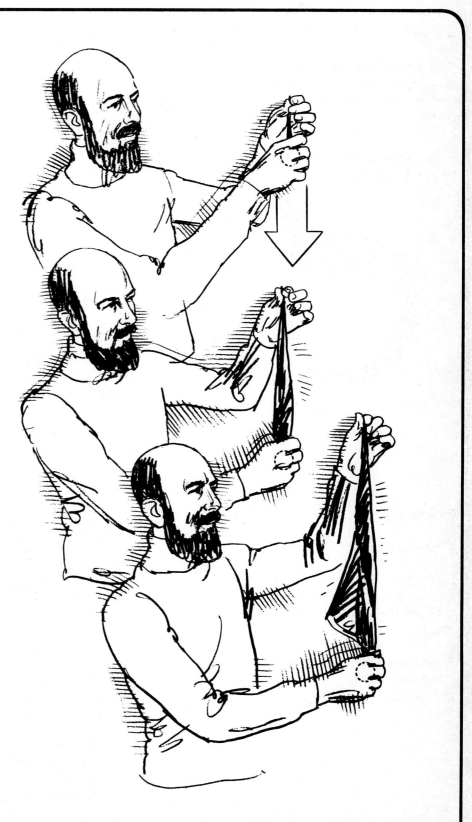

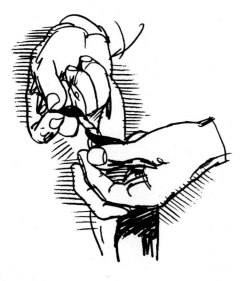

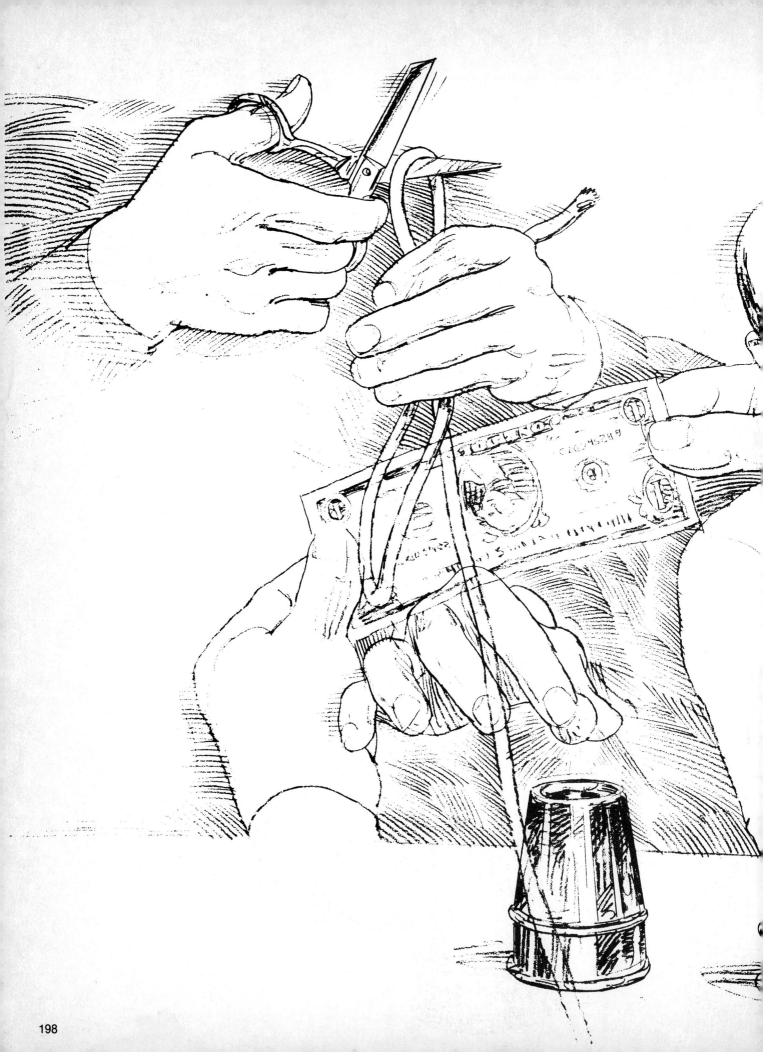

tricks

In the final analysis, mystifying your audience is really what it's all about, and in the following pages you'll learn a number of good tricks to help you do just that! They range from super-easy to quite difficult, but all of them are calculated to amuse and amaze.

torn and restored paper ★★

an old trick, tried and true, and the basis
for all of the many torn and restored paper effects . . .

to prepare

Cut a sheet of tissue paper into
two identically sized pieces,
approximately three by ten
inches, and fold one of them,
as illustrated.

Glue folded piece to the back of
the other.

to perform

Tear the paper in half and place
the left half in front of the right.

Tear in half again and place the
left pieces in front of the right.

Fold the torn edges neatly, flush
with whole packet.

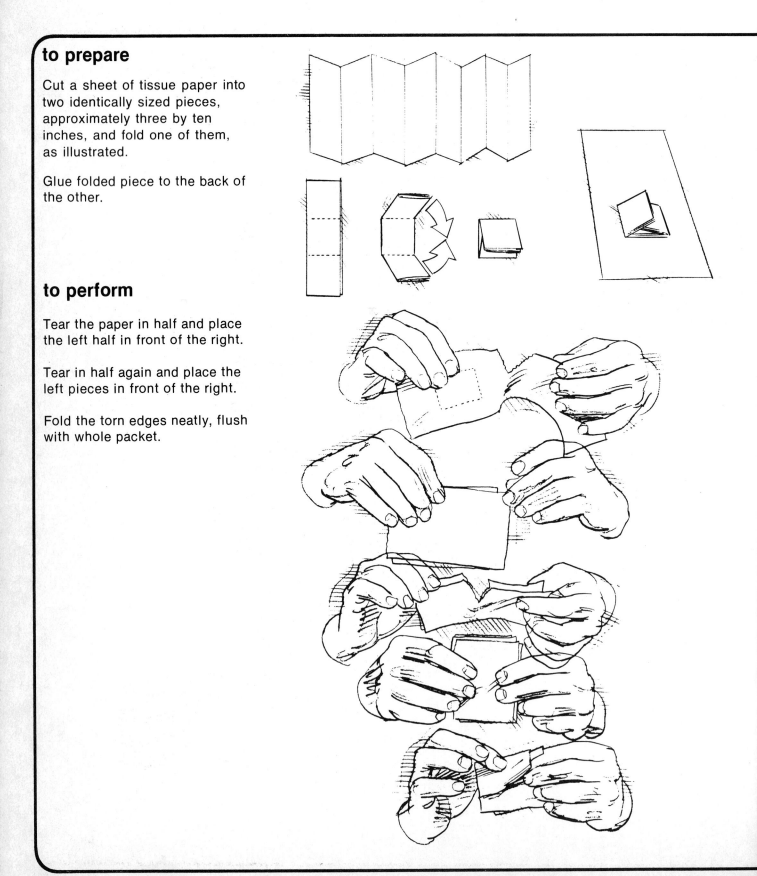

Fold the top edge even with the whole packet.

Fold the bottom edge even with whole packet.

Fold both packets in half, and in process, reverse so that whole packet faces audience and torn portion is on back.

Unfold untorn packet, and paper is restored.

This is the basic torn and restored paper trick. The variations are many—large sheets, small sheets, strips, newspapers, and on and on—but the principle is always the same.

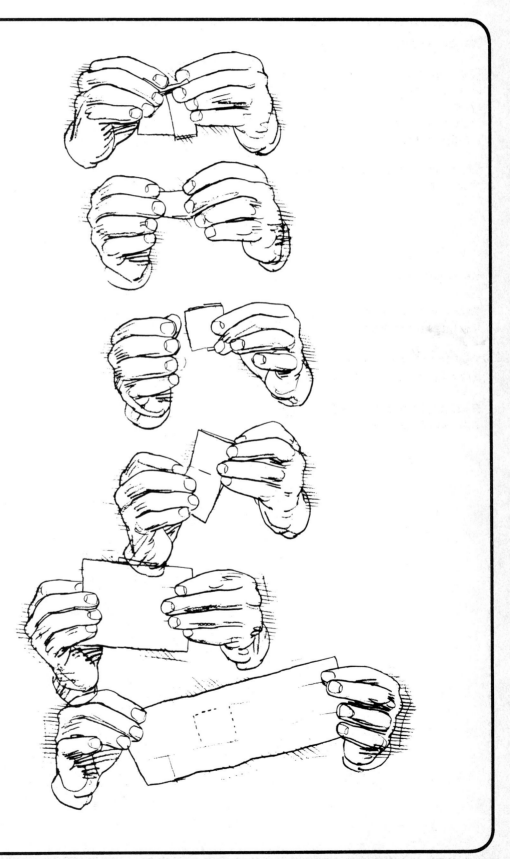

torn and restored cigarette paper ★★★

a beautiful close-up mystery . . .

the effect

Magician shows a pack of cigarette papers, removes one, tears it into eighths and then restores it. He invites spectator to initial restored pieces, place it on ashtray and set it aflame. He restores the charred embers and the spectator confirms that the initials are his.

to prepare

Place a light dab of rubber cement on corner of a pack of cigarette papers and allow to dry. Ball up one sheet of paper and press on to corner of pack.

Place in R. jacket pocket along with a pencil stub and a book of matches.

to perform

Remove pack from pocket along with matches and pencil stub, securing balled paper between R. 1 and 2 as you do so.

Place pack of paper on table and open with L. hand.

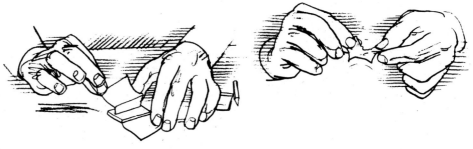

Roll ball between tips of R. thumb and R. 1 and remove paper. Roll ball between R. 1 and R. 2 and tear paper in half.

Place left piece in front of right.

Tear into quarters and place left pieces in front of right.

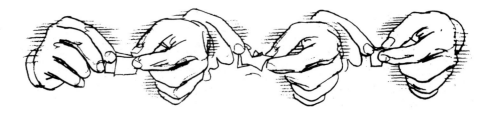

Tear into eighths and place left pieces in front of right.

Ball up pieces.

Squeeze into tight ball.

During process, switch positions of balls.

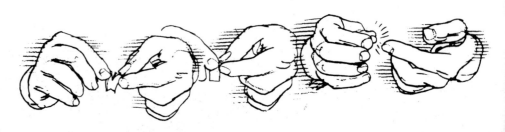

Wave finger over ball.

Grasp corner and pull out.

Roll torn ball back between R. 1 and 2 and finish opening paper.

Roll ball back between R. thumb and R. 1 and hold restored paper by tip.

Place on table and have someone initial paper.

Roll up paper and switch for torn pieces exactly as you did above.

Pull out paper, being careful not to expose torn pieces.

Ask someone to strike a match for you.

Drop paper on ashtray and place burning match alongside it or paper will not flame away.

Rub tips of R. thumb and R. 1 in ashes and slowly open paper and show initials to spectator.

If you prefer you can end this trick after you have restored the paper the first time, and you will still have a fine close-up effect.

You may also eliminate the rubber cement if you prefer and simply place a couple of rolled-up paper balls in your jacket pocket alongside the cigarette paper pack, and steal one when you remove the pack.

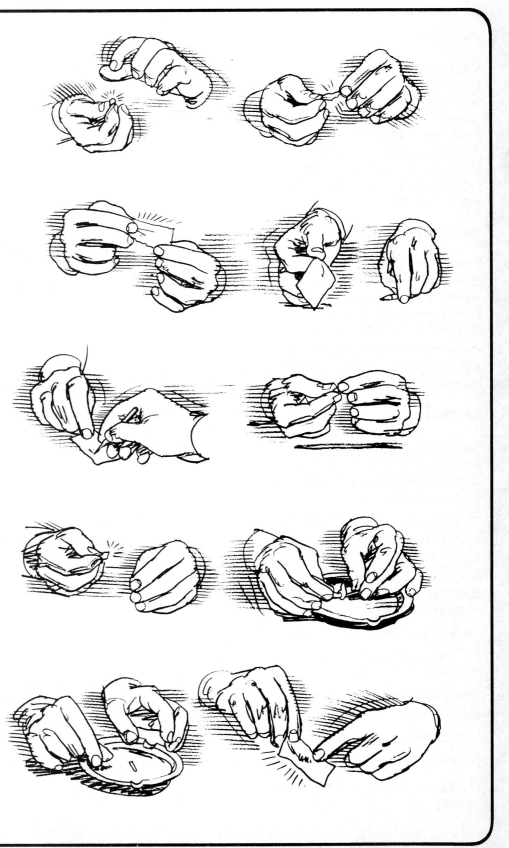

bits and tricks with matches ★

matches, perhaps because they are so easily available, are widely used by sleight-of-hand artists . . .

wood through wood

Break the heads off two wooden matches and hold as illustrated. Separate the R. fingers so that the match pulls away from the thumb but remains affixed to the tip of R. 1. Adjust the location of the matches or reverse ends until this happens.

Hold matchsticks firmly and bring hands toward each other. Just before matchsticks touch, separate R. thumb and R. 1 sufficiently to allow match in L. fingers to pass through gap at R. fingers. The instant the matches "penetrate," close the gap.

Show the matches linked together and then reverse the process.

If matches aren't available, round toothpicks from which both ends have been broken will work almost as well.

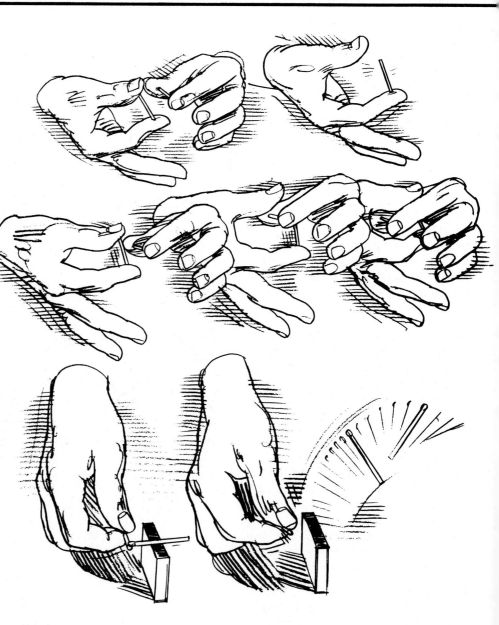

Place a match (or toothpick) on the edge of a box or book or whatever, and gently touch a second match underneath it, and the first will jump a foot or two into the air.

The secret is your fingernail. As the matches make contact (always at right angles), flick the end of the match you are holding with your fingernail.

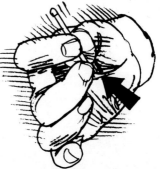

Wrap a small piece of metal-foil around the head of a match, place match on a match-box, or whatever, and ignite with a second match and it will hurl itself through the air. (Don't do this near curtains, carpets, etc.)

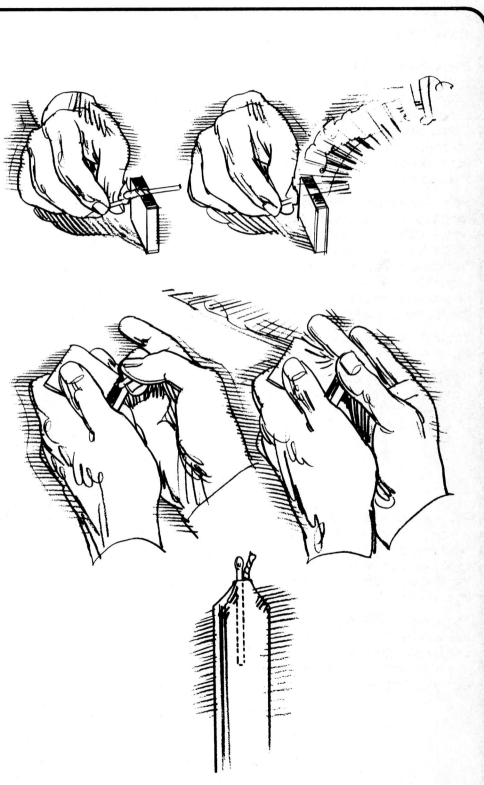

Hold a match between the R. thumb and R. 2, strike, and immediately flick forward. The match will arc through the air for ten or fifteen feet. This is a good bit for a cigarette production routine.

Magician places cigarette in mouth and attempts to light, but match flies away. He tries again, with similar results. Disgusted, he reaches under his jacket, pulls out a lit candle and lights up.

Work a wooden match into the tip of a candle and place it upside down in your inside jacket pocket. Glue a piece of fine sandpaper to a piece of cardboard and pin it inside your jacket next to the candle. When you remove the candle, rub the match against the sandpaper and it will come out lit.

This is not an impromptu trick, but rather is used as a bit during a stage routine. Excercise care when doing it or any trick with matches.

changing spots ★

a quickie trick, very easy to do, but absolutely baffling when it is properly presented . . .

First do this

Hold a die between R. thumb and R. 1.

Push thumb forward and R. 1. back, thus twisting the die one facet.

Reverse the movement, bringing the die back to its original position.

Now practice the same moves as you turn your whole hand over and back, and practice it in front of your mirror until the move is absolutely undetectable.

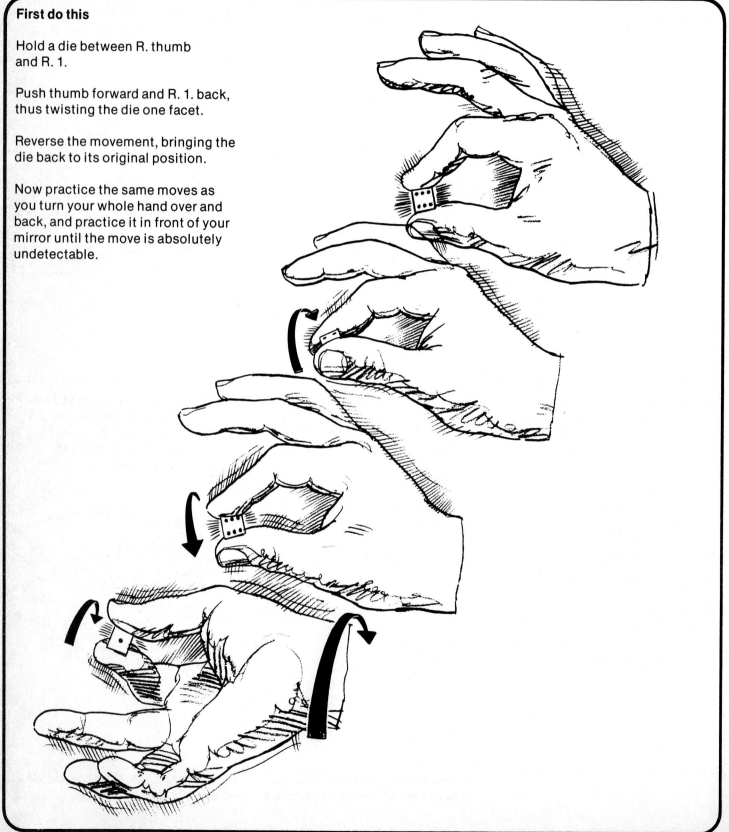

Now do this

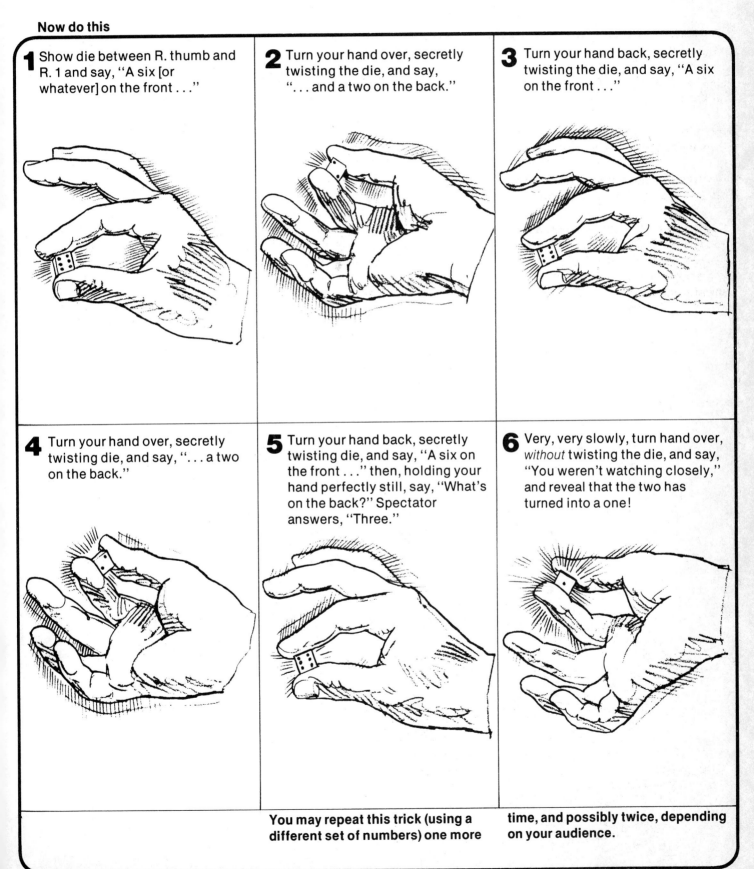

1 Show die between R. thumb and R. 1 and say, "A six [or whatever] on the front . . ."

2 Turn your hand over, secretly twisting the die, and say, ". . . and a two on the back."

3 Turn your hand back, secretly twisting the die, and say, "A six on the front . . ."

4 Turn your hand over, secretly twisting die, and say, ". . . a two on the back."

5 Turn your hand back, secretly twisting die, and say, "A six on the front . . ." then, holding your hand perfectly still, say, "What's on the back?" Spectator answers, "Three."

6 Very, very slowly, turn hand over, *without* twisting the die, and say, "You weren't watching closely," and reveal that the two has turned into a one!

You may repeat this trick (using a different set of numbers) one more time, and possibly twice, depending on your audience.

cut and restored rope ★★

an old classic but still as baffling as ever . . .

The effect: Magician cuts an unprepared rope in half, ties the end together, and restores the rope.

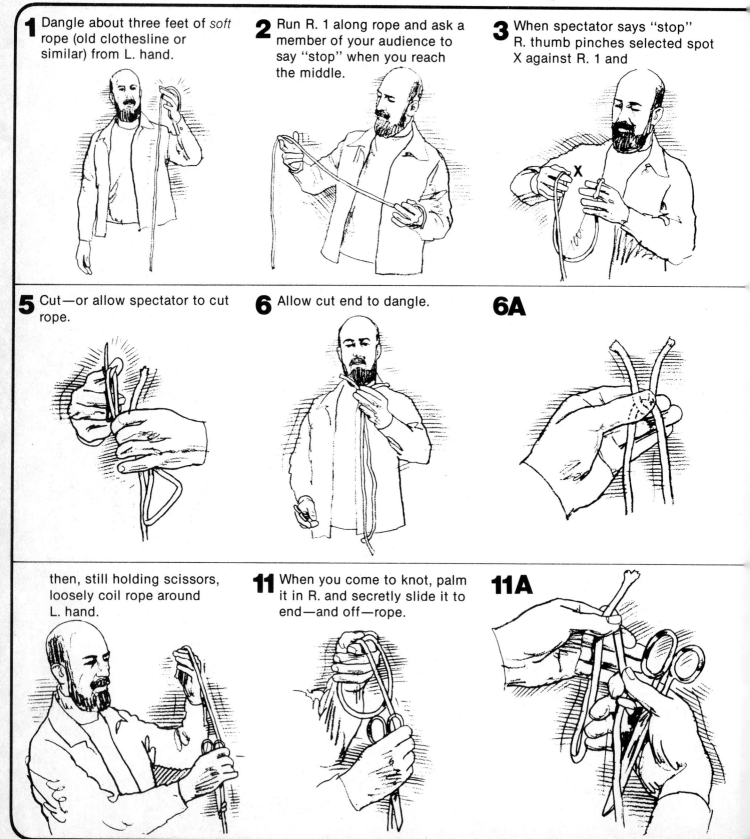

1 Dangle about three feet of *soft* rope (old clothesline or similar) from L. hand.

2 Run R. 1 along rope and ask a member of your audience to say "stop" when you reach the middle.

3 When spectator says "stop" R. thumb pinches selected spot X against R. 1 and

5 Cut—or allow spectator to cut rope.

6 Allow cut end to dangle.

6A

then, still holding scissors, loosely coil rope around L. hand.

11 When you come to knot, palm it in R. and secretly slide it to end—and off—rope.

11A

3A

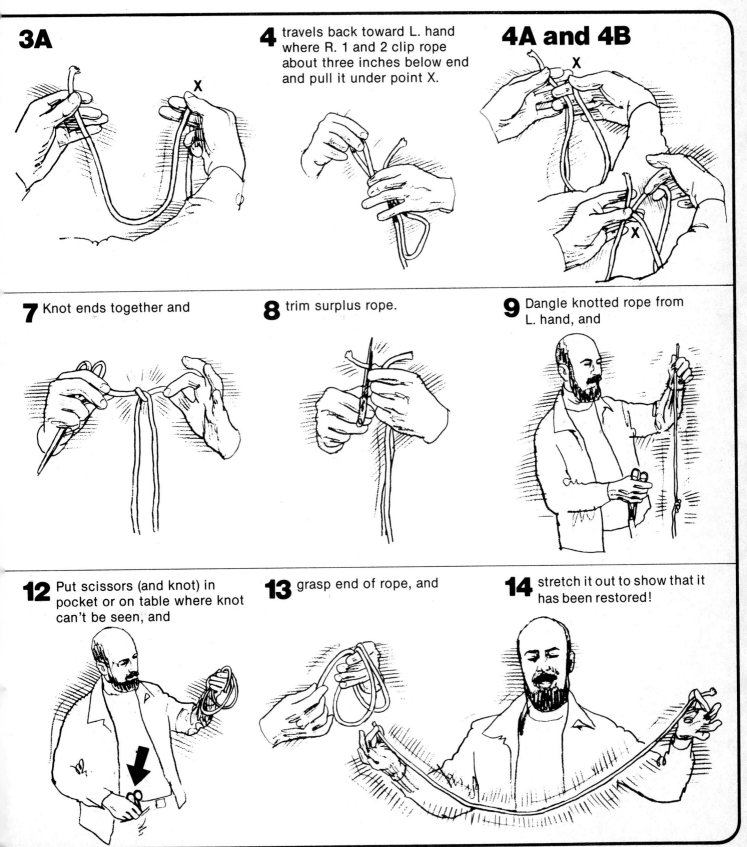

4 travels back toward L. hand where R. 1 and 2 clip rope about three inches below end and pull it under point X.

4A and 4B

7 Knot ends together and

8 trim surplus rope.

9 Dangle knotted rope from L. hand, and

12 Put scissors (and knot) in pocket or on table where knot can't be seen, and

13 grasp end of rope, and

14 stretch it out to show that it has been restored!

three shell game ★★★

the old con game, still as fascinating as ever,
and a fine close-up trick . . .

required

Three walnut shells, a very fine-grained sponge-rubber pea approximately one quarter inch in diameter, and a good, not too slick surface to work on.

Handsome plastic shells and good rubber peas are available at magic supply houses, but you can make your own if you like.

Obtain three large walnut shell-halves as similar in size and appearance as possible. Clean out the inside well. Although unprepared shells will work, you will get better results if you line the inside surface with wax or plastic wood.

the basic move

the basic move

Hold shell between the R. thumb at back and R. 1. Curl R. 2 behind, as illustrated.

Place pea on table and cover with shell. Push shell forward about two inches. Ball automatically squeezes through tiny opening in back of shell and is caught and held between thumb and tip of R. 2, from which position it cannot be seen.

If your pea is the proper consistency (not too hard, not too soft), and the opening at the rear of shell is not too small, it will not be necessary to raise the shell to allow the pea to exit.

to load pea into shell

Hold pea in basic position. Pull shell back an inch or so. Pea will flatten between thumb and table and roll into shell without it having to be raised.

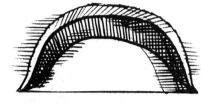

cross section

back view

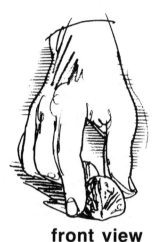

front view

side view

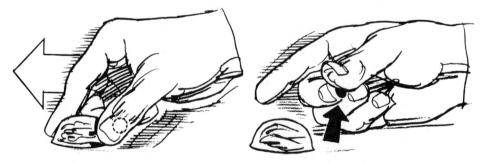

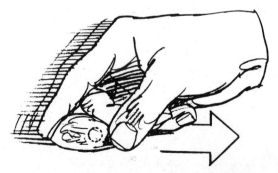

a typical series of moves

Line up shells A, B and C three or four inches apart.

Place pea about two inches in front of B, with R. hand.

Cover pea with B, with R. hand.

Push A level with B, with L. hand.

Push C level with A and B, with R. hand.

Simultaneously push A three inches forward with L. and B three inches forward with R., stealing pea in R.

Push C level with A and B, with R.

Push A to right of C, with R.

Push C to left of B, with R.

Simultaneously pull C back three inches with L. and A three inches back with R., at same time loading pea into A.

Pull B level with A and C, with R.

Ask your audience where they think pea is and show where it really is, or
point to B and say, "The pea is here . . . Right?" Your audience will agree. Pick up B and say, "Wrong! You weren't watching closely. It's right over here . . ." Pick up A and show pea.

Say, "Let's try that again," and do a different combination of moves.

It is best *not* to improvise as you go along. The top sleight-of-hand men work out their moves—and their patter—in advance and present them as part of a definite routine, and they quit while they're ahead and always leave their audience wanting more!

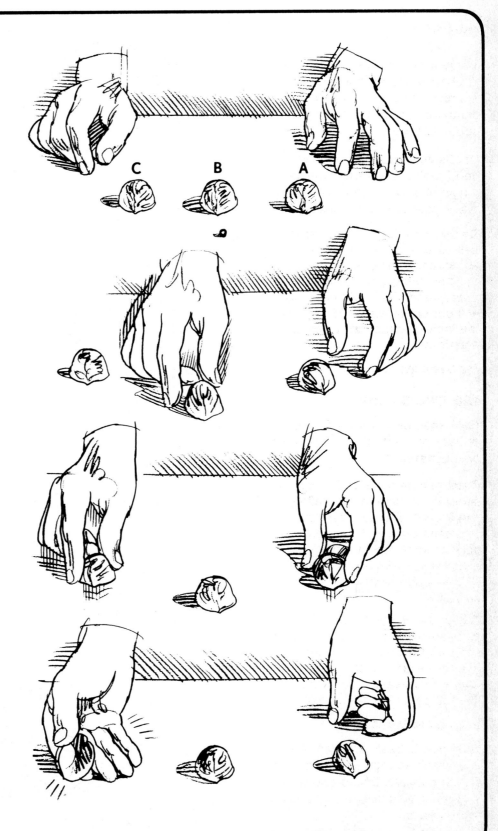

C   B   A

the stretching thumb trick ★

more of a stunt than a trick, but when it's well done it keeps little kids as amazed and amused as anything you'll ever do

try this in front of a mirror until you get it just right

Make several hypnotic passes with R. hand

and put thumb to sleep.

Bring R. hand over

and slowly slide the tip of your thumb forward and back two times . . .

Straighten out thumb,

rub R. 1 fingertip over thumb joint as though to heal it, raise thumb, and flex it several times.

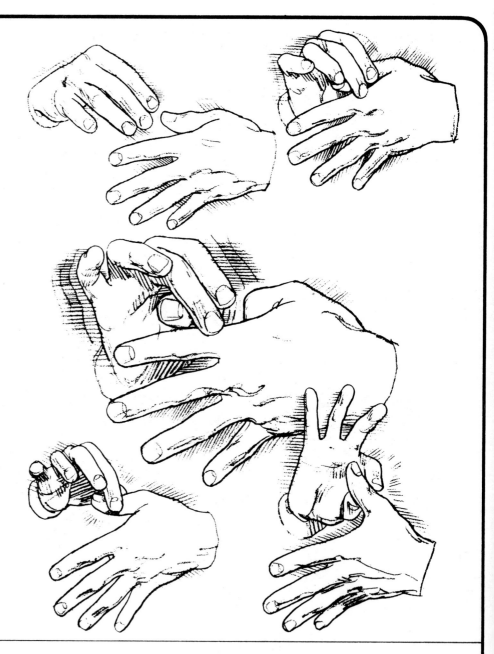

from the back it looks like this

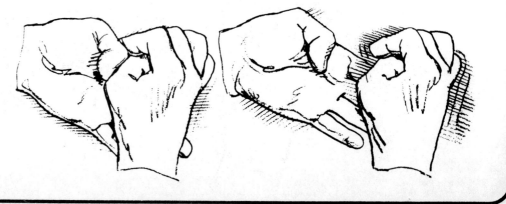

upside-down george ★

*kids love this little impromptu trick, but
it will amuse anyone*

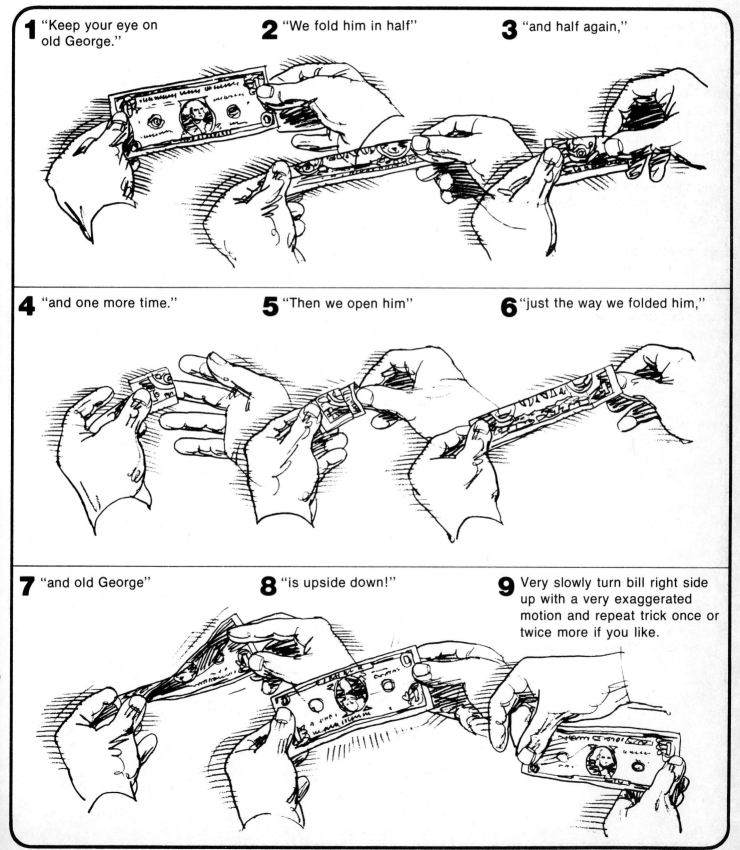

1 "Keep your eye on old George."

2 "We fold him in half"

3 "and half again,"

4 "and one more time."

5 "Then we open him"

6 "just the way we folded him,"

7 "and old George"

8 "is upside down!"

9 Very slowly turn bill right side up with a very exaggerated motion and repeat trick once or twice more if you like.

magical stunts ⋆

a few light—but amusing—quickies

The effects on these pages more closely approximate stunts than tricks, but they are all good ones. As a magician, you should at least be aware of them, and ideally, able to to do them well should the occasion arise.

the bent spoon

Grip spoon as shown, hold at angle indicated, and with apparent effort, appear to bend spoon almost in half. Then snap your fingers over the spoon and show that it is restored.

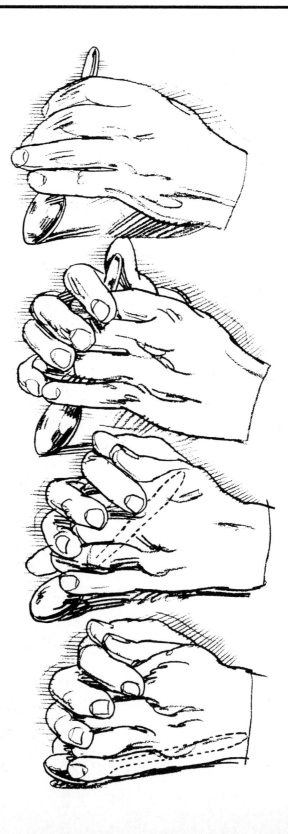

burning sugar cube

If sugar cubes are ever placed on tables again, this will be a good stunt to know. Challenge your dinner companions to light a sugar cube. They won't be able to, but you will because you have secretly tapped your fingertips in cigarette or cigar ashes and when you pick up your lump of sugar, you transfer the ashes to it and hold the match at that point.

rubber pencil

Hold the pencil as illustrated, move your hand up and down about four inches in each direction, and when you get the proper rythm, the pencil will appear to sway like a stick of soft rubber.

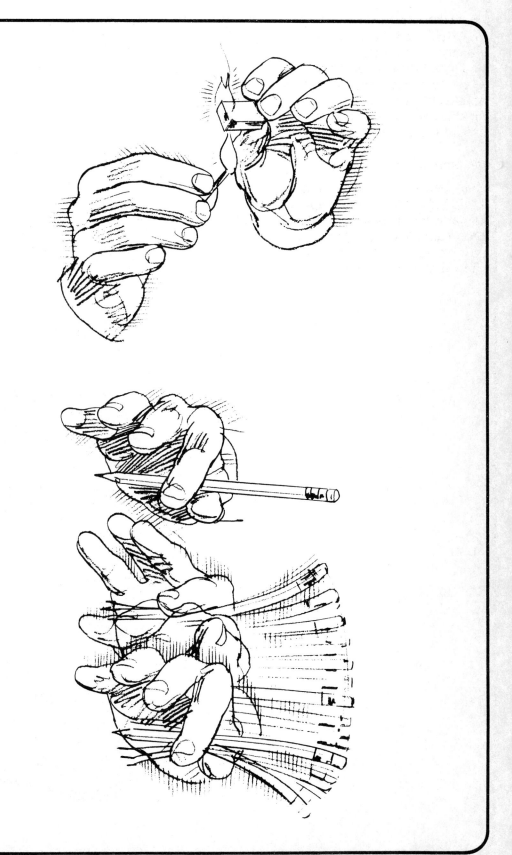

215

the vanishing salt shaker ★★

a simple, perplexing dinner table trick, and a perfect example of applied misdirection . . .

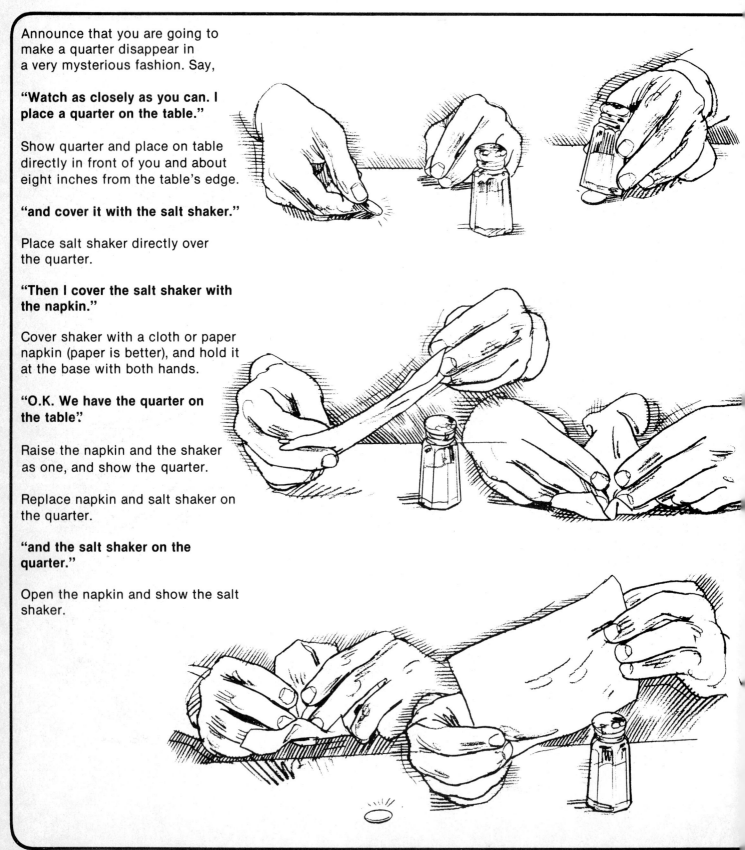

Announce that you are going to make a quarter disappear in a very mysterious fashion. Say,

"Watch as closely as you can. I place a quarter on the table."

Show quarter and place on table directly in front of you and about eight inches from the table's edge.

"and cover it with the salt shaker."

Place salt shaker directly over the quarter.

"Then I cover the salt shaker with the napkin."

Cover shaker with a cloth or paper napkin (paper is better), and hold it at the base with both hands.

"O.K. We have the quarter on the table."

Raise the napkin and the shaker as one, and show the quarter.

Replace napkin and salt shaker on the quarter.

"and the salt shaker on the quarter."

Open the napkin and show the salt shaker.

Replace the napkin.

"Watch. A snap of the fingers and the quarter disappears!"

At the word "disappears," raise the napkin and the salt shaker as one, bring it toward you and unhesitatingly drop the shaker in your lap, retaining the form of the shaker in your napkin. The instant it drops, carry the shaker-form back over the table and come to rest back over the quarter, which you and your audience have noted with surprise is still there. Say

"That's funny. Something must have gone wrong . . . Of course, I remember. It's not the quarter that's supposed to disappear."

At that, raise your R. hand and slap the napkin flat against the table as you say,

"It's the salt shaker!"

Allow the salt shaker to remain on your lap through dinner and then leave it behind your napkin or pass it to a trusted confederate to dispose of for you. If salt is required, ask the waiter for another shaker.

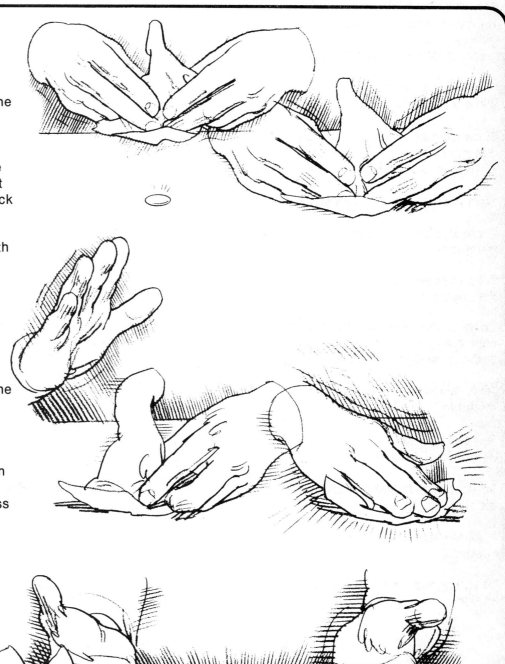

stretching a rope ★

a different—and very good—trick but
it must be the first in your program . . .

required

ten or twelve feet of soft rope
—ideally the light, braided cotton
type sold in magic shops

to prepare

Hold both ends of the rope in
your R. hand and put on jacket.
Fold the balance of the rope and
place it in your inside jacket
pocket.

to perform

Hold what appears to be a short
length of rope in R. hand.

Grasp end A in L. hand, and
holding that arm motionless, slide
R. hand over rope, pulling rope
out of sleeve. When you have
stretched rope two feet or so,
open L. hand, bring R. over to L.
and take another grip and
continue to stretch rope in this
fashion until you reach the end.

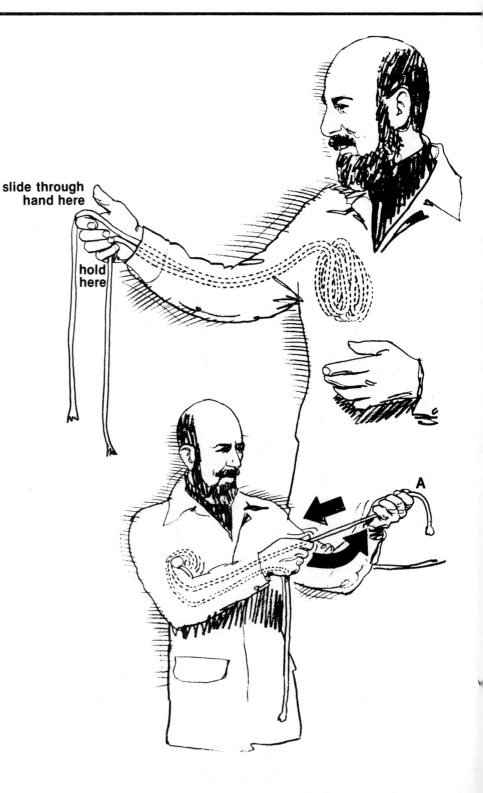

slide through
hand here

hold
here

A

Your L. hand must remain stationary throughout this trick. If you pull with your L. it becomes obvious that the rope is coming out of your R. sleeve. Pull with your R. and do so in a somewhat downward direction to further dispel the notion that the rope is coming from your sleeve.

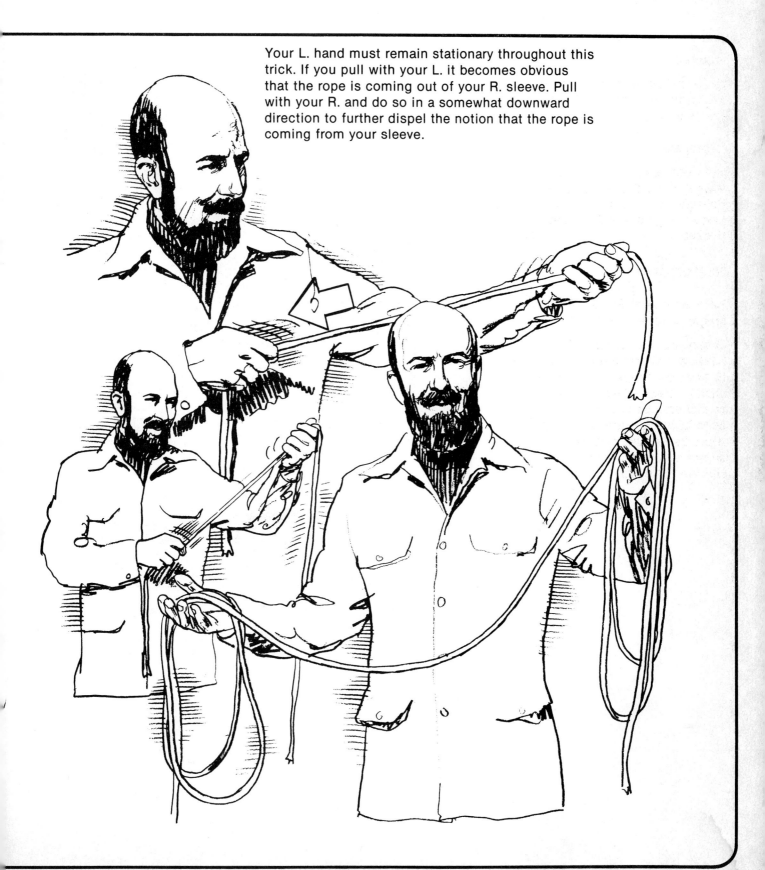

glossary

Apparatus The visible equipment magicians use in the performance of their tricks.

Acquitment A sleight in which a palmed object is secretly passed from hand to hand so as to make the hands appear to be empty.

Back-Palm A palming technique in which the object — generally a card(s) or coin(s) — is concealed behind the fingers of either hand.

Bit A fragment of a sleight or magical effect.

Break A slight opening secretly held in a deck of cards.

Change The magical transformation of one object into another.

Color Change A sleight which changes the color of an object.

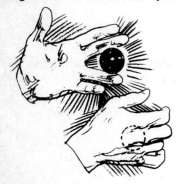

Conjurer A magician.

Crimp A very slight and hence almost invisible bend secretly placed in a card or group of cards by the magician.

Daub A dab of a greasy substance secretly administered to a card to mark it or make it slick, thus enabling the magician to locate it at a future moment.

Disappear An act by which a formerly visible object is rendered nonexistent.

Discovery The revelation of a playing card whose identity was unknown to the magician.

Double Lift Two cards held together and exhibited as one.

Effect A sleight or trick.

Finger-Palm A palming technique in which the object is concealed behind the partially closed fingers of either hand.

Force A technique in which the selection of an object—generally a card—is forced on a spectator who is under the impression that he is making a free choice.

Flash Paper Tissue paper treated with nitric acid that flares into flame upon contact with a glowing cigarette or lit match.

Gimmick A secret device used in the execution of a magic trick.

Glimpse To secretly note the suit and denomination of a card.

Illusion A stage effect using large apparatus.

Jog A card sleight in which a card is made to secretly protrude from the deck to a slight extent, thus enabling the magician to secretly locate it or the card next to it at a future moment.

In Jog A jog held on the side of the deck closest to your body during an overhand shuffle.

Out Jog A jog held on the side of the deck away from your body during an overhand shuffle.

Key Card A card, generally gimmicked, which is used to locate a particular card or cards in the deck.

Legerdemain A French term for magic of the hands or sleight of hand.

Load An object or group of objects concealed on the person (or elsewhere) and ready to be stolen for subsequent production or use.

The act of secretly introducing an object into another location.

Location The act of secretly locating a particular card in the deck.

Magician A performer of magic tricks or illusions.

Marked Cards A deck of cards secretly marked so as to enable the magician to read the suit and denomination from the back.

Move A sleight or portion of a sleight.

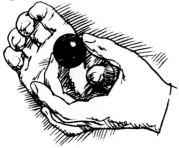

Palm To secrete from view by hiding in the palm of the hand, behind the fingers, at the root of the thumb, behind the hand, etc.

Pass A sleight.

Patter The talk a magician uses to accompany a trick.

Penetration The magical passing of one solid object through another.

Prestidigitation A French term for magic or sleight of hand performed by a prestidigitator or magician.

Produce To make an object or objects that were formerly nonexistent suddenly appear.

Production A trick in which objects are produced from an empty receptacle (rabbit from the hat) or from the air (cards, fans), etc.

Riffle The noise and motion created when the magician depresses the corner of a deck of cards with his thumb and suddenly releases it.

Shell A hollow half-object, such as a ball, shell or a hollowed-out backless coin, in which a smaller coin may be concealed.

Short Card A playing card previously cut about 1/64th of an inch shorter then the other cards in the deck, thus enabling it to be easily located by the magician when the deck is riffled.

Shuffle The process of mixing a deck of cards.

Side Steal A method of palming off one or several cards from the deck.

Silk A colorful square of very thin, compressible cloth, formerly China silk, now generally nylon, ranging in size from 12"x12" to 36" x 36".

Split Fan Production of a fan of cards from the BACK PALM position, and then the re-palming of a portion of those cards in the process of discarding them.

Steal To secretly gain possession of an object, generally from somewhere on your person.

Stripper Deck A gimmicked deck in which all the cards have been trimmed to a wedge shape, thus enabling the magician to locate a card by having it replaced into the deck in reverse position.

Switch A sleight or move in which one object is secretly substituted for another.

Talk The telltale sound an object makes when it accidentally strikes against another during the course of a trick.

Trick A deception in which the audience is fooled.

Vanish The act of making an object suddenly become nonexistent.

a few magical references . . .

Magicians are prolific book writers. The number of books on the various aspects of magic is staggering! Some are books of broad appeal aimed at the general public (magicians call them "laymen"). Most, however, are highly specialized works written for the exclusive use of their fellow magicians. Following are a number of books that I think have special merit. If you are really interested in magic, they can help you on your way. I believe most are available at any good magic supply house.

Greater Magic by John Northern Hilliard

An encyclopedic work . . . over 1000 pages of mostly good magic. The emphasis is on cards, but there are sections on balls, silks, cigarettes, coins, sponge balls, etc., and there are lots of tricks you can do with simple props you can scrounge up around the house. A good reference work too.

Modern Coin Magic by J. B. Bobo (His grandfather spelled it Beauxbeaux!)

Written in the forties, this book is already considered *the* classic work on coins, and deservedly so! It tells you everything you
should know about every aspect of the subject and contains enough fine sleights and superb tricks and routines, many contributed by top magicians, to keep you busy for a lifetime. If coins are your passion, Bobo is a must.

The Tarbell Course by Harlan Tarbell

The original course was put out long years ago. Since then it has been added to, revised, gone through a great many editions and several different publishers, and is still going strong! There are seven volumes in the set, and together they comprise a complete and very good course in magic.

The Illustrated History of Magic by Milbourne Christopher

A fascinating history of magic and magicians written by one of our foremost conjurors and magical historians. If you are going to be involved in magic, you certainly will be intrigued by its grand traditions and the fascinating people who were its stars and super-stars. This lavishly illustrated book tells you a great deal about them. I enjoyed it thoroughly and I am sure you will too.

Dai Vernon's Magic Book by Dai Vernon and written by Lewis Ganson.

Dai Vernon, an avid practitioner of magic for over 70 years (!) and still incredible, is probably the most highly regarded sleight-of-hand man in all the world, and deservedly so. A purist in every sense of the word, he has devoted his life to the furtherance of the art of magic not for fame or material rewards, but like the true artist he surely is, for the sheer love of it.

Every sleight in his book is difficult and most of the tricks are fairly complex, but each is a masterpiece, carefully worked out and presented in meticulous detail by his good friend, well-known magician Lewis Ganson.

This is certainly not a book for the beginner, but I thought you should know about it. Someday you may want to become involved.

Stars of Magic

This is a brilliant series of thirty-nine sleight-of-hand effects, each the pet trick of a highly regarded sleight-of-hand artist . . . Dai Vernon, Slydini, the late Francis Carlyle and Dr. Jacob Daly, Leo Horowitz and a number of others, including several brilliant effects by long-departed masters, Nate Liepzig and Max Malini, worked out and presented by Mr. Vernon. Again, these effects are far too involved for beginners, but someday, who knows . . .?

The Memoirs of Robert Houdin

The still fascinating memoirs of the nineteenth century French magician many consider to be the father of modern conjuring. Watch and automaton maker, inventor, dabbler in electricity, and the most successful magician of his era, Houdin's story is a must for any lover of magic.

Houdini's Escapes and Magic by Walter Gibson

This is a fairly old book (originally published over forty years ago), and there isn't really too much material that you can personally use to advantage unless you are contemplating the Chinese Water Torture Escape or have aspirations to walk through brick walls, but it does make fascinating reading and present a keen insight into the art—and science— of magic, particularly escapes and illusions. Walter Gibson, one of our foremost and most prolific writer-scholars on the magic arts, presents this and everything he does in highly readable, highly enjoyable fashion.

The Encyclopedia of Card Tricks by Jean Hugard

The late Jean Hugard was perhaps the foremost writer of magic books for magicians. Generally thin paperbacks, virtually devoid of illustrations, and not too highly detailed, they are nevertheless authoritative and all-inclusive. His books cover the gamut . . . thimbles, silks, dinner-table magic, and especially cards. His encyclopedia is a superb collection over four hundred pages long, and certainly worth having if card-magic intrigues you.

About the Author

Like a great many magicians, Bill Tarr has been interested in magic from a very early age. He did his first tricks at the age of nine, spent the greater part of his youth with a deck of cards in his hands, and eventually did a manipulative act — cards, billiard balls and cigarettes—professionally . . . a brief interlude he most thoroughly enjoyed. After a hitch in the navy he entered the arts, and for many years has been a dedicated full-time sculptor.

He is a former Guggenheim Fellow, a Municipal Art Society Award winner, and creator of several of America's largest sculptures: the Martin Luther King, Jr., Memorial, the huge Morningside Heights piece and some twelve other works in New York City.

Husband of prominent cookbook author Yvonne Young Tarr, and father of two sons, Jonathon and Nicolas, he works and lives in East Hampton, New York.

About the Illustrator

Barry Ross has been drawing and painting for as long as he can remember. A prize-winning member of the illustrious Society of Illustrators, his work has been seen and admired in virtually all of the leading American periodicals. Now You See It, Now You Don't, with its well over 1,500 drawings, marks his Herculean entry into the world of book illustration.

Mr. Ross is an ardent sportsman and outdoorsman — a skier, private pilot and sailplane enthusiast — but his primary interest lies in music. He is a dedicated composer of popular music, is currently involved in the production of several of his songs in which a good deal of professional interest has been manifested, and a promising career in that direction beckons should he choose to take it.

A native New Yorker, he lives with his well-known interior designer wife Barbara in the New York City studio-residence she designed, with their two children, Lee and Jenifer.